eat,
seoul

일러두기

이 책은 2009년부터 최근까지 〈럭셔리〉에 연재되었던 기사를 단행본으로 묶은 것으로
게재 순서 및 제목을 달리해 구성했습니다.
경우에 따라 메뉴, 운영 시간, 현재 모습 등이 다를 수 있습니다.

이 도서의 국립중앙도서관 출판시도서목록(CIP)은 서지정보유통지원시스템 홈페이지(http://seoji.nl.go.kr)와
국가자료공동목록시스템(http://www.nl.go.kr/kolisnet)에서 이용하실 수 있습니다.
(CIP 제어번호: 2015025297)

서울 미식 스팟 165

서울에서 미식을 즐기다

잇, 서울

글과 사진 〈럭셔리〉 편집부

design house

| prologue | 서울, 점점 더 맛있어지는 도시 | 8 |

한식

dining story	한식이 미식이다	14
dining scene	한식에 대한 일곱 가지 상상	18
place	외국인에게 소개하고 싶은 한식 레스토랑 46	26
	한정식	28
	그릴	36
	캐주얼 모던	44
	채식	52
	향토 음식	58
	별미	62

중식

dining story	한국의 중국 음식 100년사	72
dining story	대륙의 맛을 아십니까?	80
dining scene	짜장에서 만찬까지, 중식 테이블	86
place	서울에서 가장 맛있는 중식 레스토랑 32	94
	짜장면	96
	짬뽕	102
	일품요리	106
	코스 요리	114

프랑스 요리

dining story	프랑스 요리는 어떻게 미식의 최고봉이 되었나?	120
dining story	프랑스 미식을 완성하는 기본 식재료	128
dining scene	식사 매너부터 코스 요리까지, 프렌치 테이블	134
place	프랑스인도 인정한 프렌치 레스토랑 24	140
	프랑스인의 단골 레스토랑	142
	서래마을의 프렌치 레스토랑	156
	호텔 프렌치 레스토랑	162

이탈리아 요리

dining story	이탈리아 음식의 역사는 서양 음식의 역사다	170
place	5년 이상 건재하다, 믿고 가는 이탤리언 레스토랑 18	176

세계 요리

place	기분 전환을 위한 세계 요리 레스토랑 12	198
	일식	200
	태국 요리	204
	스페인 요리	208
	멕시코 요리	212

디저트 & 술

dining story	아시아 디저트 문화	218
dining scene	일상의 디저트 테이블	224
place	서울의 고급 디저트 숍 & 바 33	230
	오너 셰프의 파티세리	232
	전통 디저트 가게	252
	수제 맥주 펍	258
	주점 & 바	262

credits   270

| prologue | Seoul, a City of Gastronomes | 8 |

KOREAN CUISINE

dining story	Korean Cuisine, a New Proposal for Gourmet	14
dining scene	7 Imaginations for Korean Cuisine	18
place	46 Best Korean Restaurants	26
	Korean Table d'hôte	28
	Grill & Barbeque	36
	Casual Modern	44
	Vegetarian Meals	52
	Local Dishes	58
	Other Delicacies	62

CHINESE CUISINE

dining story	A 100-year History of Chinese Cuisine in Korea	72
dining story	Taste of the Mainland China	80
dining scene	Chinese Food in All Tastes and Kinds	86
place	32 Best Chinese Restaurants in Seoul	94
	Jajangmyeon	96
	Jjambbong	102
	À la carte dish	106
	Course Menu	114

FRENCH CUISINE

dining story	French Cuisine, a Very Diamond of Gastronomy	120
dining story	Basic Ingredients for French Gastronomy	128
dining scene	Course of French Table	134
place	24 Best French Restaurants	140
	French Restaurants French People Loves Most	142
	French Restaurants in Seorae Village	156
	French Restaurants in Hotels	162

ITALIAN CUISINE

dining story	History of Italian Cuisine, or the Story of Western Cuisine	170
place	18 Most Reliable Italian Restaurants	176

GLOBAL CUISINE

place	12 Global Cuisine Restaurants	198
	Japanese Cuisine	200
	Thai Cuisine	204
	Spanish Cuisine	208
	Mexican Cuisine	212

DESSERT & LIQUOR

dining story	Asian Dessert Culture	218
dining scene	Dessert Table for Special Days	224
place	33 Fine Dessert Shops & Bars in Seoul	230
	Expert Chef's Pâtisserie	232
	Traditional Korean Desserts	252
	Craft Beer House	258
	Bar & Pub	262

credits	270

prologue

서울,

점점 더
맛있어지는
도시

누군가를 만나는 자리에서 정치와 종교를 화제로 삼는다면, 최악입니다. 날씨에 관한 이야기는 지루하지요. 세상 거의 모든 사람이 관심을 갖고 있고 타인의 취향에 대해 비난이 아닌 인정이 가능한 영역. 제일 먼저 떠오르는 것이 바로 먹고 마시는 이야기입니다. 음식이나 음식점에 관해서는 누구나 한마디 거들 수 있습니다. 무엇이 특히 맛있는지, 어떤 음식점이 괜찮고 또 형편없는지. 이런 이야기를 나눌 때면 목소리가 커지고 얼굴은 자기도 모르게 환해집니다.

먹어본 것, 먹고 있는 것, 언젠가 먹어보고 싶은 것. 인간의 가장 원초적인 호기심이자 쾌락은 바로 무언가를 먹는 일입니다. 아주 오래전, 낯설고 무섭기까지 한 외형에 주저하지 않고 맛을 볼 용기를 냈던 선조가 아니었다면 지금 우리는 굴과 더덕과 두리안의 특별한 맛을 경험할 수 없었을 것입니다. 시간이 흐르고 다양한 문명이 등장하면서 인류의 '먹을 것' 리스트는 점점 길어졌고, 탐식과 미식에 대한 열망도 커졌습니다. 허기를 채우기 위해 먹는 것이 아니라 감각을 자극하기 위해 먹는 사람이 많아지다 보니 관련 지식과 정보에 대한 갈증 역시 커져가고 있습니다.

다행히 우리가 살고 있는 이 도시, 서울에서 음식에 대한 호기심을 채우기란 그리 어려운 일이 아닙니다. 세상의 매력적인 도시가 갖춰야 할 가장 중요한 덕목 중 하나가 바로 음식입니다. 자국의 독특한 음식을 잘 지키는 것과 더불어 전 세계 다양한 음식을 본고장과 비슷하게, 때로는 완전히 드라마틱하게 재해석할 수 있어야 합니다. 크고 화려한 레스토랑과 작고 푸근한 동네 식당이 공존하고 다양한 시도와 실험이 일어나면서 서울은 바쁘고 요란하며 사람들 많은 도시에서 '맛있는' 도시로 이름을 알려가고 있습니다. 오랜 역사를 통해 전해져 내려온 한식당과 이를 새롭게 해석한 패기 넘치는 젊은 셰프들의 레스토랑이 속속 문을 열고 있습니다. 세련된 프랑스 음식, 호쾌한 햄버거, 외식의 첫 기억이었던 중국 음식, 춤추는 칼끝에서 만들어진 회와 스시를 비롯해 전 세계 수많은 나라의 음식을 맛보는 일이 어렵지 않습니다. 지역마다 자리 잡은 '맛집'을 찾아 나선 사람들로 긴 줄이 생기고 앞치마를 입고 직접 음식을 만들어보려는 사람들 또한 그 어느 때보다 많아졌습니다.

2001년 첫 호를 낸 이래 가치 있는 다양한 삶의 방식을 소개해온 〈럭셔리〉는 이런 서울의 미식 문화를 다양한 앵글로 소개했습니다. 외국인 손님에게 소개했을 때 가장 반응이 좋았던 레스토랑, 변화무쌍한 서울의 레스토랑 문화에서 흔들림 없이 실력을 자랑하는 이탤리언 레스토랑, 개성 넘치는 바와 카페, 미식의 궁극이라 할 수 있는 디저트 전문점…. 업계 최고 미식 감별가와 까다로운 전문가, 직접 방문해 확인하고 음식을 먹어본 기자가 선정한 서울의 레스토랑과 음식점은 그 어떤 기사보다 독자의 호응이 높았습니다. 이렇게 차곡차곡 쌓인 정보를 한 권으로 묶어 펴내게 되었습니다. 앞으로도 계속 새로운 정보를 추가해 '맛있는 서울'을 한눈에 살필 수 있는 좋은 가이드북으로 만들어가겠습니다.

"음식에 대한 사랑보다 더 진실한 사랑은 없다"라고 독설가 조지 버나드 쇼마저도 말했습니다. 제대로 먹지 않는다면 제대로 생각할 수 없고 제대로 움직일 수 없으며 제대로 살 수 없을 것입니다. 사랑하는 사람들과 맛있는 음식을 나누며 세상일을 이야기하는 것은 가장 소박하면서도 가장 럭셔리한 경험입니다. 그런 소중한 시간을 만드는 데 이 책이 친근한 안내자가 되길 바랍니다.

〈럭셔리〉 편집장 김은령

prologue

Seoul, a City of Gastronomes

If you use politics or religion to break the ice when you first meet someone, it's definitely gonna be the worst try. Then weather? Still sounds boring. But if you still want an ordinary but not sensitive subject for your conversation, you can choose this option. It's talking about what you like to eat or drink. Food or restaurant, it may be a really common topic for almost everyone to feel comfortable to talk. What's your favorite food? Which restaurant is good or bad? Do you have any food or restaurant you especially prefer? Everybody has at least a word or two to put in when someone asks such questions.

We are always thinking about what people used to eat those old days, what they are enjoying to eat these days and what they will have to eat in the future. That is, the act of eating is the most basic and fundamental pleasure to human. Long ago, if our ancestors dared not try anything new because of its peculiar and rather gross appearance or smell, we could not have known a true taste of oyster, deodeok (codonopsis lanceolate) or durian. As human culture has been enriched for thousands of years, a list of food has likewise become more abundant consequently. Now, people want to eat not because of hunger but for pleasure and are very keen to get knowledge or information about eating-well.

In Seoul, fortunately, it is not much difficult for us to satisfy our curiosity for exotic and delicious food. If a city wants to become an attractive place, food is one of the important qualifications it should have. In other words, the city should have its own iconic food and at the same time can reproduce famous cuisines of other cities or countries as similar as possible. In Seoul, an invisible collaboration of big, sumptuous restaurants and small, casual eateries have made our busy and boisterous city a place of delicious and exquisite food. A deep pride of old and obstinate Korean restaurants, a young chef's creative interpretation for traditional food, exquisite French cuisines, simple yet still pleasing burgers, Chinese restaurants always popular for family's eating out, sashimi and sushi like a dancing knife's magic and other distinctive foods from various countries. Now you can taste all these foods without leaving Seoul. And it has become common for us to see people waiting in a long line in front of a famous restaurant and to see a number of people trying to do the cooking at home more than ever.

Luxury, a monthly magazine proposing diverse types of life styles, has addressed this ever-changing culinary culture of Seoul in several ways since its first issue in 2001, including restaurants especially popular with foreigners, authentic Italian restaurants, distinctive bars and cafés and dedicated dessert restaurants. Among them, restaurants acclaimed by culinary experts and reporters and gastronomes, who visited those restaurants and tasted food themselves also received much more favorable reviews from our readers. Now we compiled this long list of restaurants into a single book and continue to update this book with new and useful information

"There is no sincerer love than the love of food," said George Bernard Shaw, an Irish playwright. If we can't eat well, we can't think well and if we can't think well, we can't live well. Maybe having a conversation with good people while enjoying delicious food in a relaxed mood is the most frugal and ordinary daily life in some senses but the most special and luxurious experience in different senses. We hope that this book will guide you to such a precious moment of life.

Kim Eun-ryoung(Luxury Editor in Chief)

dining story

한식이
미식이다

"인간은 미각을 만족하지 못하면 결코 완전하게 행복해질 수 없다." 19세기 미식가 브리야 사바랭이 한 말이다. 많은 사람들이 세상에서 가장 맛있는 음식을 찾는 데 시간과 비용과 노력을 투자하길 마다하지 않는 오늘날에 꼭 어울리는 이야기다. 미식은 어느새 최상의 문화이자 세계를 움직이는 가장 중요한 문화 코드가 됐다. 그런데 '미식'이란 과연 무엇일까? 사전적 의미를 살펴보면 '좋은 음식, 또는 그런 음식을 먹는 것'을 가리킨다. 흔히 우리가 미식 하면 떠올리는 것들은 서양식 코스 요리나 진귀한 식재료 등이다. 하지만 건강에 좋고 친환경적이라 평가받는 한식 역시 빼놓을 수 없는 미식이 아닐까?

'약식동원藥食同原'이라는 옛말이 있다. '약과 음식은 그 근원이 동일하다'라는 뜻으로, 매일 먹는 음식이 얼마나 중요한지 강조하는 말이다. 이 말에 빗대보면 건강에 좋은 제철 음식을 최고로 치는 한식이야말로 몸에 가장 좋은 약이라는 의미로 해석할 수 있다. 비만 해소에 좋은 음식으로 꼽을 만큼 한식은 과학적으로도 입증된 건강식이다.

영양학적으로 이상적인 건강식은 동물성 기름과 식물성 기름이 8 대 2 비율을 이루는 것인데 육류, 해산물, 채소 등 갖가지 재료가 어우러진 한식은 이상적인 건강식에 가장 근접한 식단이라고 할 수 있다. 채식에만 치우치지 않으면서 육류와 해산물을 골고루 배합한 한식은 영양이 균형을 이루는 식단이다. 특히 우리 조상들이 즐겨 먹던 나물은 삶으면 부피가 줄어들어 채소 섭취를 늘리는 데 일등 공신이다. 말린 나물은 나중에 다시 불려 먹을 수 있으니 채소가 흔치 않은 겨울철에도 채소를 꾸준히 섭취할 수 있고 재활용성도 뛰어나다. 또 구황식이던 죽에 주로 쓰인 무, 당근, 시금치, 냉이 등은 섬유질이 풍부해 콜레스테롤 수치를 낮춰주고, 양념에 두루 쓰이는 파, 마늘, 생강, 고추 역시 약리 효과가 뛰어나다. 그뿐만 아니라 영양소 파괴를 최소화하는 삶기, 찌기 등 다양한 구성의 상차림은 영양학적으로 완벽한 조화를 자랑하며, 잘 알려졌듯 각종 장류와 김치 등의 발효 음식은 과학적으로 매우 뛰어난 식품이다.

이 정도면 한식이 좋은 음식, 즉 미식이란 사실을 충분히 뒷받침할 수 있다. 게다가 우리는 그 좋은 음식을 매일같이 먹고 산다. 늘 미식을 누리고 있다는 말이다. 파리와 뉴욕, 밀라노와 런던 등 트렌디한 도시마다 세련된 '코리안 퀴진'이 생기고 트렌드세터들이 드나드는 것이 괜한 일은 아니다. 우리 곁에 있는 미식, 한식을 다시 볼 때다.

dining story

Korean Cuisine, a New Proposal for Gourmet

"Man cannot be fully happy as long as his taste remains unsatisfied," said Jean Anthelme Brillat-Savarin, a French lawyer and politician and also a famous epicure in the 19th century. This word still remains true to people in the present day, who are spending all their time looking for the most delicious food in the world. Gastronomy has become one of the most important culture codes having a huge influence on this world and also become high culture itself at the same time. By the way, what is 'gastronomy?' According to a dictionary, it means a good food or an act of eating good food. A common impression for gastronomy is such a refined course meals on a large table or its rare, luxury food ingredients. In this sense, Korean food based on healthy and eco-friendly culinary culture could be called gourmet cuisine.

In Korea, there is an old saying that 'food and medicine have the same properties in its foundation.' This saying puts an emphasis on the importance of what we eat every day. Thus, we could say that eating Korean food, placing much value upon healthy, seasonal ingredients, can be interpreted as an act of keeping your body healthy. It is also verified in a scientific way that low-fat Korean food has contributed to relatively low fat intake and lower rate of obesity in South Korea.

The most ideal health food contains animal fat and vegetable fat in an 80:20 ratio. This ratio is almost realized in a traditional Korean meal in which meat, seafood and vegetable are well nutritionally balanced. In particular, the custom of eating a variety of boiled vegetables is the primary contributor to make Korean meals a healthy diet. In addition, vegetable, once dried and restored, can be used any time, even during a cold winter, because it is available again whenever it is soaked in water. Some vegetables such as white radish, carrot, spinach and shepherd's purse, which were used as main ingredients of Juk (a kind of Korean porridge and an emergency food in the past), contain rich fiber, which helps reduce cholesterol. Other vegetables usually used for ingredients of condiments, such as spring onion, garlic, ginger and chili pepper, have high medicinal values. A traditional Korean diet is more than often not based on a simple cooking technique, boiling or steaming, which is one of the good ways to minimize nutrient loss of food and which is in turn led to a nutritionally well-balanced meal. And fermented food like Kimchi and Jang (fermented soy products), has already been acknowledged for its many health benefits.

There is no doubt now that Korean food is a good food, namely, gastronomy food. Then it can be said that Koreans who do eat Korean food every day are gourmet. It explains why Korean cuisine restaurants are showing up in the coolest cities in the world, such as Paris, New York, Milan or London and have become one of the favorite places for trendsetters in those cities. Then what is the Korean food by the way?

dining scene
:
7
Imaginations
for
Korean Cuisine

한식에
대한

일곱
가지
상상

There is a large table on which a big pot of stew is placed in the middle and people sitting around the table are enjoying their meal together. Probably this is a quite common image that people have for a Korean-style dining. But the dining in a Korean restaurant does not need to always look like this. How about applying unusual ingredients or recipes and totally different style of food presentation for it? Its beautiful, picturesque presentation and amazing taste would fascinate anyone who tries it even for the first time.

한식 하면 큰 상차림이 떠오르고 순가락을 함께 담가 먹는 찌개 같은 구수한 맛을 상상하기 마련이다. 하지만 한식이 꼭 토속적이란 법은 없다. 이런 모습의, 이런 맛의 한식은 어떨까? 색다른 식재료와 서양식 조리법을 활용하고, 아이디어 넘치는 플레이팅으로 한식 상차림을 꾸며봤다. 외국인 친구나 한국을 방문한 외국인 바이어에게 소개한다면 서양 요리 못지않은 아름다운 모습과 놀라운 맛에 단번에 매료될 것이다.

미니멀 스타일의 한정식

상다리가 부러져라 차리는 한정식이 부담스럽다면 적은 양을 깔끔하게 담아내도 좋다. 달걀찜, 육회, 생강맛 장어구이, 갈비찜과 오곡밥, 겉절이, 삯국수, 상큼한 한라봉 화채. 애피타이저부터 디저트까지 6품만으로 전통 한정식의 맛과 질감을 살리고, 미니멀한 담음새로 완성된 세련된 한정식 한 상.

요리 / 서울 신라 호텔

MINIMALISM OF KOREAN TABLE D'HÔTE

Sometimes, a small and simple presentation of food looks more delicious rather than a table which is full of numerous plates. Dalgyal-jjim (steamed egg), Yukhoe (steak tartare), Saenggangmat Jangeogui (boiled eels flavored with ginger), Galbi-jjim (braised short ribs) & Ogokbap (five-grain rice), Geotjeori (fresh kimchi salad), Sakguksu (starch noodle dish) and fresh Hanrabong Hawchae (hanrabong punch). This table is prepared with only six dishes, focusing on a traditional yet refined style of the table. *By the Shilla Seoul*

전채 요리의 감각적 변신

김칫국물로 만든 젤리, 감귤즙과 참기름에 재운 관자, 꽃게살을 한 폭의 그림처럼 담아 삼색전, 냉채 등으로 일관했던 한식 전채 요리의 변신을 꾀했다. 접시 가운데 붓으로 펼쳐놓은 고추장 소스, 꽃잎과 함께 장식한 인삼 거품, 작은 인삼까지 곁들여 한국적인 우아함을 더했다.

요리 / 그랜드 인터컨티넨탈 서울 파르나스

A NEW STYLING OF APPETIZERS

Jellies made from kimchi juice, scallop seasoned in tangerine juice and sesame oil and blue crab meat are set in a fancy style. This table presents new types of appetizers, instead of common appetizers such as Samsaek Jeon (three-colored vegetable pancake) or Naengchae (chilled vegetables). A painting drawn with Gochujang (red pepper paste) in the middle of a plate, ginseng froth decorated with flowers and more extra small ginsengs. Korea's own beauty is well kept even on this elaborate table. *By the Grand Intercontinental Seoul Parnas*

마음대로 디자인하는 비빔밥

귀네스 팰트로도 젓가락으로 비벼가며 제대로 먹을 줄 안다는 비빔밥. 잘 지은 밥에 각종 나물과 달걀지단, 고추장을 턱 얹으면 완성할 수 있으니 한국식 패스트푸드요, 원하는 재료를 골라 토핑할 수 있는 DIY 메뉴다. 밥을 따로 준비하고 각종 나물과 해산물, 고추장과 들기름을 종지에 나눠 담아낸다면 매운맛에 익숙하지 않은 외국인은 고추장 양을 조절할 수 있고, 채식주의자라면 채소만 골라 담아 먹을 수 있다.

요리 / 롯데 호텔 서울

CUSTOMIZED BIBIMBAP

Bibimbap is already the most famous Korean food. Also, Gwyneth Paltrow showed a desirable way of mixing Bibimbap using chopsticks in her show. Bibimbap is a kind of fast food because you can enjoy by just putting and mixing just a few ingredients such as boiled vegetables, fried egg and red pepper paste with steamed rice. And it is also a kind of food D.I.Y. because you can control the quantity of each ingredient as you want and if you are a vegetarian you can put only vegetables. *By the Lotte Hotel Seoul*

한식 브런치

브런치 테이블은 꼭 서양 음식으로 꾸며야 할까? 한식으로도 경쾌하고 세련된 브런치를 즐길 수 있다면? 푸아 그라로 소를 채운 만두와 송이버섯 맑은 수프, 방어구이와 쑥갓 퓌레를 곁들인 강원도산 감자튀김, 명란젓 커스터드, 새우·갈비·채소를 넣은 밀전병말이, 피클과 칠리를 곁들인 제주산 새우꼬치를 간결한 화이트 접시에 담고 샴페인 한 잔을 더했다. 한식과 양식의 재료와 조리법이 한데 어우러진 한식 브런치 완성!

요리 / W 서울 워커힐

KOREAN-STYLE BRUNCH

A brunch doesn't need to be made up of Western foods. Mandu (dumplings) filled with foie gras and a soup made from pine mushroom, French fries made with Korean potatoes and added with grilled yellowtail and crown daisy puree, custard made with pickled pollock roe, shrimp, grilled beef and vegetables wrapped in wheat crepes, skewered Jeju-shrimp added with pickles and chili and even a glass of champagne. A combination of Korean ingredients and Western recipes creates this exquisite brunch. *By the W Seoul Walkerhill*

숯불 없이 즐기는 갈비찜

'코리안 바비큐'로 널리 알려진 불고기와 갈비. "지지직" 군침 도는 소리를 내며 불판 위에서 직접 굽는 것도 좋지만 좀 더 격식 있는 메인 요리에는 새로운 접근이 필요하다. 24시간 동안 쪄 부드러운 한우 갈비를 한 입 크기로 잘라 불고기 소스를 곁들인 후 김치만두, 청경채무침을 가니시로 담아내면 정찬이나 칵테일파티 어디에 내놓아도 손색없는 메뉴가 된다.

요리 / 그랜드 하얏트 서울

GALBI-JJIM WITHOUT A CHARCOAL GRILL

Bulgogi and Galbi are already widely known as 'Korean-style barbeque'. The usual way to cook this food is roasting beef or pork on a charcoal grill, while enjoying its sizzling sound. Of course, however, there are many options for a more refined version of these dishes. Soft and bite-sized Hanu Galbi (using Korean native beef), which is braised for 24 hours, added with bulgogi sauce and then topped with Kimchi mandu and seasoned bok choy, would show a great combination of taste and style when it is served for a formal dining or a cocktail party. *By the Grand Hyatt Seoul*

국물 없는 육개장

육개장은 우리에게 얼큰하고 친숙한 음식이지만, 이를 처음 접한 외국인은 빨간 국물과 형태를 알아볼 수 없을 정도로 푹 삶은 채소와 고기 때문에 선뜻 숟가락을 들지 못한다. 고추기름을 넣어 얼큰하게 만든 육개장 소스를 안심 스테이크 슬라이스 위에 얹어 메인 디시로 만들고, 고사리와 콩나물, 파 등을 켜켜이 쌓아 올린 다음, 깻잎과 호박으로 오곡밥을 돌돌 말아 사이드 디시로 만들었다. 차갑게 먹는 궁중 요리인 초선탕은 갖은 재료를 수직으로 쌓아 올려 프렌치식으로 담았다.

요리 / 서울 웨스틴 조선 호텔

THICK AND SPICY VEGETABLE BEEF SOUP, YUKGAEJANG

Yukgaejang is one of the most common foods for Koreans but its red hot stew and rich ingredients look quite unfamiliar to those who have never tasted it before. The main dish shows a combination of the yukgaejang sauce flavored with chili oil and tenderloin steak slice. And as the side dish, layered bracken, bean sprout and spring onion and five-grain rice rolled with perilla leaves and pumpkins are prepared. Choseontang, a chilled soup and kind of royal cuisine, is decorated with assorted ingredients in a French-style. *By the Westin Chosun Seoul*

한국식 디저트 테이블

오미자와 유자, 서양배에 비해 수분 함량과 당도가 높은 한국 배 등 제철 과일에 젤리와 서벗, 샤블레 등 서양식 제과 테크닉을 접목한 한국식 디저트 테이블. 오미자 펀치로 만든 오미자 젤리, 수정과로 만든 셔벗, 인삼으로 만든 아이스크림, 한국 배로 만든 샤블레 등 부드러움과 쫄깃함, 차가움 등 다양한 질감의 매력을 극대화했다.

요리 / 파크 하얏트 서울

KOREAN-STYLE DESSERT TABLE

Various Korean fruits meet Western baking techniques. Schisandra jelly made from schisandra berry punch, Sherbet made from Sujeonggwa (persimmon punch) and Ginseng Ice Cream, and Sable Cookies made with Korean pears. A variety of local tastes are well embodied in each dessert. *By the Park Hyatt Seoul*

place
:
46
Best
Korean
Restaurants

외국인에게
소개하고 싶은

한식
레스토랑
46

If you want a place to experience Korea's own culinary culture and taste excellent Korean food, our selection of fine Korean restaurants may satisfy you. These restaurants are acclaimed as an old yet great Korean restaurant with natural taste of Korea.

손님을 치를 때 가장 고민되는 것이 어떤 음식을 어떻게 대접할지다. 특히 그 손님이 외국인이라면 고민은 더욱 깊어진다. 외국인 손님에게 제대로 된 한국의 음식 문화를 알리고 그의 입맛과 취향에 맞는 한식 레스토랑에 데려가고 싶다면 이곳에 주목할 것. 오랫동안 사랑받으며 한국의 맛을 가장 잘 담아냈다는 평가를 받는 곳들만 꼽았다.

한정식	그릴	캐주얼 모던	향토 음식
필경재	한우리	개화옥	전원
품 서울	로즈힐	배상면주가	무돌
예당	명월관	토담골	제주항
삼청각 한식당	삼원가든	민스키친	해남천일관
큰기와집	벽제갈비	콩두	
석파랑	그릴 H	다담	별미
한미리	버드나무집	밍글스	토속촌 삼계탕
고메홈	사리원	류니끄	자하손만두
뉘조	우래옥		강서면옥
		채식	황생가 칼국수
		풀향기	서울서 둘째로 잘하는 집
		산촌	이남장
		소선재	새벽집
		백년옥	명동교자
		온마을 두부	하동관
		채근담	
		고상	

Korean Table d'Hôte	Grill & Barbeque	Casual Modern	Local Dishes
Philkyungjae	Hanwoori	Gaewhaok	Jeonwon
Poom Seoul	Rosehill	Baesangmyun Brewery	Mudol
Yedang	Myongwolgwan	Todamgol	Jeju Hang
Samcheonggak -Hansikdang	Samwon Garden	Min's Kitchen	Haenam Cheonilgwan
Keungiwajib	Byeokje Galbi	Congdu	
Seokparang	Grill H	Dadam	Other Delicacies
Hanmiri	Budnamujip	Mingles	Tosokchon Samgyetang
Gourmet-Home	Sariwon	Ryunique	Jaha Sonmandoo
Nwijo	Uraeok		Gangseo Myeonok
		Vegetarian Meals	Hwangsaengga -Kalguksu
		Pulhyanggi	Seoureseo Duljjaero -Jalhaneunjip
		Sanchon	Inamjang
		Soseonjae	SaebyeokJip
		Baeknyeonok	Myoungdong Kyoja
		Onmaeul Dubu	Hadongkwan
		Chaegundaam	
		Gosang	

한정식

정중하고 격식 있게 손님을 접대해야 할 때 가장 먼저 떠오르는 것이 바로 한정식이다. 전채부터 밥과 국, 반찬, 찜이나 구이 등의 계절 진미, 후식으로 구성해 서양의 코스 요리와 다름없는 한정식 레스토랑은 한국 음식에 익숙하지 않은 외국인과 찾기에도 부담이 없다. 궁중 요리에 담긴 역사적 의미나 재료, 만드는 법에 대해 미리 알아둔다면 요리와 함께 우리의 문화를 설명하기에 좋은 기회가 될 것이다. 한옥을 개조한 곳이나 한국적 소품으로 꾸민 곳이라면 한국의 아름다움을 소개하기에도 알맞다.

KOREAN TABLE D'HÔTE

A restaurant offering Korean table d'hôte is probably a good place for foreigners who are generally not accustomed to Korean food. Its course consists of an hors d'oeuvre, steamed rice, thin soup, some side dishes, seasonal delicacies and dessert. And the knowledge about ingredients and recipes of this Korean cuisine would give you a good chance to understand Korean culture in some aspect. As well as from food, you would see Korea's own beauty from a restaurant placed in a traditional Korean house, or decorated with unique traditional decorations.

필경재

비즈니스를 위한 한정식 레스토랑으로 첫손에 꼽히는 필경재는 주변 경관과 음식 맛, 서비스의 삼박자가 조화를 이룬 곳이다. 500년이 넘은 고택으로 조선 광평대군의 종손인 이천수가 건립해 '반드시 웃어른을 공경할 줄 아는 자세를 지니고 살라'라는 뜻을 담아 이름을 지었다. 외관은 전통 가옥의 고즈넉함을 그대로 살려 마치 시간을 거슬러 올라간 듯한 느낌이 든다. 나무가 우거진 마당과 정원을 휴식 공간으로 꾸며 식사 후 여유를 즐길 수 있어 더욱 좋다. 미정식부터 수라정식까지 여섯 가지 코스 요리를 선보이며 자연산 송이 전복죽, 궁중 신선로 등 대표적인 궁중 음식을 맛볼 수 있다.

Philkyungjae

Always the best place for inviting important guests. Its beautiful scenery and attentive service are quite impressive, not mention to their great food. An old house more than 500 years old, whose name means 'always respect your elders', will bring you back to those old days in a quiet and peaceful atmosphere. It also provides a resting place in the woods. There are six course menus including Korean royal cuisine.

Address	강남구 광평로 205
Contact	02-445-2115
Web	www.philkyungjae.co.kr
Operation	12:00~22:00(Break 15:00~18:00)
Closed	설 · 추석 당일

205, Gwangpyeong-ro, Gangnam-gu
+82-2-445-2115
www.philkyungjae.co.kr
12:00~22:00(Break 15:00~18:00)
Day of Lunar New Year's Day & Chuseok

품 서울

푸드 스타일리스트 노영희 씨가 지인들과 함께 연 곳으로 주로 양반가에서 먹던 반가 음식을 현대에 맞게 재해석해 선보인다. 점심은 두 가지, 저녁은 세 가지 코스로 이루어지며, 당뇨 환자를 위한 건강식도 있다. 신선한 제철 식재료만으로 만든 정갈한 맛도 훌륭하지만, 코스마다 그에 어울리는 한 폭의 그림같이 아름다운 프레젠테이션은 이곳에서만 누릴 수 있는 특별한 즐거움이다. 간소한 와인 리스트와 한국 음식에 어울리는 전통주도 갖추었다. 한강까지 한눈에 내려다볼 수 있는 탁 트인 전망이 일품이며, 예약 손님에 맞춰 재료를 준비하기 때문에 반드시 사전 예약해야 한다.

Poom Seoul

Poom Seoul serves up refined cuisine of a yangban class (the gentry of Joseon Dynasty) in a modernized way. They have two course menus for lunch and three for dinner. A special meal for a diabetic is available as well. You can enjoy fresh seasonal ingredients and exquisite presentation on the table is another pleasure from this restaurant. A simple wine list is included on the menu as well as traditional Korean liquors well harmonized with their cuisines. Reservations are recommended, because ingredients vary depending on a guest's choice.

Address	용산구 두텁바위로60길 49, 3층	3F, 49, Duteopbawi-ro 60-gil, Yongsan-gu
Contact	02-777-9007	82-2-777-9007
Web	www.poomseoul.com	www.poomseoul.com
Operation	12:00~22:00(Break 15:00~18:00)	12:00~22:00(Break 15:00~18:00)
Closed	일요일	Sun

예당

정·재계 인사는 물론이고 연예인도 꾸준히 찾는다는 강남의 명소. 전통 한정식보다 현대적인 콘셉트를 가미한 특색 있는 요리 위주로 선보인다. '풀 내음 밥상', '정을 담은 밥상' 등 코스 요리의 이름조차 남다르다. 청포묵을 넓게 펴 채소를 말아넣고, 말린 귤을 샐러드에 넣는 등 특색 있는 요리 궁합이 많다. 이곳을 찾는 단골들이 추천하는 대표 메뉴는 단호박과 대추를 곁들인 갈비찜. 4명부터 30명까지 들어갈 수 있는 별실이 있으며, 한 층을 통째로 이용해 단체 모임을 열 수도 있다.

Yedang

Yedang, serving a modern, distinctive cuisine, is especially popular with celebrities and figures of the economic and political worlds. Its course menus have distinctive names such as a 'table full of verdant scent' or a 'table with a warm affection'. The most popular dish is Galbi-jjim added with sweet pumpkin and jujubes. It has a private dining room accommodating up to 30 guests and you can make reservations for the whole floor for a group meeting.

Address	강남구 언주로153길 5	5, Eonju-ro 153-gil, Gangnam-gu
Contact	02-563-5085	82-2-563-5085
Operation	11:30~21:30(Break 14:00~17:30)	11:30~21:30(Break 14:00~17:30)
Closed	토요일, 설·추석 연휴	Sat, Holiday of Lunar New Year's Day & Chuseok

삼청각 한식당

북악산 기슭에 자리한 삼청각 한식당은 서울의 비경을 감상하며 궁중 한정식을 즐길 수 있는 곳이다. 북악산 약수, 국산 콩, 직접 담근 재래식 장과 김치를 이용한 궁중 요리와 반가 요리는 현대인의 입맛을 고려했으며 채식주의자를 위한 코스 메뉴도 준비돼 있다. 임금님께 진상했다는 궁중 상차림이 유명하며, 8~12가지 코스 요리로 구성된다. 일곱 개의 별실을 갖추고 있어 긴밀한 대화를 나누는 장소로도 손색이 없다. 사전 예약은 필수다.

Address	성북구 대사관로 3
Contact	02-765-3700
Web	www.samcheonggak.or.kr
Operation	12:00~22:00(Break 15:00~18:00)
Closed	연중무휴

Samcheonggak Hansikdang

Samcheonggak 'Hansikdang', which is located at the foot of Mountain Bugak, is a nice place to appreciate picturesque scenery whilst you are enjoying royal Korean table d'hôte. It transforms cuisines for royal family and a yangban class (the gentry of Joseon Dynasty) into modernized dishes yet is still based on major native ingredients including a variety of jancs (traditional Korean sauces) and Kimchi. A course menu for a vegetarian is available too. This restaurant is especially known for a set menu of royal cuisine, consisting of 8 to 12 courses. Its private dining room is suitable for a private meeting. Reservation is required.

3, Daesagwan-ro, Seongbuk-gu
82-2-765-3700
www.samcheonggak.or.kr
12:00~22:00(Break 15:00~18:00)
Open all year round

큰기와집

반가 음식 전문점인 큰기와집은 처음 한국 음식을 접하는 외국인에게 소개하기 좋을 만큼 깔끔한 맛이 돋보인다. 좌식 룸과 테이블을 갖춰 바닥에 앉는 데 익숙하지 않은 외국인과 함께 찾기에도 부담 없다. 열 가지가 넘는 요리로 구성된 코스 한정식은 죽부터 갈비찜, 떡갈비만두, 청포묵무침, 전복구이, 단호박찜, 삼색전, 탕과 고기까지 구성진 한 상으로 이루어진다. 그러나 무엇보다 큰기와집을 더욱 유명하게 만든 주인공은 간장게장과 양념게장이다. 감칠맛 나는 게장에 반해 이곳을 찾는 외국인 관광객도 많다.

Address	종로구 북촌로5길 62
Contact	02-722-9024
Operation	11:30~21:00(Break 15:30~17:30)
Closed	연중무휴

Keungiwajib

This restaurant provides an excellent cuisine agreeable to anyone who tries Korean food for the first time. Other than floor tables usually used by this kind of restaurant, they have dining tables and chairs, more familiar to those from western culture. A table d'hôte course composed of more than 10 courses boasts a numerous kinds of Korean cuisine. But Ganjang Gejang (raw crab marinated in soy sauce) and Yangnyeom Gejang (also raw crab but marinated in spicy sauce) are the best contributors which attract foreign tourists.

62, Bukchon-ro 5-gil, Jongno-gu
82-2-722-9024
11:30~21:00(Break 15:30~17:30)
Open all year round

석파랑 / Seokparang

흥선대원군이 아끼던 여름 별장의 사랑채를 지금의 세검정으로 옮겨와 복원한 곳. 넓은 정원과 운치 있는 한옥이 고풍스러운 느낌을 자아내며 전통 궁중 음식을 선보인다. 담백한 맛과 정갈한 상차림이 이곳의 특징. 수라 어만두, 칠향계, 신선로 등 귀한 음식과 해남 진양주, 한산 소곡주 등 우리나라 고유의 전통주도 맛볼 수 있다. 놋그릇과 놋수저, 나전으로 나비 문양을 새긴 테이블까지 세심한 장식이 음식 맛까지 높인다.

Seokparang, which was Prince Daewongun's favorite place, was moved to Segeomjeong and then restored as at present. But its grand garden and refined old building still keep old feeling well. Seokparang's specialty is a traditional royal cuisine with fine taste and neat presentation. Sinseollo (royal hot pot) and traditional Korean liquors are available as well. Its brassware and table made with mother-of-pearl look distinguishing.

Address	종로구 자하문로 309	309, Jahamun-ro, Jongno-gu
Contact	02-395-2500	82-2-395-2500
Web	www.seokparang.co.kr	www.seokparang.co.kr
Operation	12:00~22:00(Break 15:00~18:00)	12:00~22:00(Break 15:00~18:00)
Closed	설 · 추석 연휴	Holiday of Lunar New Year's Day & Chuseok

한미리 / Hanmiri

38가지 천연 양념만 사용해 깊고 풍부한 맛이 나는 다양한 정찬을 인간문화재 이봉주 선생의 작품인 전통 놋그릇과 도자기에 정성스럽게 담아낸다. 푸짐하다 싶을 정도로 넉넉한 양과 은은하고 부드러운 맛이 특징. 다섯 가지 코스 요리가 있으며 각종 버섯에 조랭이떡, 들깻가루를 넣어 끓인 버섯 신선로는 직접 개발한 대표 메뉴로, 고소하고 진한 맛이 일품이다. 후식으로 곁들이는 두텁떡과 오미자차도 직접 만든다고. 상견례 장소로도 유명하다.

Hanmiri serves up their cuisine with a deep, rich taste coming from 38 natural seasonings, in brassware and porcelain dishes. A hearty quantity of their meals is one of the charms they have. On their menu are five course meals. Sinseollo (royal hot pot) with various mushrooms and other ingredients based on their self-developed recipe imparts a deeper flavor. This restaurant is also a popular place for a family meeting.

Address	강남구 영동대로 333(대치점)	333, Yeongdong-daero, Gangnam-gu
Contact	02-556-8688	82-2-556-8688
Web	www.hanmiri.co.kr	www.hanmiri.co.kr
Operation	11:30~22:00(Break 15:00~17:30)	11:30~22:00(Break 15:00~17:30)
Closed	신정, 설 · 추석 전날과 당일	New Year's Day, The eve and the day of Lunar New Year's Day & Chuseok

고메홈

한국 전통 약선 한정식 레스토랑 고메홈은 한의학 이론을 근거로 생약이나 약용 가치가 높은 재료를 조합한 메뉴를 선보인다. 가정집을 개조한 12개의 방과 작은 정원을 갖춰 고즈넉한 분위기가 장점이다. 한방 재료를 사용하지만 향과 맛이 은은해서 약선 요리를 처음 접하는 사람이나 외국인도 거부감이 들지 않는다. 맛이 강한 젓갈이나 장보다 유자청이나 매실청 등 천연 조미료를 사용해 담백함이 돋보인다. 간장게장 정식도 추천한다. 선물용으로 보리굴비를 포장 판매한다.

Gourmet-Home

Gourmet-Home's medicinal cuisine is based on medicinal and therapeutic ingredients of oriental medicine. It is placed at a remodeled traditional house with 12 rooms inside and a small garden outside which makes this restaurant look quiet and peaceful. They add oriental medicine ingredients into all the food, but to the extent that anyone who first tastes this medicinal food can enjoy it. Natural seasonings are the primary factor of light and plain taste. A table d'hôte with Ganjang Gejang is popular as well.

Address	강남구 삼성로75길 26-8	26-8, Samseong-ro 75-gil, Gangnam-gu
Contact	02-568-4595	82-2-568-4595
Operation	11:30~21:00(Break 14:30~17:00)	11:30~21:00(Break 14:30~17:00)
Closed	연중무휴	Open all year round

뉘조

일 년 내내 먹을 수 있는 야생초와 제철 야생초 등 수백 가지 재료로 만든 약선 요리 전문점. 호박죽부터 10여 가지 야생초를 버무린 시절무침, 씹는 질감이 식욕을 자극하는 뿌리범벅, 홍보쌈과 편육 등이 차례로 나온다. 그중에서도 계절 나물을 버무린 시절무침이 이 집 메인 메뉴. 야생초 효소로 만든 드레싱을 사용해 음식에서 풍성한 향이 난다. 음식이 나올 때마다 직원들이 재료에 대해 자세히 설명해 궁금증을 해소해주며, 한국 문화에 익숙한 외국인 손님들이 즐겨 찾는다.

Nwijo

Another restaurant well-known for medicinal cuisines added with hundreds of ingredients. Their course meal consists of Hobak Juk (pumpkin porridge), dozens of wild grass seasoned in various way and then Hongbossam (boiled pork in cabbage wraps) and Pyeonyuk (boiled meat slices). The dressing made from wild grass enzyme gives off rich, flavorful scent. They provide a detailed explanation for each dish. This place is popular with foreign guests accustomed to Korean culture.

Address	종로구 인사동14길 27	27, Insadong 14-gil, Jongno-gu
Contact	02-730-9301	82-2-730-9301
Operation	11:30~22:00(Break 16:00~17:00)	11:30~22:00(Break 16:00~17:00)
Closed	설·추석 전날과 당일	The eve and the day of Lunar New Year's Day & Chuseok

그릴

한국을 찾은 외국인들이 가장 인상적인 한국 음식으로 꼽는 것이 불고기와 생갈비다. 나라에 따라 선호하는 육질과 양념이 다른데, 일본인은 담백한 생고기와 생갈비를 주로 찾고, 북미나 유럽인은 양념갈비와 불고기 등을 선호한다. 비즈니스 미팅을 위한 자리라면 생갈비에 레드 와인을 곁들여 좀 더 고급스러운 분위기를 연출해보자. 와인은 갈비는 물론 밑반찬과도 잘 어울린다.

GRILL & BARBEQUE

Foreigners in Korea say that Bulgogi (meat marinated in soy sauce) and Saenggalbi (non-marinated meat) are the most impressive Korean food. Unseasoned grilled meat is preferred by Japanese and seasoned or marinated one is popular with North Americans and Europeans. Ribs on s grill and a bottle of red wine would be the best combination for a formal business meeting.

한우리

한우 샤부샤부와 꽃등심으로 유명한 레스토랑. 단아한 분위기와 고급스러운 인테리어 덕분에 격식을 차려야 하는 자리에 어울린다. 전통 한정식의 틀을 유지하면서 천연 식재료를 사용해 신선하고 영양가 높은 음식을 마련한다. 로스편채와 쇠고기 버섯 국수전골, 평양냉면 등도 재료의 풍미를 그대로 살린 담백한 맛이 일품이다.

Hanwoori

Korean Beef Shabu-Shabu and Kkotdeungsim are most famous. Its elegant ambiance and luxury interiors seem to be good for a formal meeting. Fresh and nutritious cuisine is served in a form of traditional table d'hôte. Roseu Pyeonchae (pan-fried beef with vegetables), Hot Pot with Beef, Mushroom and Noodle and Pyeongyang Naengmyeon (Pyeongyang style cold noodles) are excellent as well with natural, rich taste of ingredients.

Address	강남구 도산대로 304(본점)	304, Dosan-daero, Gangnam-gu
Contact	02-545-3334	82-2-545-3334
Web	www.hwrfood.com	www.hwrfood.com
Operation	11:30~22:00	11:30~22:00
Closed	설 · 추석 연휴	Holiday of Lunar New Year's Day & Chuseok

로즈힐

'갈비와 와인'이라는 콘셉트를 선보이는 고급 바비큐 레스토랑으로 예약제로만 판매하는 질 좋은 한우 생갈비가 대표 메뉴다. 강원도 횡성과 전라도 순천에서 공수한 최상급 한우만을 고집한다. 특히 일반 등심보다 두 배 두껍게 썬 등심에 코냑을 뿌려 풍미를 더한 '코냑 등심'은 살살 녹는 육질이 일품인 한국식 퓨전 스테이크로 외국인 손님에게 인기 있다. 시원하고 아삭한 개성 보쌈김치와 함께 먹으면 개운하다.

Rosehill

Rosehill, whose concept is a mariage of Galbi and wine, is a high-class barbeque restaurant. Its unmarinated Saeng Galbi is available only when you make reservations in advance. Its premium Korean beef comes from Hoengseong and Suncheon, famous regions of quality Korean beef. Cognac Deungsim (sirloin with cognac sauce), which is a fusion steak cooked by sprinkling cognac on the sirloin thicker than usual, is especially foreigner's favorite. Gaeseong Bossam Kimchi (wrapped kimchi) would enhance the flavor of it.

Address	강남구 테헤란로 152 지하 1층	B1F, 152, Teheran-ro, Gangnam-gu
Contact	02-508-2090	82-2-508-2090
Web	www.irosehill.co.kr	www.irosehill.co.kr
Operation	11:30~21:30(Break 14:30~17:30)	11:30~21:30(Break 14:30~17:30)
Closed	설·추석 연휴	Holiday of Lunar New Year's Day & Chuseok

명월관

쉐라톤 그랜드 워커힐 내에 자리한 숯불구이 전문점. 바깥 테라스가 있어 여름에는 한강을 바라보며 이국적인 바비큐 파티를 즐길 수 있다. 호텔에서 운영하는 곳답게 깔끔한 개인용 테이블 세팅과 친절한 서비스가 돋보인다. 참숯으로 굽는 생갈비가 베스트 메뉴이며, 달지 않은 양념갈비도 인기 있다.

Myongwolgwan

In the summertime, an open-air terrace of Myoungwolgwan looking over a great view of the Han River is a good place to hold an exotic barbeque party. Its best menu is Saeng Galbi (unmarinated grill beef) grilled over a hardwood charcoal fire and Yangnyeom Galbi (marinated grilled beef) is popular as well. The friendly service of its staff is also nice.

Address	광진구 워커힐로 177	177, Walkerhill-ro, Gwangjin-gu
Contact	02-450-4595	82-2-450-4595
Web	www.sheratonwalkerhill.co.kr	www.sheratonwalkerhill.co.kr
Operation	12:00~21:30	12:00~21:30
Closed	연중무휴	Open all year round

삼원가든

성수대교 남단에 있는 삼원가든은 1976년 개업한 유서 깊은 한정식집이다. 돌솥밥, 떡갈비 정식, 매운 갈비, 한우 모둠 세트 등이 돋보인다. 생등심, 로스편채, 양념갈비 등이 대표 메뉴이며 명절에는 한우 선물 세트를 선보인다. 식사 후 물레방아와 폭포가 인상적인 정원을 산책하는 재미도 쏠쏠하다. 소규모 하우스 웨딩이나 돌잔치, 프라이빗 파티 공간으로도 손색없다. 200석 규모의 메인 홀, 한식 온돌방, 작은 모임을 위한 소규모 연회석 등 성격에 따라 자리를 고를 수 있다. 외국 바이어 접대뿐 아니라 가족 외식에도 적합한 음식점이다.

Samwon Garden

Samwon Garden dates back to 1976. Dolsotbap (hot pot rice), Table d'hôte with Tteok Galbi (grilled short rib patties), Spicy Galbi and Assorted Korean beef are their main dishes. Saeng Deungsim (unmarinated beef sirloin), Roseu Pyeonchae (pan-fried beef with vegetables) and Yangnyeom Galbi (marinated grilled beef) are especially popular and a Korean beef gift set is available for Closed. It would be nice to walk in a garden with a water mill and a cascade. This restaurant is recommendable for a formal business as well as a family event such as a small house wedding or first-birthday party.

Address	강남구 언주로 835
Contact	02-548-3030
Web	www.samwongarden.com
Operation	11:50~22:00
Closed	연중무휴

	835, Eonju-ro, Gangnam-gu
	82-2-548-3030
	www.samwongarden.com
	11:50~22:00
	Open all year round

벽제갈비

일반 고깃집에서는 느끼기 힘든 우아한 인테리어와 와인 바를 연상시키는 방대한 와인 리스트로 눈길을 끈다. 〈월스트리트 저널〉의 '아시아 5대 음식'에 선정된 곳인 만큼 외국인들에게 소개하기 좋다. 저녁에 찾는다면 고기와 함께 식사를 즐길 수 있는 코스 요리를 주문해보자.

Byeokje Galbi

Remarkable is its elegant interior design not common in an ordinary barbecue restaurant. Its extensive wine list is also astonishing. This place has been selected as one of the '5 Asian cuisines' by the Wall Street Journal. A course menu serving both meat dish and meal together is great for dinner.

Address	강남구 언주로30길 26
Contact	02-2058-3535
Web	www.ibjgalbi.com
Operation	11:30~22:00
Closed	연중무휴

	26, Eonju-ro 30-gil, Gangnam-gu
	82-2-2058-3535
	www.ibjgalbi.com
	11:30~22:00
	Open all year round

그릴 H

한국식 숯불구이와 서양식 스테이크를 한자리에서 즐길 수 있는 퓨전 그릴 레스토랑. 한국과 서양의 고기구이 문화를 비교해볼 수 있다. 스테이크를 먹은 후 동치미 국물로 맛을 낸 시원한 냉면으로 입가심하면 개운하다. 스테이크는 500℃ 이상의 화덕에서, 최상급 한우 등심은 무연 직화 테이블에서 구워 낸다.

Grill H

A fusion grill house you can enjoy an original steak and Korean charcoal-grilled beef and see the differences between two styles. A bowl of Naengmyeon (cold noodles) flavored with Dongchimi (radish water kimchi) would refresh your mouth after eating steak. The wood oven beyond 500 degrees Celsius is used for steak while a Korean premium beef is grilled on the smokeless, direct gas-fired table.

Address	강남구 도산대로 439, 8층
Contact	02-3446-5547
Web	www.grillh.com
Operation	11:30~22:00(Break 15:00~18:00)
Closed	설·추석 연휴

Address	8F, 439, Dosan-daero, Gangnam-gu
Contact	82-2-3446-5547
Web	www.grillh.com
Operation	11:30~22:00(Break 15:00~18:00)
Closed	Holiday of Lunar New Year's Day & Chuseok

버드나무집

30년 이상 한결같이 최상급 한우를 선보이는 고깃집. 한우 암소의 등심과 천연 양념이 어우러진 주물럭이 대표 메뉴다. 연한 암소 갈비에 칼집을 내 구우며 특수 부위인 제비추리도 맛볼 수 있다.

Budnamujip

For more than 30 years, they have served a Korean premium beef. Jumulleok (grilled short steak), made with sirloin and natural seasonings, is most popular. Neck chain, a special beef cut, is also available.

Address	서초구 효령로 434(서초동 본점)
Contact	02-3473-4167
Web	www.budnamujip.com
Operation	11:30~22:00
Closed	연중무휴

Address	434, Hyoryeong-ro, Seocho-gu
Contact	82-2-3473-4167
Web	www.budnamujip.com
Operation	11:30~22:00
Closed	Open all year round

사리원

양념한 고기와 버섯, 채소를 익혀 먹는 야채불고기, 사골을 고아 만든 육수에 고기를 재워 양념한 육수불고기 등이 인기 메뉴이며 3대째 전해 내려온 비법으로 만든다. 12가지 과일과 야채즙으로 만든 소스의 은근한 단맛이 고기와 잘 어우러진다.

Sariwon

A marinated beef broiled with mushrooms and vegetables and a beef marinated in ox bone broth are popular. They use recipes that have been handed down through three generations. Its specific house sauce, which is made by mixing 12 fruits and vegetable juice, is wonderfully harmonized with beef.

Address	강남구 남부순환로 2712(도곡점)
Contact	02-573-2202
Web	www.sariwon.co.kr
Operation	11:30~22:00
Closed	연중무휴

	2712, Nambusunhwan-ro, Gangnam-gu
	82-2-573-2202
	www.sariwon.co.kr
	11:30~22:00
	Open all year round

우래옥

쇠고기만으로 우려낸 육수와 메밀면의 구수함이 매력적인 우래옥은 전통 평양냉면으로 유명하다. 자고로 냉면은 동판에 구운 불고기와 함께 먹을 때 환상적인 맛의 조화를 이루는 법. 불고기는 2인 이상 주문이 가능하며, 가격은 3만 원대다.

Uraeok

A well-known restaurant for its traditional cold noodle, Pyeongyang Naengmyeon. Its delicate flavor from beef broth and buckwheat noodle is great and when you try it with Bulgogi (grilled meat), you would find that Naengmyeon enhance the taste of Bulgogi. But Bulgogi is available only when you order more than 2 person's portion.

Address	중구 창경궁로 62-29(본점)
Contact	02-2265-0151
Web	우래옥주교점.com
Operation	11:30~21:30
Closed	월요일

	62-29, Changgyeonggung-ro, Jung-gu
	82-2-2265-0151
	11:30~21:30
	Mon

캐주얼 모던

파스타집 일색이던 압구정동과 청담동, 가로수길에 '밥집'이 생겼다는 소식이 심심찮게 들려온다. 양식당도 고급 레스토랑과 캐주얼한 비스트로가 있듯 한식당에도 비스트로 같은 캐주얼 모던 바람이 불고 있다. 맛은 정통을 유지하되 담음새와 식기, 테이블 세팅에 현대적인 감각을 더한 것. 와인 한잔을 곁들이기에도 잘 어울리는 세련된 공간이다.

CASUAL MODERN

Around Apgujeong, Cheongdam and Garosu-gil where were formerly dotted with Italian restaurants, Korean modern bistros are starting to spring up, which has form a kind of trend in culinary scenery. These restaurants keep an authentic taste of their food but use a modern table setting with stylish tableware. They are also a nice place to enjoy a glass of wine with their meals.

개화옥

개화옥은 가장 멋스럽게 한식을 즐길 수 있는 곳으로 정평이 나 있다. 경기와 호남 지방의 반가 음식을 요즘 사람들의 입맛에 맞춰 내며, 질 좋은 등심으로 만든 불고기와 직접 만든 개화옥 순대는 담백한 맛이 으뜸이다. 된장국수와 김치말이국수, 제주도산 흑돼지로 만든 보쌈과 시원한 동치미 맛도 일품. 벽을 가득 채운 미술 작품과 도자기에 정갈하게 담은 음식은 시각적인 아름다움도 전한다.

Gaewhaok

Probably the most stylish Korean restaurant. They serve traditional cuisines of Gyeonggi and Honam areas but adjust the flavor to young people's taste. Bulgogi using a premium sirloin and Sundae (Korean sausage) based on their own recipe are the best menu. Other cuisines including diverse noodle dishes with variation in ingredients, Bossam (boiled pork) using Jeju black pork and Dongchimi (water based radish kimchi) offered as side dish are truly enjoyable.

Address	강남구 압구정로50길 7(1호점)		7, Apgujeong-ro 50-gil, Gangnam-gu
Contact	02-549-1459		82-2-549-1459
Web	www.gaewhaok.com		www.gaewhaok.com
Operation	24시간		24 hours
Closed	연중무휴		Open all year round

배상면주가

애주가들이 좋아할 만한 곳으로 인근 외국계 기업 직원들이 외국인 바이어와 미팅하기 위해 많이 찾는다. 은은한 조명과 깔끔하게 정돈된 인테리어가 현대적인 한국미를 물씬 풍긴다. 3월 냉이주, 6월 매실주, 9월 국화주, 12월 도소주 등 계절마다 한시적으로 세시주를 출시해 철 따라 즐기던 선조들의 술 문화를 느낄 수 있다. 점심때는 식사만 할 수도 있는데 이때 활인 18품, 흑미주 등 다섯 가지 전통주 중 한 잔을 무료로 서비스한다.

Baesangmyun Brewery

A pub of Baesangmyun Brewery Company is popular as a business meeting place with foreign buyers. They release a special spirit called Sesiju each season. During lunch time, you can have a meal only but a glass of traditional liquor is served for free.

Address	서초구 강남대로27길 7-9(양재점)		7-9, Gangnam-daero 27-gil, Seocho-gu
Contact	02-579-7710		82-2-579-7710
Web	www.soolsool.co.kr		www.soolsool.co.kr
Operation	11:30~다음 날 01:00		11:30~The next day 01:00
Closed	일요일, 공휴일		Sun, Public Holidays

토담골

떡 벌어진 한 상 차림보다 소담한 가정식 백반을 선호하는 이들이 좋아할 만한 곳이다. 여주에서 직접 가져온 붉은 흙을 이용해 한국적 인테리어로 꾸몄으며, 소박한 항아리와 절구 등 전통 소품이 분위기를 더한다. 민속 주점과 한식집을 겸하는데 20여 가지 산나물로 맛을 내는 토담골 정식, 취쌈과 호박쌈 등 시골정취를 듬뿍 느낄 수 있는 꽁보리밥이 인기. 손맷돌로 직접 갈아 만든 녹두전이나 제육 굴보쌈 등은 술안주로 제격이다.

Todamgol

If you prefer a simple home-style cooking over a big table d'hôte, you would like this place. You can see Korea's unique charm through their interiors using red dirt brought from Yeoju and other traditional stuff like jars and a mortar. Todamgol Set Menu with around 20 vegetable side dishes is most popular and Kkongboribab (steamed barley rice) is famous. Nokdujeon (mung bean pancake) and Bossam (boiled pork) with oysters are also well matched with traditional liquors they offer.

Address	강남구 삼성로 766		766, Samseong-ro, Gangnam-gu
Contact	02-548-5115		82-2-548-5115
Operation	11:00~22:00		11:00~22:00
Closed	설 · 추석 연휴		Holiday of Lunar New Year's Day & Chuseok

민스키친

주인의 성을 따 이름 붙인 레스토랑으로 모던하고 심플한 카페 분위기에서 한식을 즐길 수 있다. 매콤한 고추장찌개와 청포묵무침, 비빔밥 같은 친숙한 가정식부터 된장 소스로 맛을 낸 삼겹살구이, 연어 무초말이, 파무침을 곁들인 닭안심 등 독특한 고기와 생선 요리를 맛볼 수 있다. 음식은 모두 정갈하게 담아내며 파티션으로 좌석을 나눠 조용한 분위기에서 식사할 수 있다.

Min's Kitchen

Taking the name from its chef, Kim Min-Ji, this restaurant serves up Korean cuisines in a modern, simple ambiance. Their menu shows great diversity, from home-style cuisine to beef, pork and fish dish. As each table has a divider, you can have your meal in a quiet and private space.

Address	강남구 도산대로45길 10-4(강남점)		10-4, Dosan-daero 45-gil, Gangnam-gu
Contact	02-544-1007		82-2-544-1007
Web	www.minskitchen.kr		www.minskitchen.kr
Operation	11:30~22:00(Break 15:00~17:30)		11:30~22:00(Break 15:00~17:30)
Closed	일요일		Sun

콩두

10년 넘게 모던 한식 레스토랑으로 사랑받아온 곳. 2013년 덕수궁으로 이전해 새로운 둥지를 틀었는데 맛은 물론이고 아름다운 인테리어로 미식가를 유혹한다. 콩두에서는 지역 장인이 만든 최고의 고추장, 된장, 국간장을 사용한다. 메뉴는 가격대와 음식 가짓수에 따라 초록빛 · 햇빛 · 물빛 코스로 구성된다. 전채 요리는 샐러드, 견과류로 맛을 낸 타락죽 등으로 비슷하지만 메인 메뉴는 선택의 폭이 넓다. 서산 바다에서 잡은 게장 정식, 은대구구이, 저온 숙성한 흑돼지구이, 연잎 흑돼지보쌈 등을 맛볼 수 있다. 한국의 프리미엄 전통주나 와인을 갖췄으며 자체 개발한 막걸리 칵테일도 선보인다.

Congdu

Congdu has served a modern Korean cuisine more than 10 years. In 2013, it moved to Deoksugung-gil and was been refurbished. The excellent flavor of their cuisines comes from a variety of Korean fermented sauces made by a master. Their menus are categorized into three course meals depending on its price and the number of plate. Wine and traditional premium liquors including their special Makgeolli cocktail is available as well.

Address	중구 덕수궁길 116-1	116-1, Deoksugung-gil, Jung-gu
Contact	02-722-7002	82-2-722-7002
Web	congdu.com	congdu.com
Operation	11:30~22:00	11:30~22:00
Closed	연중무휴	Open all year round

다담

정재덕 헤드 셰프의 정갈한 음식을 맛볼 수 있는 곳. 강릉 선교장에서 영감을 얻은 단아한 인테리어가 돋보인다. 전국 각지의 종가에서 전수된 집안 고유의 레시피와 발효 음식을 연구해 더욱 섬세하고 정교한 한식을 만든다. 철이 바뀔 때마다 새로운 메뉴가 등장하는데, 알이 꽉 찬 섬진강 참게의 살을 발라 게 국물과 달걀을 넣어 찐 뒤 알과 내장을 얹어 다시 한 번 찐 '참게 알찜'은 다담이 자랑하는 별미다. 각종 재료를 연꽃 위에 올린 '연꽃 구절판'은 흡사 예술 작품처럼 아름답다. 열 가지 내외의 음식으로 구성한 점심과 저녁 코스도 마련돼 있다.

Dadam

Based on study for traditional food recipes and Korean fermented food, they serve a more delicate and elaborate Korean cuisine. Each season, they present a new dish, among which Mitten Crab Roe Soufflé is considerably great. Plus, the dish like Lotus Platter of Nine Delicacies would please your eyes. They also have a course menu for both lunch and dinner, respectively consisting of around 10 courses.

Address	강남구 도산대로 445 지하 1층	B1F, 445, Dosan-daero, Gangnam-gu
Contact	02-518-6161	82-2-518-6161
Web	www.thedadam.co.kr	www.thedadam.co.kr
Operation	12:00~22:00(Break 15:00~18:00)	12:00~22:00(Break 15:00~18:00)
Closed	연중무휴	Open all year round

밍글스

"한식에 와인을 곁들여도, 서양 음식에 전통주를 곁들여도 어색하지 않은 식탁을 차리고 싶었어요." 밍글스의 강민구 셰프는 한국의 제철 자연 식재료에 서양식 조리법을 가미해 요리한다. 메뉴는 아뮤즈부슈와 애피타이저, 메인, 디저트로 구성하며 매달 바뀐다. 흑초와 다시마로 새콤하고 담백한 맛을 낸 푸아 그라, 찰옥수수의 쫀득한 맛을 함께 즐기는 먹물 리소토, 된장을 발라 숯불에 구운 양갈비, 송로버섯으로 풍미를 낸 장 등 어느 것 하나 쉽게 만든 메뉴가 없다. 도자 그릇과 소반으로 장식한 홀은 아늑한 분위기를 풍긴다.

Mingles

Chef Kang Min-Gu's dish uses seasonal Korean ingredients and his cooking technique is borrowed from western cultures. Mingles' menu is composed of amuse bouche, appetizer, main dish and dessert, which are changed each month. His sophisticated and delicate cuisines such as foie gras or lamb chop based on his specific recipes are totally impressive.

Address	강남구 선릉로 758 지하 1층	B1F, 758, Seolleung-ro, Gangnam-gu
Contact	02-515-7306	82-2-515-7306
Web	www.restaurant-mingles.com	www.restaurant-mingles.com
Operation	월~금 Mon to Fri 12:00~22:30(Break 15:00~18:00), 토 Sat 18:00~22:00	
Closed	일요일	Sun

류니끄

부산 출신 류태환 셰프가 일본, 호주, 영국에서 요리하다 돌아와 가로수길에 낸 레스토랑. 세이지, 로즈메리, 바질을 재배하는 미니 가든을 지나 레스토랑에 들어서면 널찍한 홀과 분주한 오픈 키친이 한눈에 들어온다. 류니끄의 메뉴는 시즌에 따라 테마가 달라지는 것이 특징. 김치로 만든 퓌레, 간장에 절인 골뱅이, 페이스트리로 감싼 인절미, 자색 고구마로 만든 와플 등의 메뉴를 류태환 셰프가 장을 보면서, 여행하면서, 책을 보면서 영감을 얻은 것이라고. 메인 요리를 고를 수 있는 런치 세트와 디너 코스, 한입거리 음식과 빵, 날생선, 앙트레, 메인 요리로 구성한 테이스팅 메뉴가 있다.

Ryunique

Chef Ryu Tae-Hwan, who worked as a chef in Japan, Australia and England, came back to Korea and settled in Garosu-gil. Ryunique changes its theme each season. He says his unique and unusual recipes are based on inspiration he gets during grocery shopping, traveling or reading. Ryunique has lunch and dinner courses, also offering tasting menus.

Address	강남구 강남대로162길 40	40, Gangnam-daero 162-gil, Gangnam-gu
Contact	02-546-9279	82-2-546-9279
Web	www.ryunique.co.kr	www.ryunique.co.kr
Operation	12:00~22:30(Break 15:30~18:00)	12:00~22:30(Break 15:30~18:00)
Closed	연중무휴	Open all year round

채식

비빔밥을 비롯한 전통 한식은 갖가지 나물, 버섯, 두부 등을 주로 사용하므로 채식 요리로도 퍽 잘 어울린다. 특히 사찰 음식점이나 두부 전문점 등 특화된 한국식 채식 레스토랑은 외국인의 입맛을 사로잡을 만하다. 채식주의자에게 자신 있게 소개할 만한 서울의 대표적인 채식 메뉴와 레스토랑 일곱 곳.

VEGETARIAN MEALS

Traditional Korean cuisines also become good vegetarian meals as various vegetables are used in their recipes. In particular, Buddhist temple cuisine and food of tofu restaurants would be well accepted by a foreigner's taste.

풀향기

각종 꽃과 나무를 심은 앞마당을 지나 한지와 황토로 꾸민 실내장식을 마주하는 것만으로도 푸근한 느낌이 든다. 입구에서부터 눈길을 끄는 크고 작은 항아리에는 전국 각지에서 엄선한 콩과 고추로 만든 간장, 된장, 고추장이 담겨 있다. 이곳 음식의 대부분은 재료 본연의 맛과 향을 느낄 수 있도록 천연 조미료로 간하는 것이 특징. 산나물 전문점으로 시작했지만 육류요리를 추가하면서 전통 한정식과 궁중 요리 메뉴까지 갖추었다. 채식주의자나 한국 문화에 관심이 많은 이들과 함께 찾기에 적합하다.

Pulhyanggi

Large jars you can see at the entrance contain assorted fermented sauces made from carefully selected soy beans and chili peppers. Natural seasonings are used for most cuisine of this restaurant to emphasize taste and smell of each ingredient and material. It was started as a vegetable cuisine restaurant first but now serves Korean table d'hôte and royal cuisine as well with some meat dishes.

Address	용산구 한남대로 146(한남점)	146, Hannam-daero, Yongsan-gu
Contact	02-796-3490	82-2-796-3490
Web	www.pulhyanggi.co.kr	www.pulhyanggi.co.kr
Operation	11:30~22:00	11:30~22:00
Closed	설 · 추석 연휴	Holiday of Lunar New Year's Day & Chuseok

산촌

인공 조미료를 배제하고 마늘, 파, 달래, 부추, 흥거 등 다섯 가지 양념 겸 채소인 '오신채'를 사용하지 않으며 사찰 음식의 전통대로 김치 외에는 고춧가루도 삼간다. 이곳 음식에 익숙하지 않은 이들은 밋밋하다고 말할 정도. 일곱 가지 야생 나물을 각기 다른 양념으로 무친 산채 모둠나물, 당면에 버섯, 우엉, 목이버섯, 푸른 나물 등을 넣어 만든 잡채와 제철 재료로 만든 튀김, 전 등이 인기 있다. 저녁에는 공연도 펼쳐 외국인 손님에게 한국 문화를 알려주기에 적합하다.

Sanchon

In principle, it is not allowed to use five pungent vegetables (spring onions, garlic, chives, green onions and leeks) in temple food. Sanchon, however, allows them for general customer's taste but still does not use artificial additives and limits use of chili pepper power as well except kimchi. This may make some people feel that their food is a little too plain and simple. An evening performance provided in this restaurant would be a good opportunity for foreigners to glance Korean culture.

Address	종로구 인사동길 30-13	30-13, Insadong-gil, Jongno-gu
Contact	02-735-0312	82-2-735-0312
Web	www.sanchon.com	www.sanchon.com
Operation	12:00~22:00	12:00~22:00
Closed	설 · 추석 연휴	Holiday of Lunar New Year's Day & Chuseok

소선재

산야초와 10년 묵은 약된장을 이용한 한식 코스 요리로 유명하다. 철 따라 산과 들에서 나는 열매와 꽃으로 만든 효소를 양념으로 쓰기에 음식을 먹은 뒤 속이 편안하고 개운하다. 산나물로 담근 장아찌를 갈아 넣은 버섯 비빔밥, 전통 떡갈비구이 등이 있다. 단아한 담음새와 깔끔한 맛 덕분에 일본인 관광객도 많이 찾는다. 한옥 특유의 아늑함을 최대한 살린 인테리어도 돋보인다.

Soseonjae

A course meal using wild grass and 10 year-old mild soybean paste is their specialty. They use various wild fruits and flowers for their stomach-friendly sauce, which would be good for your digestion. A neat presentation and distinguishing taste of their meals are especially preferred by Japanese. Its interior design maximizing Hanok's own beauty is great.

Address	종로구 삼청로 113-1	113-1, Samcheong-ro, Jongno-gu
Contact	02-730-7002	82-2-730-7002
Operation	11:00~21:30(Break 15:00~17:00)	11:00~21:30(Break 15:00~17:00)
Closed	연중무휴	Open all year round

백년옥

예술의전당 맞은편에 있는 백년옥은 강원도에서 키운 콩으로 만든 순두부로 유명한 곳이다. 맷돌로 간 자연식 순두부는 인공 조미료는 물론 고춧가루 등 양념을 넣지 않아 우윳빛이 감돈다. 순두부와 콩비지 요리부터 들깨순두부, 두부비빔밥, 뚝배기순두부 등 다양한 두부 요리와 부침개, 팥칼국수 등을 맛볼 수 있다. 김치와 콩나물무침, 미역무침, 무생채와 깻잎 등이 기본 반찬으로 나온다. 현관 앞에서 두부를 만들고 남은 콩비지를 봉투에 담아 무료로 나눠주기도 한다. 종일 붐비는 편이라 편한 사람들과 간편하게 식사할 때 찾기를 권한다.

Baeknyeonok

This restaurant, which is located across the street from Seoul Arts Center, is well known for its soft tofu that shows milky-white color as it is made in a natural way using a millstone but excludes chili pepper powders from it. You can find a variety of tofu cuisine such as soft tofu and pureed soybean stew on the menu along with Korean pancake and red bean noodle soup. Note that this place is always crowded with many people and thus would be more appropriate for casual dining.

Address	서초구 남부순환로 2407
Contact	02-523-2860
Operation	10:00~22:00
Closed	설 · 추석 연휴

	2407, Nambusunhwan-ro, Seocho-gu
	82-2-523-2860
	10:00~22:00
	Open all year round

온마을 두부

하루가 다르게 카페와 레스토랑이 새롭게 문을 여는 삼청동길 끝자락에 있는 온마을 두부는 삼청동이 알려지기 전부터 자리 잡은 터줏대감이다. 자체적으로 작은 두부 공장을 두고 매일 직접 두부를 만든다. 온마을 두부의 별미는 두부젓국찌개와 서리태콩두부. 두부젓국찌개는 새우젓으로만 간하고 명란젓을 올리는데 양념이 진하지 않아 두부의 담백한 맛을 느낄 수 있다. 소박한 인테리어에 가격도 저렴한 편이다.

Onmaeul Dubu

It is an old eatery placed at the end of Samcheong-dong-gil, long before Samcheongdong became one of the popular places in Seoul. This restaurant has its own small tofu factory that produces fresh tofu every day. You can enjoy fresh taste of various tofu cuisines in a reasonable price.

Address	종로구 삼청로 127
Contact	02-738-4231
Operation	11:00~21:00
Closed	설 · 추석 연휴

	127, Samcheong-ro, Jongno-gu
	82-2-738-4231
	11:00~21:00
	Holiday of Lunar New Year's Day & Chuseok

채근담

전통 사찰 음식과 각 지역의 특산물을 이용한 채식을 맛볼 수 있는 곳. 실내는 오방색과 전래 민화를 모티브로 차분하게 꾸몄다. 채식주의자를 위한 코스 요리와 육식을 포함한 코스 요리를 따로 선보이고 있으며, 젓갈류나 향신료를 절제하고 담백하게 요리한다. 전통주와 와인 등 채식 상차림과 곁들이기 좋은 술도 구비하고 있으며 상견례 장소로 인기가 좋다.

Chaegundaam

Chaegundaam serves up traditional temple foods and vegetarian meals made with indigenous ingredients from each region in Korea. In this restaurant, you can see the interior decorated with Obangsaek and old Korean folk paintings. On their menu, there are course meals both for vegetarians and non-vegetarians, for which use of jeotgal (salted seafood) and spices are limited. They also serve traditional alcohol beverage and wine which would go well with vegetarian meals. With all these merits, Chaegundaam is popular as a meeting place between families of the bride and the bridegroom before their marriage.

Address	강남구 역삼로98길	23, Yeoksam-ro 98-gil, Gangnam-gu
Contact	02-555-9173	82-2-555-9173
Web	www.chaegundaam.com	www.chaegundaam.com
Operation	12:00~22:00(Break 14:30~18:00)	12:00~22:00(Break 14:30~18:00)
Closed	설·추석 연휴	Holiday of Lunar New Year's Day & Chuseok

고상

사찰 음식을 현대인의 입맛에 맞춰 선보이는 곳. '음식은 청결하고 부드러우며 법도에 맞아야 한다'는 '삼덕三德'을 기본 철학으로 한다. 이곳의 음식은 마늘, 파, 부추, 달래, 흥거 등 오신채를 사용하지 않아 뒷맛이 깔끔하다. 계절별로 다르게 준비되는 주전부리, 주방장이 엄선한 재료로 만든 건강죽인 약선죽, 항암효과가 뛰어난 버섯으로 만든 건강탕인 열구자탕 등 건강식을 맛볼 수 있다.

Gosang

This restaurant serves a Buddhist temple food changed to make it more palatable to general people these days, based on the principle of 'Three Virtues,' meaning cleanliness, softness and thoroughness of food and food preparation. For a fresh aftertaste, they do not use five pungent spices (spring onions, garlic, chives, green onions and leeks). Diverse healthy dishes such as refreshment prepared with seasonal ingredients, medicinal herb porridge made with ingredients strictly selected by a chef and royal chafing dish using mushrooms with anti-cancer effect are available in this place.

Address	중구 을지로5길 26 지하 2층	B2F, 26, Eulji-ro 5-gil, Jung-gu
Contact	02-6030-8955	82-2-6030-8955
Web	www.baru-gosang.com	www.baru-gosang.com
Operation	월~토 Mon to Sat 11:30~22:00(Break 15:00~17:00), 일 Sun 11:30~21:00	
Closed	설·추석 당일	Day of Lunar New Year's Day & Chuseok

향토 음식

고춧가루와 젓갈로 양념한 맛깔스러운 전라도 음식과 맵고 짠맛이 강한 경상도 음식, 된장으로 간을 맞추는 충청도 음식은 같은 재료를 쓰더라도 확연히 다른 맛을 낸다. 지방으로 일일이 찾아가기 어렵다면 각 지역 요리가 총집합한 서울에서 대표적인 향토 음식점을 찾아보자.

LOCAL DISHES

In Jeolla Province food is flavored with a wide range of seasonings and in Gyeongsang Province you can experience hot and salty taste from their food. In Chungcheong Province, people season their food with soybean paste, which make the taste obviously different from other provinces. For you who cannot go to each region to taste its food, we have listed some local food restaurants in Seoul.

전원

규모가 작지만 예약하지 않으면 자리가 없을 정도로 단골이 많다. 경상남도 진해 출신인 이곳 대표는 해산물을 주재료로 한 부산 요리를 선보인다. 점심에는 된장찌개와 생선구이, 쌈을 기본으로 갖가지 반찬이 나온다. 저녁에는 신선한 제철 재료로 만든 요리를 메인으로 매일 다른 메뉴를 선보인다. 신발을 벗고 올라가는 2층은 계단과 앉는 자리가 협소해 체구가 큰 외국인 손님이라면 불편할 수도 있다.

Jeonwon

This restaurant is so small and crowded that reservations are required. Its owner, who was born in Jinhae, South Gyeongsang Province, serves up cuisines of Busan, whose primary ingredient is seafood. For lunch, bean paste stew and grilled fish are on the table with various side dishes. For dinner, food using fresh seasonal ingredients is offered as a main dish, but the menu is changed every day. You would take off your shoes on the second floor, where is relatively small.

Address	중구 동호로 284	284, Dongho-ro, Jung-gu	
Contact	02-2278-3096	82-2-2278-3096	
Operation	12:00~22:00	12:00~22:00	
Closed	토·일요일	Sat & Sun	

무돌

무등산의 옛 이름을 딴 무돌은 남도 향토 음식 전문점이다. 알맞게 익은 김치와 홍어, 돼지고기를 함께 먹는 삼합, 싱싱한 낙지와 육회가 조화를 이루는 육낙무침, 연한 갈비와 쫄깃쫄깃한 낙지가 감칠맛 나는 갈낙탕, 비린내가 전혀 나지 않는 고등어 김치조림, 연포탕 등 전라남도의 갖가지 메뉴를 갖췄다. 간장에 졸인 백김치, 완도산 감태, 다시마무침 등 밑반찬도 맛깔스럽다. 남도 음식의 기본인 낙지젓, 새우젓, 조기젓도 기본으로 나온다.

Mudol

Mudol's specialty is local food of South Jeolla Province, such as Samhap (the fermented skate, steamed port slices and kimchi) or Yuknakmuchim (longarm octopus mixed with raw beef, soup of beef rib and longarm octopus, mackerel braised with kimchi and octopus soup). Many side dishes provide excellent flavors as well. Several kinds of jeotgal (salted seafood) are basically served on the table.

Address	강남구 선릉로 748	748, Seolleung-ro, Gangnam-gu
Contact	02-515-3088	82-2-515-3088
Operation	11:30~23:00	11:30~23:00
Closed	일요일, 설·추석 연휴	Sun, Holiday of Lunar New Year's Day & Chuseok

제주항

한국 사람이 가장 좋아하는 생선이 갈치와 고등어일 것이다. 집에서도 쉽게 해 먹을 수 있지만 숯불이나 석쇠로 조리한 구이나 맛깔스럽게 끓인 조림은 제주 요리 전문점에서 먹는 편이 확실히 맛있다. 제주항은 제주도에서 잡은 은갈치와 고등어를 당일 비행기로 직송해 싱싱한 맛을 보장한다. 생선 상태가 좋은 날에는 생선회나 초절임도 맛볼 수 있다. 특히 22가지 재료로 만든 양념 맛이 일품인 갈치조림과 고등어조림은 큼지막한 생선과 함께 무, 호박, 고구마 등을 듬뿍 넣어 매콤하면서도 시원한 맛을 낸다.

Jeju Hang

This restaurant is serving cutlass fish and mackerel caught in Jeju and then delivered through flight on the same day. If fish is fresh enough, sashimi and pickled fish would be available. A braised cutlass fish and braised mackerel, which are flavored with a special sauce made from 22 ingredients, would taste a little spicy but white radish, pumpkin and sweet potato accompanied in them would refresh your taste.

Address	강남구 언주로 811(신사점)
Contact	02-512-7071
Operation	월~금 11:30~22:30, 토·일 11:30~22:00
Closed	설 · 추석 당일

	811, Eonju-ro, Gangnam-gu
	82-2-512-7071
	Mon to Fri 11:30~23:00, Sat & Sun 11:30~22:00
	Day of Lunar New Year's Day & Chuseok

해남천일관

유홍준 교수가 《나의 문화유산 답사기》에서 극찬한 남도 음식점 '천일식당'의 진가를 서울에 재현한 곳. 천일식당 주인의 딸이 운영하는 해남천일관에서는 해남 음식을 그대로 선보인다. 갈빗살을 다진 뒤 갖은 양념을 더해 숯불에서 구운 떡갈비부터 마른 굴비구이, 삼합 등 이곳에서만 맛볼 수 있는 음식은 특유의 싱싱한 맛이 살아 있다. 갓김치, 파김치, 열무김치, 묵은 배추김치 등 갖가지 김치에 토하젓, 톳, 돔배젓, 갈치속젓, 밴댕이젓, 황석어젓 등 제철 젓갈을 기본 반찬으로 내는 한 상 차림을 보면 넉넉한 인심까지 짐작할 수 있다.

Haenam Cheonilgwan

Cheonilgan realizes the authentic taste of 'Cheonil', which is the southern Korean restaurant, highly acclaimed by Professor Yu Hong-June in his book 《My Exploration of Cultural Heritage》. Grilled short rib patties, grilled dried yellow corvina and samhap fully keep distinctive flavors of this restaurant. Side dishes including assorted kimchi and seasonal jeotgal (salted seafood) would also satisfy your mouth.

Address	강남구 테헤란로13길 21
Contact	02-568-7775
Web	www.해남천일관.kr
Operation	11:30~21:30(Break 15:00~17:00)
Closed	일요일

	21, Teheran-ro 13-gil, Gangnam-gu
	82-2-568-7775
	11:30~21:30(Break 15:00~17:00)
	Sun

별미

격식을 차린 한정식과 지방색을 살린 반가 요리뿐 아니라 서민의 애환이 담긴 '별미' 역시 빼놓을 수 없는 한식이다. 여름 보양식으로 으뜸인 삼계탕과 추운 겨울 몸을 녹여주는 단팥죽 한 그릇, 설렁탕과 곰탕 한 그릇이면 푸짐하고 맛깔 나는 한국의 맛을 제대로 전달할 수 있을 것이다. 다만 한국을 처음 찾은 이에게는 지나치게 소박한 인테리어와 상차림이 성의 없어 보일 수 있으니 한식을 많이 먹어본 이와 함께하는 것이 좋다.

OTHER DELICACIES

Korean cuisine does not always mean a formal table d'hôte or exquisite food of the royal family and the local gentry. Various delicacies usually enjoyed by ordinary people take up a considerable part of the Korean cuisine. Samgyetang (chicken soup with ginseng) to invigorate your weary body in the summertime, Danpatjuk (sweet red bean soup) to keep you warm in a cold weather and Seolleongtang or Gomtang (traditional beef soup), all of these foods keep Korea's own taste in them very well.

토속촌 삼계탕

서촌의 터줏대감 토속촌은 약이 되는 한국 음식인 삼계탕을 선보인다. 전통 한옥을 개조해 입구부터 눈길을 끈다. 살이 보드라운 영계에 들깻가루와 호박씨, 흑임자 등 약재와 견과류를 듬뿍 넣어 푹 끓여 고소하고 진한 맛이 일품이다. 청와대 근처라는 지리적 특성상 정치인들 사이에서도 보양식으로 인기를 끈다. 기름기를 쏙 뺀 전기구이 통닭도 맛볼 수 있다.

Tosokchon Samgyetang

Its specialty, Samgyetang, is the healing food in the summertime. A tender pullet boiled with various medicinal herbs and nuts in a pot for a long time is always fantastic. As it is located closed to Cheongwadae (the Blue House), politicians are primary customers. A non-greasy rotisserie chicken is also a popular dish.

Address	종로구 자하문로5길 5	5, Jahamun-ro 5-gil, Jongno-gu
Contact	02-737-7444	82-2-737-7444
Operation	10:00~22:00	10:00~22:00
Closed	연중무휴	Open all year round

자하손만두

부암동의 여유로운 전경을 내려다보며 형형색색 얌전하게 빚은 만두로 만든 만둣국과 만두전골을 맛볼 수 있는 곳. 고즈넉한 분위기와 가정집을 개조해 꾸민 푸근한 내부가 잘 어우러진다. 조랭이떡을 넣은 떡만둣국, 쇠고기와 표고버섯, 숙주로 맛을 낸 여름 메뉴인 편수만두 등 자칫 평범할 수 있는 만두를 제대로 즐길 수 있다. 맵지 않은 양배추김치와 식후에 나오는 오미자차는 속을 든든하게 해준다. 만두는 포장 판매도 한다.

Jaha Sonmandoo

Looking over the peaceful scenery of Buam-dong, you can enjoy Mandutgut (dumpling soup) and Manju jeongol (dumpling hot pot). Its quiet surroundings and cozy interiors are well matched and give off comfortable ambiance. They serve diverse mandu dishs, which seem ordinary in some way, but with variations in recipes. As they provide a take-out service, you can enjoy their food at home or elsewhere.

Address	종로구 백석동길 12	12, Baekseokdong-gil, Jongno-gu	
Contact	02-379-2648	82-2-379-2648	
Web	www.sonmandoo.com	www.sonmandoo.com	
Operation	11:00~21:30	11:00~21:30	
Closed	설·추석 전날과 당일	The eve and the day of Lunar New Year's Day & Chuseok	

강서면옥

1960년대 중반 서울 명보극장 옆에서 새콤달콤한 육수 맛으로 명성을 날린 평양식 냉면 전문점. 남북 적십자회담 당시 북측 대표가 찾은 냉면집으로도 유명하다. 강원도 토종 메밀과 전분을 알맞은 비율로 섞어 만든 구수하고 부드러운 면발, 양지를 푹 고아서 낸 국물과 동치미를 섞은 육수가 일품이다. 역대 대통령 모두 단골인 덕에 여름철 별미로 청와대에 출입하던 귀하신 몸이라고.

Gangseo Myeonok

This place has been well known for its Pyeongyang Naengmyeon in an excellent chilled broth (Pyeongyang-style cold noodles) for over 50 years. It is also famous because representatives of North Korea visited here during the South-North Red Cross Conference. Its noodles made from the native buckwheat of Gangwon Province properly mixed with starch enhance deep flavors to the dish, along with a wonderful broth.

Address	중구 세종대로11길 35(서소문점)
Contact	02-752-1945
Operation	11:30~22:00
Closed	설 · 추석 연휴

35, Sejong-daero 11-gil, Jung-gu
82-2-752-1945
11:30~22:00
Holiday of Lunar New Year's Day & Chuseok

황생가 칼국수(구 북촌 칼국수)

삼청동 일대를 찾은 이들에게 추억의 맛을 떠올리게 하는 곳. 사골을 넣어 푹 우려낸 육수의 진한 맛을 즐길 수 있는 사골 손칼국수가 대표 메뉴다. 자극적이지 않은 겉절이와 고기를 듬뿍 넣어 만든 왕만두는 환상의 콤비를 이룬다. 이외에도 얼큰한 버섯전골과 보쌈, 모둠전 등 든든한 식사 메뉴까지 다양하게 즐길 수 있다.

Hwangsaengga Kalguksu (formerly 'Bukchon Kalguksu')

Their specialty is Sagol Sonkalguksu (hand-rolled noodles in ox bone broth) from which you can taste a truly deep flavor of its ox bone broth boiled for a long time. Wang Mandu (king-sized dumpling) would have better taste when you eat with Geotjeori, (rather bland and fresh kimchi salad). Other dishes like Beoseot-jeongol (mushroom hot pot), Bossam (napa wrap with pork) and Modeumjeon (assorted pan-fried delicacies) are available as well.

Address	종로구 북촌로5길 78		78, Bukchon-ro 5-gil, Jongno-gu
Contact	02-739-6334		82-2-739-6334
Operation	11:00~21:30		11:00~21:30
Closed	설 · 추석 연휴		Holiday of Lunar New Year's Day & Chuseok

서울서 둘째로 잘하는 집

빠르게 트렌드가 변하는 삼청동이지만 옛날 모습 그대로 일대를 지키는 곳이 바로 서울서 둘째로 잘하는 집이다. 1976년 개업 당시만 해도 십전대보탕 등 한방차 전문 다방이었지만, 이 일대를 찾는 연인들이 많아지면서 달콤한 단팥죽과 식혜, 수정과 등 먹을거리를 갖추었다. 구운 밤을 얹고 계핏가루를 뿌린 단팥죽이 대표 메뉴다.

Seoureseo Duljjaero Jalhaneunjip (The Second Best in Seoul)

It was originally opened in 1976 as a traditional Korean medicinal teahouse. But as Samcheong-dong, a place where it is located, has become one of the most popular date places in Seoul, they started to serve some light meals and beverages such as Danpatjuk (sweet red bean soup), Sikhye (sweet drink made from fermented rice), Sujeonggwa (cinnamon punch with dried persimmon), etc. Of course, their best menu is Danpatjuk garnished with roasted chestnut and cinnamon powder.

Address	종로구 삼청로 122-1	122-1, Samcheong-ro, Jongno-gu	
Contact	02-734-5302	82-2-734-5302	
Operation	11:00~21:00	11:00~21:00	
Closed	월요일	Mon	

이남장

30년 전통을 자랑하는 설렁탕 전문점. 48시간 동안 가마솥에 푹 끓여낸 진한 육수와 푸짐하게 올린 고기가 일품이다. 무료로 제공하는 추가 공깃밥과 국수사리 덕분에 한국인의 정을 느낄 수 있다. 진한 국물에 최상의 양지와 우설, 머리 고기를 듬뿍 넣어 보양식으로 좋다.

Inamjang

They have served Seolleongtang (traditional beef soup) as their main dish for 30 years. Its deep broth boiled in a large iron pot for 48 hours and hearty amount of beef on it add more flavor. If you request a bowl of steamed rice or noodle more, you can have it without charge. A variety of beef cut and deep broth would make it a good health food.

Address	중구 삼일대로12길 16(을지로점)
Contact	02-2267-4081
Operation	09:00~22:00
Closed	설·추석 연휴

Address	16, Samil-daero 12-gil, Jung-gu
Contact	82-2-2267-4081
Operation	09:00~22:00
Closed	Holiday of Lunar New Year's Day & Chuseok

새벽집

외국인에게 '24시간 영업'이라는 독특한 한국 문화를 스개할 수 있는 곳. 꽃등심을 비롯한 한우 전문점으로, 즉석에서 고기를 썰어 감칠맛이 난다. 국물이 진한 해장국을 맛볼 수 있으며 선짓국과 함께 나오는 육회비빔밥 역시 해장용으로 먹기에 좋다.

SaebyeokJip

This place is distinguishing in a sense that it is open 24 hours. They serve various Korean beef cuisines including rib eye. Cutting meat on the table makes it taste fresher. Haejangguk (hangover soup) with its thick broth is available and Beef tartare bibimbap served with Seonjitguk (ox blood soup) is also good to treat a hangover.

Address	강남구 도산대로101길 6(청담동점)
Contact	02-546-5739
Operation	24시
Closed	연중무휴

Address	6, Dosan-daero 101-gil, Gangnam-gu
Contact	82-2-546-5739
Operation	24 hours
Closed	Open all year round

명동교자

전통 고명인 알쌈을 올린 칼국수가 대표 메뉴다. 구수하면서도 진한 국물과 부드러운 면발의 조화가 환상적이다. 마늘을 듬뿍 넣은 김치는 매운 편이지만 칼국수와 아주 잘 어울린다.

Address	중구 명동10길 29(명동점)
Contact	02-776-5348
Web	www.mdkj.co.kr
Operation	10:30~21:30
Closed	설 · 추석 당일

Myoungdong Kyoja

Kalguksu (hand-rolled noodle soup) garnished with its own traditional material is their main dish. A deep and flavorful broth and soft noodles are wonderfully harmonized. Kimchi added with rich garlics is also good to eat with Kalguksu.

Address	29, Myeong-dong 10-gil, Jung-gu
Contact	82-2-776-5348
Web	www.mdkj.co.kr
Operation	10:30~21:30
Closed	Day of Lunar New Year's Day & Chuseok

하동관

곰탕, 특곰탕과 수육이 하동관 메뉴의 전부. 이 중 일반 곰탕에 양지, 차돌박이, 포 뜬 내장인 내포 중 원하는 고기 두 가지를 선택할 수 있는 특곰탕을 추천한다. 개업한 이래 70여 년간 한우 암소 고기를 사용하며, 놋그릇에 푸짐하게 담아낸다. 곰탕을 처음 먹는 외국인은 내장이나 양지 등을 빼고 먹는 편이 좋다.

Address	서울 중구 명동9길 12(명동점)
Contact	02-776-5656
Web	www.hadongkwan.com
Operation	07:00~16:30
Closed	첫째 · 셋째 주 일요일

Hadongkwan

They serve only three dishes, Gomtang (traditional beef soup), Teuk Gomtang (special Gomtang) and Suyuk (boiled beef slices), among which Teuk Gomtang is most popular as it is served with 2 kinds of meat you choose. They have used Korean beef only since they opened 70 years ago and served their soup in a brass pot. If it is the first time that you try Gomtang, it would be better to remove brisket before eating.

Address	12, Myeong-dong 9-gil, Jung-gu
Contact	82-2-776-5656
Web	www.hadongkwan.com
Operation	07:00~16:30
Closed	1st and 3rd Sun

dining story
:
A 100-year
History of Chinese Cuisine
in Korea

한국의
중국 음식

100년사

세계 최고의 미식을 논할 때 가장 먼저 손꼽는 중식. 온갖 진귀한 식재료와 현란한 조리법으로 완성하는 중식은 대중적인 친근함부터 럭셔리함까지 다채로운 면모로 전 세계에 영향을 끼쳤다. 우리나라에서 중식은 인천의 차이나타운으로 들어와 배달 음식, 호텔의 고급 중식, 청담동 차이니스 레스토랑으로 변화했다. 통계에 따르면 한국의 중식당 수는 무려 2만 4000개에 이른다. 100년이 넘도록 우리의 입맛을 사로잡은 중식의 매력은 무엇일까?

Chinese cuisine is always considered the best gastronomy food in the world with its unique characteristic such as various yet rare ingredients and a chef's spectacular cooking skills. Chinese food is a very friendly food for ordinary people but it is sometimes transformed into the most sumptuous cuisine in the world. In Korea, Chinese food appeared first in the Chinatown of Incheon and then was evolved into various forms such as a small eatery providing delivery service, a fine restaurant in a hotel or a luxury Chinese restaurant in Gangnam. The number of all these Chinese restaurants is roughly 24,000. What makes Korean people fascinated to Chinese food for over a century?

인천에 상륙한 짜장면

1883년 인천이 개항하면서 산둥 지방 출신 근로자들이 만들어 먹던 고향 요리가 한국식 중국 요리의 근간이 되었다는 것은 모두가 아는 사실이다. 중국 요리가 본격적으로 자리 잡은 것은 무역업자, 공장 경영자 등 경제적으로 여유가 있는 이들을 위한 고급 중식당이 등장하면서부터. 인천 차이나타운의 '공화춘', '중화루', '동흥루'는 당대 미식가들이 즐겨 찾는 3대 청요릿집으로 손꼽혔다. 특히 음식점과 호텔의 혼합형인 '산둥회관'은 1912년 공화춘으로 이름을 바꾼 뒤 돼지고기, 양파, 생강 등을 춘장에 함께 볶아 국수에 얹은 중국식 짜장면을 선보이다가 한국전쟁 전후 양파와 고기를 넣고 춘장을 좀 더 묽게 해 한국식 짜장면을 만든 것으로 알려져 있다.

인천에 공화춘이 있었다면 서울의 가장 대표적인 중국 음식점은 을지로의 '아서원'이었다. 1907년 설립된 것으로 알려진 이곳은 1970년 문을 닫을 때까지 약 60년간 서울에서 화교가 경영하는 대표적인 음식점이었다. 이곳을 거친 수많은 화교 출신 요리사들이 서울의 호텔 중식당에 자리 잡으면서 국내 중국 요리의 근간을 이뤘다. 이외에도 수제 만두 전문점으로 유명한 '취천루', '안동장' 등 많은 중식당이 명동에 생겨난 것은 인근에 중국대사관(당시 대만대사관)과 화교학교가 있었기 때문이다. 마치 작은 차이나타운처럼 몰려 있던 중국 음식점은 당시 사교와 유흥의 장소일 뿐만 아니라 집회장, 예식장, 연회장으로 활용되었으며, 대부분 밀실을 따로 둬 '밀실 정치'의 무대가 되기도 했다.

리틀 차이나타운, 연희동과 연남동

인천과 명동이 1세대 중식당의 근간이라면 1970년대 이후부터는 연희동과 연남동 일대의 중식당이 그 명맥을 이었다. 화교 3000여 명이 모여 살아 '리틀 차이나타운'으로 불리던 연희동과 연남동에는 1969년 한성 화교학교가 명동에서 옮겨 오며 본격적으로 차이나타운이 조성되었다. 이 골목에 있는 중식당만 10여 곳. 어느 지역의 음식이라는 표기는 찾아보기 힘들지만 막상 먹어보면 쓰촨(사천), 하얼빈, 타이완, 베이징 등 지역별로 맛의 차이를 느낄 수 있다. 또 겉모습이나 인테리어는 허름하다고 할 정도로 소박한 편이다. 중식 셰프나 칼럼니스트 등 전문가들은 연희동과 연남동의 중식당은 대부분 맛과 질에 큰 차이가 없다고 평한다. 집집이 주특기로 내세우는 요리는 있으나, 기본 음식 수준이 대동소이하다는 것. 다만 중식당이 한곳에 집중되어 있다 보니 평균적으로 맛의 질이 높은 편이다.

비즈니스의 장, 호텔 중식당

인천 차이나타운과 연희동, 연남동이 화교가 만드는 대중적 중식당의 일면을 보여준다면 고급 요리는 호텔을 중심으로 발달했다. 최초의 호텔 중식당이 문을 연 곳은 명동의 세종 호텔이었다. 그 후 옛 반도 호텔(현 롯데 호텔 서울의 전신)의 중식당 '용궁'이 대만인 셰프를 영입하면서 국내 호텔 중식당이 활기를 띠었다. 이후 더플라자 호텔의 '도원', 서울 신라 호텔의 '팔선', 서울 웨스틴 조선 호텔의 '호경전(현 '홍연'의 전신)'이 그 계보를 이어나갔다. 특히 도원은 현대그룹 정주영 회장을 비롯해 정·재계 명사가 즐겨 찾던 곳으로 큰 인기를 모았다. 별실이 많아 정·재계 주요 인사들이 회동하기에 좋았을 뿐 아니라 담백한 광둥식 요리로 그들의 입맛을 사로잡았기 때문. 1976년 오픈한 도원의 맛은 1980년대 초반 합류한 유방녕 주방장의 손끝에서 완성되었는데, 그는 한국인의 입맛에 맞게 중국 요리를 개발한 것으로 정평이 나 있다.

1980년대 중반 이후에는 팔선이 고급 중식당의 새로운 기준을 제시했다. 1979년 오픈한 팔선은 초창기 도원의 명성에 미치지 못했으나 신선한 식재료와 정중한 서비스가 조화를 이루며 급부상한 후 지금까지 국내 최고의 중식당으로 인정받고 있다. 특히 팔선의 총주방장 후덕죽 상무가 국내 최초로 선보인 불도장은 1980년대 중반 최고의 화젯거리였다. 전복, 바닷가재, 돼지 발굽의 힘줄 등 20가지 재료를 넣고 3~4시간 동안 찐 것으로, 여전히 인기와 명성을 이어가고 있다.

중식당 아닌 차이니스 레스토랑

2000년대 초반 청담동이 레스토랑 트렌드를 주도하면서 중국 음식도 새로운 국면을 맞이했다. '연경', '이닝', '온더록', '빠진', '리산' 같은 고급 중식당을 비롯해 '홀리차우', '칸지고고' 등의 아메리칸 차이니스와 '난시앙' 등의 중국 본토 브랜드까지 등장하면서 다채로운 중식의 세계가 열렸다. 대중적인 고급 중식을 내놓은 옛 안세병원 뒤 '동천홍'이나 24시간 배달하며 쟁반 짜장과 볶음 짬뽕 등 히트 메뉴까지 양산한 '현경' 역시 강남을 기점으로 영역을 확대했다. 중식이 지금처럼 다양하고 다채로워진 데는 강남의 차이니스 레스토랑 역할이 컸다. 동네 중국집과 호텔 중식당이 전부인 중식의 한계를 뛰어넘은 것이다. 이들은 여전히 다양한 주류 리스트와 특색 있는 요리를 선보이며 서울의 중식 문화를 이끌고 있다.

JAJANGMYEON LANDED IN INCHEON

As widely known, Jajangmyeon originated from immigrants who came from Shandong, China after an opening of the Incheon port in 1883. Then Chinese food was more popularized by traders and factory managers who were financially stable at that time. As Chinese restaurants kept their pace with this trend, the number of a fine Chinese restaurant increased as well. Gonghwachun, Junghwaru and Dongheungru were considered the most famous Chinese restaurant of the Chinatown in those days. Gonghwachun, which was formerly 'Sandunghoegwan,' a kind of restaurant cum hotel, changed its name in 1912 and started to serve a Chinese-style Jajangmyeon which was made by sautéing pork, onion, ginger and other ingredients with chunjang (black bean paste). But after the Korean War, Gonghwachun invented a Korean-style Jajangmyeon, using thinner chunjang.

In the meanwhile Aseowon in Euljiro became the most popular Chinese restaurant in Seoul. Since it was opened in 1907 by a Chinese owner, Aseowon was the best Chinese restaurant in Seoul until it was closed in 1970. And many Chinese chefs who worked at Aseowon settled in other Chinese restaurants to form a culture of domestic Chinese restaurants. The majority of Chinese restaurants including Chwicheonru (famous for its hand-made dumplings) and Andongjang were located around Myeong-dong because the Chinese Embassy (Taiwan Embassy in those days) and the school for Chinese people in Korea were situated in Myeong-dong too. This small version of the Chinatown played an important role as the center of social life and entertainment in those days and Chinese restaurants were used for various purposes, for example, a meeting, a party or even a wedding ceremony. Most of these restaurants had private dining rooms, which provided a secret space for closed-door politics.

A LITTLE CHINATOWN, YEONHUI & YEONNAM

The first generation of the Chinese restaurant was formed in Incheon and Myeong-dong. Since the 1970s, the next generation's main stage was Yeonhui-dong and Yeonnam-dong. Two towns where roughly 3,000 Chinese people already settled down began to form a 'little Chinatown' after Hanseong School for Chinese people in Korea moved in this area in 1969. About 10 Chinese restaurants still remained in the alley. There is no explanation for origin of their food but you can find various styles of Chinese food including Sichuan, Harbin, Taiwan and Beijing styles. These eateries are not much a fine restaurant but rather a humble place.

Several Chinese chefs and food columnists say that Chinese restaurants in Yeonhui-dong and Yeonnam-dong do not show much difference in the taste or quality. Each restaurant has its own specialty but basic items are not much different in their tastes. Compared to Chinese restaurants in other places, however, they are still distinguishing.

CHINESE RESTAURANTS IN HOTEL AS A BUSINESS FIELD

Chinese restaurants mentioned until now are places for ordinary people while a Chinese restaurant in a hotel is characterized by a high-class Chinese cuisine. The first hotel that launched a Chinese restaurant was the Sejong Hotel in Myeong-dong. Then Yonggung, a Chinese restaurant of the Bando Hotel (old name of the Lotte Hotel Seoul), accelerated a development of Chinese restaurants of hotels, by inviting a Taiwanese chef. This trend was followed by 'Tao Yuen in the Plaza Hotel, 'Palsun' in the Shilla Seoul and 'Ho Gyeong Jeon' (currently, Hong Yuan) in the Westin Chosun Seoul.

Tao Yuen was especially popular with figures from economic and political fields, including Chung Ju-Yung, the founder of Hyundai Groups. The private dining rooms of this restaurant were preferred by businessmen and politicians, but the most important reason of this popularity was their amazing Cantonese cuisine. In the early 1980, when Chef Yu Bang-Nyeong joined Tao Yuen, he completed the specific taste of Tao Yuen and has been regarded as the one who found the best taste Korean people love.

In the mid-1980s, Palsun became a new standard of a high-class Chinese cuisine. Right after it was opened in 1979, Palsun just stayed in the second place following Tao Yuen but later, with fresh food materials and attentive service it took over the first place from Tao Yuen. In particular, Buldojang (also known as 'Buddha Jumps Over the Wall', a kind of shark's fin soup) first introduced by Hu Deok-Juk, the executive chef of Palsun, became a big issue at that time. Buldojang which is cooked by braising 20 kinds of ingredients including abalone and lobster for three to four hours remains the best cuisine in this restaurant.

NEW GENERATION OF CHINESE RESTAURANTS

In the early 2000s, a central stage of Chinese cuisine in Seoul moved to Cheongdam-dong with a new culinary trend around this town. From modern Chinese restaurants such as Yeun Kyung, Yining, On the Rock, Pazin and Lisyan to American-Chinatown style's Ho Lee Chow and Congee GoGo, to Nan Xiang from the mainland China, Chinese restaurants in Korea have been diversified more than ever. Dongcheonhong with the concept of a fine Chinese cuisine for ordinary people, Hyunkyung, well-known for its 24 hour delivery service and some other Chinese restaurants were booming around the Gangnam area. With their own characteristic and merits, these Chinese restaurants have contributed to the current diversity of a Chinese restaurant, going beyond the limits of Chinese restaurants in neighborhood and in hotels. They are still a leading group that forms a culinary culture of Chinese dining in Seoul.

dining story
:
Taste of
the
Mainland
China

대륙의
맛을

아십니까?

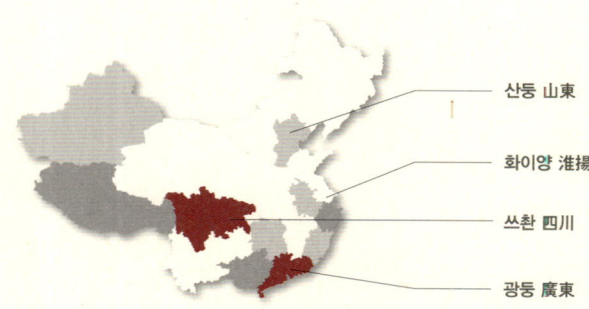

"South is sweet, North is salty, East is spicy and West is sour." This quote sounds like a magic spell but is usually used to explain in the simplest way a food of China, consisting of over 56 ethnic groups. Now let's take a look at many styles of Chinese cuisine which can be classified into four main regions: Huaiyang, Sichuan, Guangdong (or Canton) and Shandong.

"남쪽은 달고 북쪽은 짜고 남첨북함, 南甛北鹹 동쪽은 맵고 서쪽은 시다 동랄서산, 東辣西酸." 주문처럼 느껴지는 이 말은 56개가 넘는 민족으로 이루어진 중국의 음식을 한마디로 표현할 때 등장한다. 화이양, 쓰촨, 광둥, 산둥까지 대표적인 중국의 네 개 지역별 중국 요리의 특징을 살펴보았다. 아는 만큼 더 맛있어지는 법이다.

요리와 공간 / 마오

화이양 淮揚

양쯔강 중·하류에서 발달한 화이양 음식은 명·청 시대에 전성기를 맞았다. 청나라의 건륭제는 강남 지역을 유람하며 맛본 화이양 음식에 매료되어 국빈이 찾을 때마다 이 지역 음식을 대접했다. 그 전통은 오늘날까지 이어져 국가적 경축 행사나 국빈 대접의 만찬에 항상 화이양 전통 음식을 올린다. 화이양은 물의 고장이라는 의미의 '수향'과 쌀과 생선이 풍족하다는 의미의 '어미지향'이라는 별칭으로 불릴 만큼 생선과 새우, 게 등 수산물을 사용한 미식이 발달했다. 쏘가리 살을 저며 꽃 모양으로 손질한 후 다람쥐와 비슷한 모양으로 탕수육 양념을 한 '쑹수구이위', 송나라 문호 소동파가 즐겨 먹었다고 알려진 삼겹살찜 '동파육', 거지들이 훔쳐온 닭에 진흙을 발라 숨겨두었다가 구워 먹었다는 '자오화지'는 화려한 화이양 음식을 대표한다. 새우 살을 다져 완자를 만들어 튀겨내는 '자샤추'와 같이 민물새우의 살을 다져 과일이나 꽃 등 아름다운 모양을 만드는 데 집중하는 것도 특징이다. 가을이 되면 미식가를 흥분시키는 민물게 이야기를 빼놓을 수 없다. 10월에는 알이 밴 암컷, 11월에는 살이 오른 수컷을 먹어야 제맛을 즐길 수 있다고.

HUAIYANG

The Huaiyang cuisine that developed along the lower and middle reaches of the Yangtze River flourished most during the Ming and Qing Dynasties. It is said that the Qianlong Emperor of the Qing Dynasty was so captivated by the food of Huaiyang while he travelled around the country that he always served up this Huiyang cuisine to foreign guests. This tradition has been handed down and the Huiyang cuisine is still served either on the table for a national guest or on a national celebration day. Huiyang, also called a 'home of water' or a 'home of rice and fish,' is famous for its fine dining using a variety of seafood such as fish, shrimp or crab. For example, Songshuguiyu is made by shaping a finely chopped mandarin fish into a squirrel-like form and then adding tangsuyuk sauce. Dongpo Pork is famous with a legend that Su Dongpo, the famed Song Dynasty poet, relished it. Jiaohuaji, also known as 'Beggar's Chicken,' has a story that a beggar covered the chicken he stole with mud because he didn't want to let others know he was cooking a chicken. All these foods are the typical cuisine of Huaiyang. In addition, another characteristic of the Huaiyang cuisine is a flower-shaped food adorned with chopped meat, for instance, Zha xia qiu, a fried shrimp dumpling made with finely chopped shrimps. And freshwater crab in season in autumn is a specialty of this region. Egg-bearing female crabs are the best in October and male crabs are in their best conditions in November.

쓰촨 四川

장시江西, 후난湖南 등 양쯔강 중·상류와 쓰촨 분지의 여름은 덥고 습하며, 겨울은 한파가 몰아친다. 한겨울의 추위와 식량난을 극복하기 위해 이곳 사람들은 독특한 음식 저장법을 개발했으며, 음식이 부패되는 것을 막기 위해 향신료를 많이 사용했다. 또 습한 환경 속에서 살아남기 위해 그 열을 땀으로 배출해주는 매운 음식을 주로 먹는다. 명나라 말기에 혁명기를 거치며 인구 대부분이 사망하고, 청나라 말기와 일제 침략기를 지나면서 내란을 피해 전국 각지에서 사람들이 모여들었다. 그 결과 중국 각지의 식문화가 결합했고, 이와 같은 다양성 덕에 중국 내에서 홍콩과 마카오 못지않은 미식 지구로 발전했다. 쓰촨 요리는 서민 가정의 식탁에 자주 오르는 음식이기도 하며 매콤한 맛을 즐기는 한국인의 입에도 잘 맞는다. 마파두부, 닭고기를 마른 고추와 볶아낸 '궁바오지딩', 돼지고기를 삶아 익힌 다음 양념과 함께 볶아내는 '후이궈러우'는 중국의 된장찌개와 다름없는 음식. 쓰촨 음식은 고추나 후춧가루를 쓰지 않고 '화자오'라는 산초나무 열매를 사용해 혀가 얼얼할 정도로 매운맛이 압도적이다. 이 매운맛을 '마라'라고 하는데, 쓰촨식 샤부샤부의 검붉은 국물에서 진하게 느낄 수 있다.

SICHUAN

In Jiangxi and Hunan around the upper and middle reaches of the Yangtze River and in the Sichuan Basin, the weather is very hot and humid in summer and extremely cold in winter. To overcome such an extreme weather and resulting food shortage problem, people in this region developed their own way to preserve food and used a great deal of spices to prevent food from being spoiled. And they usually take in very spicy food to release heat through their skin by sweating, as one of the ways to adjust humid weather. The majority of people died when the revolt broke out in the end of the Ming Dynasty and then a number of people flocked into this region from all parts of the country in the end of the Qing Dynasty and during the period of Japanese occupation. As a result, culinary cultures of various regions were mixed in this region and this diversity helped Sichuan become a famous gastronomic city like Hong Kong and Macau. The Sichuan cuisine is ordinary people's everyday food and also quite agreeable to the taste of Korean people who love spicy food very much. Mapo Doufu, Kung Pao Chicken (stir-fried chicken with dried chili peppers) and Twice-Cooked Pork (stir-fried steamed pork with a sauce) are the most typical and common food in Sichuan. Instead of chili peppers or black peppers, they use Sichuan peppers, characterized with its fiery taste. You can taste it from Sichuan Hot Pot (Sichuan-style shabu shabu).

광둥 廣東

중국인은 '경치 좋은 쑤저우에서 태어나 미인 많은 항저우에서 비단옷을 입고 호사하며 광둥에서 좋은 요리를 즐기는 것'이 남자로 태어나 누릴 수 있는 최고의 삶이라고 믿었다. 광둥은 중국에서 제일 먼저 개방된 곳으로 바다에서 갓 잡아 올린 풍부한 해산물과 동서 문화가 융합된 조리법이 발달해 중국에서 가장 풍요로운 음식 문화를 꽃피웠다. 너구리, 고양이, 원숭이, 뱀 등 야생 희귀 동물을 가리지 않고 식재료로 삼아 다채로운 식문화가 발달했다. 기상천외한 요리는 오늘날 '음식 천국' 광둥의 원동력이다. 그중 뱀과 고양이, 닭고기를 각종 양념과 함께 끓인 '룽후더우', 금방 젖을 뗀 새끼 돼지구이 '추이피루주'가 대표적. 광둥의 상징인 상어 지느러미와 제비집, 전복 등을 사용한 요리는 고급 식재료의 색과 맛을 살리기 위해 양념과 기름을 비교적 적게 사용한다. 광둥 요리 하면 빼놓을 수 없는 것이 아침과 저녁 식사 중간에 먹는 딤섬이다. 서양식 베이커리 문화에서 영향을 받아 한입에 먹을 수 있는 다양한 맛과 모양이 발달했다. 이를 차와 함께 즐기는 행위를 일컫는 '얌차' 문화는 전 세계로 널리 퍼졌다.

GUANGDONG (CANTON)

According to an old Chinese saying, the best life of a man is to be born in the beautiful Suzhou, live in Hangzhou, a city of beautiful women and silk, and eat good food in Guangdong. Guangdong, which was known for fresh and rich seafood and was the first region opened to Western culture, developed their own recipes in which Chinese and Western cultures were well blended. The food ingredients such as raccoon, cat, monkey and snake are distinctive as well. Long Hu Dou (Dragon Fighting against the Tiger), made with snake meat, cat meat and chicken, and Roast Suckling Pig are most famous among Cantonese cuisines. As for cuisine using shark's fin, bird's nest or abalone, relatively less condiments and oil are used to keep an original flavor of these ingredients. Dim Sum is also the one of the most famous Cantonese foods. Plus, desserts in this region, as was influenced by Western bakery, are much various in its kind. In particular, Yum Cha, a way of drinking Chinese tea with various desserts, has widely been known all over the world.

산둥 山東

한국의 중국 음식 문화에 가장 많은 영향을 끼친 지역이 바로 베이징과 텐진을 포함한 산둥 지역이다. 청나라 시대에 이르러 황궁의 많은 요리사가 산둥 출신임이 밝혀졌고, 화이양 요리와 함께 궁정 요리의 중요한 계보를 이어갔다. 현재까지 전해지는 베이징의 궁정 요리 체계에는 산둥 요리의 조리법에 짙게 남아 있다. 중국 요리의 대명사 탕수육의 새콤달콤한 '탕추' 조리법이 지역을 대표하는 맛이다. 산둥 지역의 음식은 북방 내륙 지역의 음식인 '지난차이'와 해안가에 위치한 지역의 음식 '자오둥차이'로 나뉜다. 지난차이는 밀과 함께 옥수수와 육류 등을 주재료로 하며, 자오둥차이는 풍부한 해산물을 주재료로 삼는다. 하지만 남부 지역과 비교했을 때 식재료가 풍부하지 않기 때문에 밀가루만으로도 찌고, 튀기고, 굽고, 삶고, 지지고, 볶는 등 다양한 조리법을 응용해 만두, 국수, 전병, 수제비 등 수많은 음식을 만들어낸다. 대표 요리로 말린 해삼을 불려 대하와 함께 간장으로 양념한 '훙사오 하이선', 황허에서 잡아 올린 잉어로 탕수육 양념을 한 '탕추리위', 돼지 내장을 양념과 함께 졸이는 '주잔다창'과 중국식 고구마 맛탕 '바쓰디과'가 있다.

SHANDONG

The Chinese food in Korea was largely affected by the cuisine of Shandong, the northern area of China including Beijing and Tianjin. Most of chefs who worked in the imperial palace came from Shandong and the Shandong cuisine has played the most important role to continue the tradition of Chinese Imperial cuisine together with the Huaiyang cuisine. The unique recipes of the Shandong cuisine are well kept in the Beijing Imperial cuisine. Tang Cu Pai Gu (Sweet and Sour Spare Ribs) is the most typical dish in this region. The cuisine in Shandong is simply divided into two styles: Jiaodong style using seafood as main ingredients and Jinan style encompassing dishes from eastern Shandong. One of the features of Jinan style is to use wheat, corn and meat as main ingredients. In Jinan, where food materials were not enough or diverse, cooking techniques were remarkably developed in so much diverse ways that people in this area make a wide range of food only from flour by braising, frying, roasting, steaming and sautéing it. The delicacies of Shandong are Sea Cucumber and King Shrimp seasoned with soy sauce, Tang Cu Li Ji made with carp flesh instead of pork fillet, Jiuqu Dachang made with pig's large intestine boiled in a sauce and Basi Digua, a dish of sweet potato with caramelized sugar.

dining scene
:
Chinese Food
in
All Tastes
and
Kinds

짜장에서
만찬까지,

중식
테이블

Chinese food is not the food for Chinese people only and has been evolved into various forms and styles all over the world. In Korea, you can enjoy Jajangmyeon which does not exist in China and you can also see a delivery man always carrying a small steel box. Despite all these variations and diversities, however, each Chinese food has its best moment to enjoy it.

전 세계 어디에서나 만날 수 있는 중국 음식. 본토에서는 볼 수 없는 짜장면부터 전화 한 통이면 한 그릇도 배달해주는 '철가방'까지 한국의 중국 음식 역시 고유한 문화를 지녔다. 중국 하면 생각나는 대표 음식과 함께 어떤 순간 즐기면 좋을지, 그 찰나의 장면으로 초대한다.

가장 한국적인 중국 음식, 짜장면

중국 음식 하면 가장 먼저 떠오르는 짜장면은 볶음장을 얹은 국수인 짜장미엔炸醬麵이 원조다. 발효시켜 찐 밀가루와 대두, 캐러멜을 섞은 '사자표 춘장' 덕에 달고 반질반질한 윤기가 나는 짜장면은, 비록 중국에서 유래했지만 남녀노소 누구나 어떤 날이건 부담 없이 즐기는 우리나라의 대표적 외식 메뉴가 됐다.

요리 / 서울 웨스틴 조선 호텔 홍연

JAJANGMYEON, A CHINESE FOOD IN A VERY KOREAN WAY

The Korean-style Jajangmyeon is derived from Zhajiangmian, a Chinese dish of thick wheat noodles and zhajiang (fermented soybean paste). Jajangmyeon, made with fermented wheat flour, soybean and the famous 'Lion Soy Bean Sauce' mixed with caramel sauce, has become one of the most common foods in Korea. *By Hong Yuan of the Westin Chosun Seoul*

광둥 대표 요리, 딤섬

'마음에 점을 찍는다'는 뜻의 딤섬點心은 이름처럼 간단하고 정갈한 음식이다. 중국에서는 코스의 중간 식사로 먹고 홍콩에서는 전채 음식으로 먹는 것이 일반적이지만, 한국에서는 후식의 의미가 더 강하다. 요리를 시키면 서비스로 주는 군만두나 물만두 역시 한국식 딤섬 문화의 일면이라고 생각할 수 있다. 요즘에는 '딘타이펑', '웨스턴 차이나' 등 딤섬을 전문적으로 다루는 레스토랑도 많아졌다.

요리 / 서울 웨스틴 조선 호텔 홍연

DIM SUM, A DELICACY FROM GUANGDONG

Dim Sum, with the meaning of 'touching the heart' or 'marking a dot in the heart,' is simple and orderly-made food. Generally, it is served between course meals in China while it is an appetizer in Hong Kong. In Korea, however, Dim Sum is served as a kind of dessert after a meal. This custom is not familiar because Gun Mandu (fried dumplings) and Mul Mandu (boiled dumplings) are served as a complimentary dish. There are Dim Sum restaurant like Din Tai Fung and Western China these days. *By Hong Yuan of the Westin Chosun Seoul*

차이니스 패스트푸드, 볶음밥과 볶음국수

한국으로 건너와 정착한 중국 요리가 짜장면, 짬뽕이라면 미국으로 건너간 중국 요리는 '차오판', 즉 볶음밥이다. 찰기 적은 쌀로 지어 밥알이 서로 붙지 않아 더욱 맛있는 볶음밥과 쉽게 붙지 않는 볶음국수는 영화나 드라마에도 자주 등장하는 차이니스 패스트푸드. 2000년대 이후 국내에서도 미국처럼 간단히 사 갈 수 있는 테이크아웃 메뉴로 선보이고 있다.

요리 / 서울 웨스틴 조선 호텔 홍연

STIR-FRIED RICE & NOODLES, THE CHINESE FAST FOOD

If Jajangmyeong or Jjambbong is a Korean variation, Chao Pan, a kind stir-fried rice, is an American variation. This Chinese-American food is very popular because the stir-fried rice is less sticky and the stir-fried noodles are not swollen soon. These Chinese foods have become a common fast food in the U.S. A take-out service for some Chinese foods is available in Korea from the early 2000s. *By Hong Yuan of the Westin Chosun Seoul*

기름기 많은 중식에는 역시 배갈

중국 음식과 가장 잘 어울리는 술은 단연 배갈, 즉 수수를 원료로 빚은 증류주인 '바이주白酒'다. 중국 음식점에서 파는 캐주얼한 독한 술로만 알고 있었다면 오산이다. 중국에는 국가 공인 검정 대회에서 수상한 여덟 가지 술을 가리켜 8대 명주라고 하는데, 배갈 역시 명주로 손꼽힌다. 대부분 도수가 50도 안팎이라 취하기 쉽지만 잔이 매우 작고 식사 때 뜨거운 차와 함께 마시기 때문에 부담이 적다.

요리 / 서울 웨스틴 조선 호텔 홍연

BAIJIU, THE BEST MARIAGE WITH CHINESE FOOD

Baijiu, a strong distilled spirit made from fermented sorghum, is the best alcoholic beverage for Chinese food. But Baijiu is not just common liquor. There are eight famous Chinese liquors certified by the Chinese government and Baijiu is one of them. Though Baijiu has significantly higher alcohol content, you can enjoy it during your meal as a kind of light accompaniment along with a hot cup of tea. *By Hong Yuan of the Westin Chosun Seoul*

모던하게 재해석한 황실 만찬

청나라 시대 건륭제는 지방을 순회할 때 그 지방의 요리를 음미했을 뿐 아니라, 많은 요리사를 궁중으로 불러들여 궁중 요리를 더욱 발전시켰다고 한다. 그중 양저우 출신의 한 요리사가 만족滿族 요리와 한족漢族 요리를 통합했다는 의미의 만한전석滿漢全席을 만들었다. 산해진미를 모두 맛볼 수 있는 만한전석은 사흘에 걸쳐 180가지나 되는 요리를 먹는 성대한 만찬이다.

요리 / 서울 신라 호텔 팔선

IMPERIAL BANQUET WITH A MODERN TWIST

In particular, the Qianlong Emperor who enjoyed various delicacies of each region while travelling all the regions of China invited a number of chefs to his palace to improve the taste and diversity of Chinese Imperial cuisine. Among them, one chef who came from Yangzhou created Manhan Quanxi (Manchu Han Imperial Feast) by integrating roughly 180 unique delicacies out of Manchu and Han cuisines. It is not possible to cook the whole dish of Manchu Quanxi now, for some of those exotic ingredients are not available any more and recipes of some cuisines disappeared. *By Palsun of the Shilla Seoul*

갖은 재료로 우려낸 고급 보양식, 불도장

청나라 시대에 완성된 '불도장'은 최고의 보양식으로 손꼽힌다. 상어 지느러미와 자연산 송이, 오골계, 관자, 화고버섯, 사삼해삼의 일종 등 갖은 재료를 육수와 함께 용기에 담고 밀봉해 3~4시간 동안 찌는, 탕과 찜 중간 형태 요리다. 재료가 저마다 고유의 깊은 맛을 내며 환상의 하모니를 연출한다. 단백질과 칼슘이 풍부하고 소화 흡수가 빠르며 식욕 증진과 원기 회복에 탁월한 보양식이다.

요리 / 서울 신라 호텔 팔선

BUDDHA JUMPS OVER THE WALL, A TRUE & EXQUISITE HEALTH FOOD

Buddha Jumps Over the Wall, created during the Qing Dynasty, is considered the one of the best health foods. Thicker than soup but thinner than stew, this dish is cooked by braising shark's fin, mushroom, silkie chicken, scallop, sea cucumber and other ingredients in a broth for three to four hours. Deep, rich tastes of each ingredient are beautifully harmonized. This dish also contains rich protein and calcium and is an easily digestible health food to help you increase your appetite and recover your strength. *By Palsun of the Shilla Seoul*

뜨겁게 우려낸 중국차와 디저트

기름진 음식을 자주 먹는 중국인이 살이 찌지 않는 것은 차를 즐겨 마시기 때문이라는 연구 결과가 있을 만큼 중국인에게 차는 빼놓을 수 없는 생활 습관이다. 국내에는 용정차와 보이차가 널리 알려져 있다. 특히 보이차는 발효차의 특성상 차가운 몸을 따뜻하게 해주어 건강과 다이어트를 염두에 둔 이들에게 인기가 높다. 마실 때 매그럽게 넘어가고 마신 뒤 단맛이 은은하게 도는 것이 최상품이다.

요리 / 서울 웨스틴 조선 호텔 홍연

HOT BREWED TEA & DESSERT

A study said that the habit of enjoying tea helps Chinese people prevent obesity although most Chinese foods are much greasy. That's why we cannot help but mention their tea drinking habit when we talk about China and Chinese people. Longjing tea and Pu-erh tea (or Pu'er tea) are well-known traditional Chinese teas in Korea too. Pu-erh tea is especially popular with those who want to lose weight because it, as a sort of fermented tea, is good to keep your body warm. The finest Pu-erh tea leaves a good feeling and sweet fragrance in the back of throat. *By Hong Yuen of the Westin Chosun Seoul*

place
:
32
Best
Chinese Restaurants
in
Seoul

서울에서 가장 맛있는

중식 레스토랑 32

There are various types of Chinese restaurants in Seoul from a small store providing a delivery service in your neighborhood to a fancy restaurant of a five star hotel. But they all have similar items on their menu including ordinary meals like Jajangmyeon (black bean sauce noodle) and à la carte dish like Ohyang Jangyuk (braised thinly-sliced pork). Of course, however, it is true that each restaurant has its own specialty.

동네 중국집부터 고급 호텔의 전문 중식당까지, 중국집이라면 짜장면 같은 식사류부터 오향장육 같은 일품요리까지 두루 갖추고 있지만 자신 있게 내세우는 필살기가 있는 법. 서울 최고의 중식당과 그곳의 필살기 메뉴를 꼽았다.

짜장면
신성각
동화반점
이품
주
장순루
홍운장
오모리찌개
매화
일품향

짬뽕
동천홍
마담 밍
홍콩반점 0410
차이엔
용정
야래향

일품요리
호화반점
목란
개화
리샨
태가원
경발원
명화원
브루스 리
루이
송가
크리스탈 제이드 상하이 딜라이트

코스 요리
청
홍보각
팔선
홍연
타이판
가향

Jajangmyeon
Sinseonggak
Donghwabanjeom
Ipum
Ju
Jangsunru
Hongunjang
Omori Jjigae
Maehwa
Ilpumhyang

Jjambbong
Dongcheonhong
Madam Ming
Hong Kong
-Banjeom 0410
Chaiyen
Yongjeong
Yaraehyang

À la Carte Dish
Hohwa Banjeom
Mokran
Gaehwa
Lisyan
Taegawon
Gyeongbalwon
Myeonghwawon
Bruce Lee
Luii
Songga
Crystal Jade Shanghai
-Delight

Course Menu
Chung
Hong Bo Gak
Palsun
Hong Yuan
Taipan
Gahyang

짜장면

"지금까지 당신이 중식당에서 가장 자주 시킨 메뉴는 무엇인가?"라고 묻는다면 그 대답은 단연 '짜장면'이 아닐까? 큼지막한 감자와 양파를 넣은 옛날짜장, 면과 소스를 볶아 진한 맛을 즐길 수 있는 쟁반짜장, 돼지고기를 잘게 다진 유니짜장까지. 다소 지저분하고 교통이 불편한 골목길에 위치해도 기꺼이 찾아갈 수밖에 없는 최고의 짜장면 집을 공개한다.

JAJANGMYEON

If someone asks you "what is your favorite Chinese food?" then you would definitely answer it's Jajangmyeon. But there are all the sorts of Jajangmyeon with different recipes and flavors, for example, Yetnal Jajang (old-style) with largely cut pieces of potato and onion, Jaengban Jajang (jumbo-sized) made by roasting noodles and sauce, Yuni Jajang with minced pork. Some restaurants serve up so wonderful Jajangmyeon that you have no choice but to visit there again and again, even though their store is not much clean and located in an area with poor transportation.

신성각

마포에 위치한 1960년대식 수타 짜장 전문점. 외진 곳에 있지만 일부러 찾는 이가 많을 정도로 미식가들 사이에서 소문난 곳. 주문 후 바로 손으로 면을 뽑아내고, 춘장에 갖은 재료를 볶아내 정성이 느껴진다. 다만 화학조미료 맛에 길든 이들은 맛이 심심하게 느껴질 수 있다.

Sinseonggak

This restaurant, located in Mapo, serves Suta Jajang (whose noodles are made entirely by hand, not by machines) made in a 1960 style. Even though it is not easy to find this restaurant on the street, many people frequently visit there. Once an order is made, they start to make noodle by hand and then roast all the ingredients with chunjang (spring paste). If you are more familiar with artificial ingredients, you would feel their food is rather bland.

Address	마포구 임정로 55-1		55-1, Imjeong-ro, Mapo-gu
Contact	02-716-1210		82-2-716-1210
Operation	11:30~16:00		11:30~16:00
Closed	일요일, 신정, 설·추석 연휴		Sun, New Year's Day, Holiday of Lunar New Year's Day & Chuseok

동화반점

동대문 쇼핑몰 밀리오레 옆 골목을 약 40년간 지켜온 곳으로 1960년대부터 정·재계 인사들의 발길이 끊이지 않았다. 다른 중국집보다 면발이 살짝 가는데 이 때문에 양념이 골고루 잘 배어 있다. 돼지고기 완자에 해산물을 넣은 '팔보완자' 역시 대표 메뉴.

Donghwabanjeom

This restaurant has been situated at the alley next to Migliore, the large shopping mall, for over 40 years and in the meantime, has become a popular place with many figures in the economic and political worlds. Their noodles are slightly thinner than those of other Chinese restaurants and this is their secret to have their noodles fully seasoned. Palbo Wanja (pork meatball fried with seafood) is also their best selling item.

Address	중구 장충단로13길 7		7, Jangchungdan-ro 13-gil, Jung-gu
Contact	02-2265-9224		82-2-2265-9224
Operation	11:00~다음 날 05:00		11:00~The next day 05:00
Closed	연중무휴		Open all year round

이품

연희동에 위치하며, 테이블 다섯 개가 전부이므로 손님이 많으면 합석해야 할 때도 있다. 면 요리는 짜장과 간짜장, 짬뽕, 굴짬뽕겨울 메뉴이 대표적. 다른 중식당에 비해 깨끗한 기름에 재료를 볶아 깔끔한 불 맛과 진한 양념이 조화를 이룬다. 식어도 바삭한 군만두를 곁들여보자.

Ipum

This restaurant, located in Yeonhui-dong, has only five tables, which sometimes make you sit together with other people on one table. Jajangmyeon, Ganjajangmyeon (served with noodle and sauce in a separate bowl), Jjambbong (spicy noodle soup) and Gul Jjambbong (with oysters) are main dishes. Their food roasted in fresh cooking oil is well suitable with their thick sauce. Gun Mandu (fried dumpling) is also worth eating, for it is still crispy even long after it is fried.

Address	서대문구 연희로11길 20	20, Yeonhui-ro 11-gil, Seodaemun-gu	
Contact	02-322-6172	82-2-322-6172	
Operation	11:00~21:00	11:00~21:00	
Closed	둘째·넷째 주 화요일	2nd and 4th Tue	

주

서울 웨스틴 조선 호텔 최초의 중식당 '홍연'의 창립멤버인 주덕성 조리장이 운영하는 곳으로 걸쭉하고 고소한 옛날 짜장이 일품이다. 캐러멜 소스를 넣지 않은 깔끔한 맛이 돋보인다. 튀김 요리에서 느껴지는 내공이 만만치 않아 깐풍기, 칠리새우 등의 요리 역시 훌륭하다.

Ju

Ju is run by Chef Ju Deok-Seong, who was one of the founding members of Hong Yuan, the first Cantonese restaurant of the Westin Chosun Seoul Hotel. Yetnal Jajang (old-style black bean sauce noodle) with thick and savory sauce and without caramel sauce is their excellent main dish. Fried dishes such as Kkanpunggi (deep-fried chicken in hot pepper sauce) and Chili shrimp are also wonderful.

Address	서초구 동광로19길 16	16, Donggwang-ro 19-gil, Seocho-gu
Contact	02-3482-3374	82-2-3482-3374
Operation	11:30~21:30(Break 15:00~17:00)	11:30~21:30(Break 15:00~17:00)
Closed	월요일	Mon

장순루

쉐라톤 그랜드 워커힐 건너편 골목에서 인심 좋은 화교 남매가 운영하는 중식당. 30년이 넘는 전통을 자랑하는 곳으로 처음에는 작게 시작했지만 맛집으로 소문나면서 아예 건물 전체로 가게를 넓혔다. 붉은 간판과 홍등이 달린 화려한 외관이 눈길을 사로잡는다. 양파를 큼지막하게 썰어 넣은 짜장면이 대표 메뉴.

Jangsunru

Jangsunru is run by the Korean-Chinese brother and sister and located at the alley across the street from the Sheraton Grand Walkerhill. It has been over 30 years after it was opened as a small eatery. But as it was known for their delicious food and more and more people visited it, Jangsunru came to take up the whole building. Its red sign and red lamp are impressive. Jajangmyeon with largely cut onion is their specialty.

Address	광진구 아차산로76길 11	11, Achasan-ro 76-gil, Gwangjin-gu
Contact	02-3436-2000	82-2-3436-2000
Operation	11:30~21:30	11:30~21:30
Closed	설 · 추석 연휴	Holiday of Lunar New Year's Day & Chuseok

홍운장

1925년 북한 신의주 경찰서 앞 '신강루'에서 시작해 지금의 홍운장에 이르기까지 3대에 걸쳐 화교 출신 셰프가 운영하는 곳. 짬뽕, 생굴짬뽕, 삼선짬뽕, 삼선짜장, 옛날짜장 등 간단한 면 메뉴가 눈에 띈다. 채소를 많이 넣어 뒷맛이 개운한 옛날식 짜장과 칼칼한 짬뽕을 함께 맛볼 것.

Hongunjang

Singangru situated in front of Sinuiju Police Station in 1925 has led to this restaurant, run by three generations of the Korean-Chinese family. Simple noodle dishes such as Jjambbong (spicy noodle soup), Saenggul Jjambbong (with raw oysters), Samseon Jjambbong (with diverse seafood) and Yetnal Jajang are served. Yetnal Jajang with abundant vegetables and spicy Jjambbong are good to eat together.

Address	강남구 삼성로 341	341, Samseong-ro, Gangnam-gu
Contact	02-558-3666	82-2-558-3666
Operation	11:40~20:50	11:40~20:50
Closed	월요일	Mon

오모리찌개

석촌호수 주변에 위치한 김치찌갯집이지만 별미로 시작한 수타 짜장이 메인 메뉴만큼 인기를 끄는 곳. 돼지비계를 볶아 만든 진한 짜장 소스와 차지게 뽑아낸 수타식 면발이 어린 시절 향수를 불러일으킨다.

Omori Jjigae

Omori Jiigae was opened as a Kimchi stew bistro near Seokchon Lake as you can guess from its name but Suta Jajang (using noodle made by hand), once their extra dish, has now become popular as much as the main dish. A thick jajang sauce made from roasted pork fat and hand-made sticky noodles have some similarities with Jajangmyeon in the past.

Address	송파구 송파대로 473		473, Songpa-daero, Songpa-gu
Contact	02-416-0067		82-2-416-0067
Web	www.omori.co.kr		www.omori.co.kr
Operation	24시		24 hours
Closed	연중무휴		Open all year round

매화

연남동에서 3대째 중국집을 운영하는 곳. 각종 채소와 고기를 길게 잘라 만드는 유슬짜장을 맛볼 수 있다. 면은 수타로 뽑아 쫄깃하다. 여름에는 비취 냉면, 겨울에는 매생이 굴짬뽕 등 별미 메뉴를 한정적으로 선보인다. 고소하고 깔끔한 짜장면을 좋아하는 이들의 입맛에 딱 맞는 곳이다.

Maehwa

It has been run by three generations of a family in Yeonnam-dong. Yuseul Jajang made by cutting various vegetables and meat into thin strips is available. Its noodle made by hand, not by a machine, is sticky. They offer seasonal dishes in a limited period, for example, Naengmyeon (cold noodles) for summer and Maesaengi Gul Jjambbong (spicy noodle soup with seaweed fulvescens and oysters) for winter. If you like savory taste of Jajangmyeon, this place is worth the visit.

Address	마포구 성미산로 192		192, Seongmisan-ro, Mapo-gu
Contact	02-332-0078		82-2-332-0078
Operation	11:30~22:00(Break 15:00~17:00)		11:30~22:00(Break 15:00~17:00)
Closed	설 · 추석 연휴		Holiday of Lunar New Year's Day & Chuseok

일품향

돼지고기를 넣은 짜장면을 부담스러워하는 이들을 위한 곳. 왕새우를 듬뿍 넣어 고소한 맛이 나는 짜장면이 일품이다. 중국 전통 의상인 치파오를 맞춰 입고 서툰 한국말로 서비스하는 중국 직원들도 인상적이다. 명동 중국대사관 앞 골목에 위치.

Ilpumhyang

If you don't prefer Jajangmyeon with too much pork, this restaurant would satisfy your taste. Jajangmyeon with a great deal of king prawn is their specialty. Chinese waiting staff in qipao, a traditional Chinese dress, is much impressive though they use broken Korean. It is located at the alley in front of the Chinese Embassy in Myeong-dong.

Address	중구 남대문로 52-13	52-13, Namdaemun-ro, Jung-gu
Contact	02-753-6928	82-2-753-6928
Operation	11:00~21:30	11:00~21:30
Closed	첫째 · 셋째 주 일요일	1st and 3rd Sun

짬뽕

비가 오는 날이나 숙취 때문에 고생한 날 한 번쯤 떠올려봤을 짬뽕. 우리가 즐기는 짬뽕은 중국이 아닌 일본 나가사키의 '시카이로'라는 중식당에서 유래했다. 닭 뼈를 우려낸 육수에 돼지고기, 해산물까지, 육해공陸海空의 모든 재료가 들어 있다는 의미에서 '잔폰 뒤섞여 있다는 뜻의 일본어'이라 불렀으며, 우리나라에는 짬뽕으로 소개되었다. 고춧가루를 넣어 칼칼한 맛을 낸 한국식 짬뽕은 짜장면과 함께 중국 음식을 대표하는 메뉴가 되었다. 숙취 해소용 홍합짬뽕, 화끈한 불 맛을 느낄 수 있는 볶음짬뽕은 한국에서만 맛볼 수 있는 메뉴다.

JJAMBBONG

When it rains or when you suffer from hangovers, somehow it whets our appetite for a spicy meal like Jjambbong. Jjambbong we are enjoying these days originates from Shikairō, a Chinese restaurant in Nagasaki, Japan, not from China. It was called Champon or Chanpon (meaning 'mixed' in Japanese), because pork and seafood were put together into a chicken bone broth. Later it was introduced into Korea, with the name of Jjambbong. A Korean-style jjambbong flavored with lots of chili pepper powder has become one of the best Chinese cuisines. Honghap Jjambbong (adding mussels into Jjambbong) appropriate for relieving hangovers and Bokkeum Jjamgbbong (sauteed one) with pungent taste are only found in Korea.

동천홍

압구정동과 청담동을 주 무대로 활동하는 패션 피플과 셀러브리티 사이에서 독보적인 인기를 얻는 곳. 얼큰한 짬뽕과 계절 특선 굴짬뽕 덕이다. 주방장의 솜씨도 훌륭하지만 신선한 재료에서 우러나오는 국물 맛이 개운하고 깊다.

Dongcheonhong

This place is particularly popular with fashion people and celebrities around Apgujeong-dong and Cheongdam-dong. This popularity is attributable to its spicy Jjambbong and its seasonal delicacy, Gul Jjambbong (with oysters) based on its chef's excellent recipes as well as fresh ingredients. There are many branches in several places but the main restaurant behind the Gangnam Eulji Hospital is the best.

Address	강남구 언주로173길 14(압구정점)	14, Eonju-ro 173-gil, Gangnam-gu
Contact	02-548-8887	82-2-548-8887
Web	www.dongchunhong.com	www.dongchunhong.com
Operation	11:30~21:30	11:30~21:30
Closed	연중무휴	Open all year round

마담 밍

강남 선릉역 근처에 있으며 인근 직장인들이 즐겨 찾는다. 전날 과음을 한 이들이 숙취를 해소하기 위해 찾는 대표 메뉴는 단연 시원한 짬뽕. 이곳의 짬뽕은 일반 짬뽕보다 더 매운 편인데 고추기름으로 매운 정도를 조절할 수 있다. 봄에는 냉이짬뽕, 여름에는 매콤한 냉짬뽕 등 이색적인 계절 메뉴를 선보인다.

Madam Ming

Madam Ming is one of the favorite restaurants of office workers around Seolleung Station. The spicy Jjambbong is always the best item for those who want to cure their hangovers. Madam Ming serves Jjambbong spicier than ordinary Jjambbong and if you want far spicier one, you can add some hot chili oil. They also have distinctive seasonal dishes for each season.

Address	강남구 선릉로86길 5-4	5-4, Seolleung-ro 86-gil, Gangnam-gu
Contact	02-567-6992	82-2-567-6992
Web	www.madamming.com	www.madamming.com
Operation	11:30~21:30	11:30~21:30
Closed	일요일, 설·추석 연휴	Sun, Holiday of Lunar New Year's Day & Chuseok

홍콩반점 0410

오로지 짬뽕으로 승부를 거는 짬뽕 전문점. 주문 후 바로 조리하는 짬뽕, 짬뽕밥, 볶음짬뽕이 대표 메뉴다. 바삭한 군만두와 찹쌀 탕수육을 곁들여도 좋다. 여러 명이 간다면, 시원한 맥주와 해물 누룽지탕도 추천한다. 여름 한정 메뉴로 차가면과 냉짬뽕도 판매하니 참고하자.

Hong Kong Banjeom 0410

They put all of their efforts only for delicious Jjambbong. It is cooked right after an order is made and Jjambbong, Jjambbong Bap (with steamed rice) and Bokkeum Jjambbong (sauteed) are their main dishes. With these spicy noodle soups, a crispy Gun Mandu (fried dumplings) or Chapssal Tangsuyuk (sweet and sour pork) is well matched. If you visit with several people, Haemul Nurungji Tang (scorched sweet rice soup with seafood) and a glass of cool beer would be great. Note that Chagamyeon (noodle soup in chilled broth with various toppings on it) and Naeng Jjambbong (cold spicy noodle soup) are available for the summer months only.

Address	강남구 강남대로122길 15(논현 본점)		15, Gangnam-daero 122-gil, Gangnam-gu
Contact	02-540-0410		82-2-540-0410
Web	www.zzambbong.com		www.zzambbong.com
Operation	24시간		24 hours
Closed	설 · 추석 당일		Day of Lunar New Year's Day & Chuseok

차이옌

진하고 담백한 국물이 그리운 날 주방장의 특선 짬뽕을 주문해볼 것. 전복까지 아낌없이 넣은 온갖 해물 잔치에 속이 확 풀린다. 간장, 식초, 다진 파 등 여덟 가지 소스 재료가 함께 나와 원하는 대로 소스를 만들어 먹을 수 있는 빙화 군만두도 빼놓을 수 없는 별미다.

Chaiyen

If you are tempted by a thick and plain soup, Chef's special dish of Chaiyen would be great. The assorted seafood including a great deal of abalones would make your stomach feel satisfied. Binghwa Gunmandu (snowflake-shaped fried dumplings), to which you can add several ingredients as much as you want, is also special.

Address	용산구 이촌로88길 8		8, Ichon-ro 88-gil, Yongsan-gu
Contact	02-792-0872		82-2-792-0872
Operation	11:30~22:00(Break 15:00~17:00)		11:30~22:00(Break 15:00~17:00)
Closed	연중무휴		Open all year round

용정

산책하기 좋은 북촌길에 위치해 데이트 후 들르기 좋다. 사계절 내내 먹을 수 있는 삼선짬뽕, 신선한 제철 굴 맛을 즐길 수 있는 굴짬뽕, 고추와 춘장을 함께 넣어 칼칼하게 볶은 고추 짜장까지, 어떤 메뉴를 시켜도 후회가 없다. 코스 요리도 수준급이다.

Yongjeong

As this restaurant is located on the walking trail of Bukchon, it would be nice to put it on your list of date places. Samseon Jjambbong is served all year round and you can enjoy fresh taste of oysters in season from Gul jjambbong. Gochu Jajang (noodle roasted with chili pepper and black bean sauce) is also available. Whatever you choose among these dishes, you would never regret your choice. Their course cuisine is also wonderful.

Address	종로구 창덕궁1길 12	12, Changdeokgung 1-gil, Jongno-gu
Contact	02-747-3000	82-2-747-3000
Operation	11:00~21:00	11:00~21:00
Closed	일요일, 설 · 추석 연휴	Sun, Holiday of Lunar New Year's Day & Chuseok

야래향

회현동 일대 직장인들의 숙취 해소집으로도 알려진 곳. 시원한 짬뽕 국물은 유명 해장국 못지않다. 송이와 전복을 볶아 만드는 보양 요리 '전가복'은 신선한 재료의 맛이 그대로 살아 있다. 다만 손님이 몰리는 식사 시간대의 불친절한 서비스가 아쉽다.

Yaraehyang

This restaurant is well known as a good place to cure hangovers by nearby office workers. Its spicy noodle soup seems to have no rival in curing hangovers. Jeongabok, fried with abalones and pine mushrooms, is popular because of its flavor from fresh ingredients. But it would be better if their unfriendly service during busy lunch time would be improved.

Address	중구 퇴계로10길 14	14, Toegye-ro 10-gil, Jung-gu
Contact	02-752-3991	82-2-752-3991
Operation	11:30~22:00	11:30~22:00
Closed	설 · 추석 연휴	Holiday of Lunar New Year's Day & Chuseok

일품요리

한국인에게 가장 인기 있는 일품요리는 단연 탕수육. 중식당의 수준을 가늠하기 위해 시키기 좋은 메뉴이기도 하다. 바삭한 튀김옷과 육즙이 살아 있는 고기, 신맛과 단맛이 조화를 이루는 소스의 맛과 농도를 통해 주방장의 요리 실력을 엿볼 수 있기 때문이다. 그다음 인기 있는 메뉴는 깐풍기. 단시간에 양념을 더하고 튀김 고유의 바삭함을 잃지 않는 것이 포인트다. 허름한 탕수육 명소부터 중국 현지 요릿집을 옮겨놓은 듯한 연남동의 정통 중국집까지 한자리에 모았다.

À LA CARTE DISH

Korean's most favorite Chinese dish on à la carte menu is probably Tangsuyuk (sweet and sour pork). The taste of Tangsuyuk is sometimes a good standard to evaluate a Chinese restaurant. Its crispy batter, succulent meat and sweet yet sour sauce are much depending on a chef's skills. Kkanpunggi may follow Tangsuyuk in popularity. It is important to pour sauce right after frying chicken so that it does not lose crispy texture of its batter.

호화반점

갤러리아 백화점 맞은편에 위치한 곳. 튀김옷을 적당히 입혀 바삭한 탕수육이 일품이다. 새콤달콤한 소스는 기름진 음식을 좋아하지 않는 어른들 입맛에도 잘 맞는다. 기름진 식사 후 짬뽕으로 마무리하면 속이 편안하다.

Hohwa Banjeom

This restaurant is located across the street from the Galleria Department Store. Tangsuyuk with crispy batter is their specialty and its sweet and sour sauce is well agreeable to people who does not like greasy food. Finishing with a bowl of spicy Jjambbong after eating greasy food would make your stomach comfortable.

Address	강남구 압구정로54길 4		4, Apgujeong-ro 54-gil, Gangnam-gu
Contact	02-511-2125		82-2-511-2125
Operation	12:00~22:00		12:00~22:00
Closed	설·추석 당일		Day of Lunar New Year's Day & Chuseok

목란

TV 출연으로 인기몰이를 하고 있는 중식 대가 이연복 셰프가 운영하는 곳. 초기에는 모든 메뉴를 그가 직접 만들 정도로 정성을 들였다. 한국인의 입맛에 맞는 칼칼한 깐풍기와 부드럽게 튀긴 탕수육이 일품이다. 몇 시간이 지나도 탕수육의 튀김옷이 바삭바삭 살아 있다.

Mokran

Chef Lee Yeon-Bok, one of the most famous chefs these days, is the owner and head-chef of Mokran. In early days he cooked almost all dishes by himself. Kkanpunggi with fiery taste loved by almost all Koreans and Tangsuyuk with long lasted crispy texture of its batter are both their specialty.

Address	서대문구 연희로15길 21		21, Yeonhui-ro 15-gil, Seodaemun-gu
Contact	02-732-0054		82-2-732-0054
Operation	11:30~22:00		11:30~22:00
Closed	월요일		Mon

개화

명동 중앙우체국 옆 골목에 자리 잡은 곳으로, 음식 대부분이 자극적이지 않고 기름도 적게 사용하는 편이다. 고추잡채, 팔보채 등의 정갈한 칼질만 봐도 주방장의 내공을 알 수 있다.

Gaehwa

Located at the alley next to the Myeong-dong Central Post Office, this restaurant use less cooking oil and their dishes are not much spicy. The chef's excellent skills are well shown on neatly cutting ingredients of Gochu Japchae (sauteed chili peppers and pork) and Palbochae (sauteed mixed seafood and vegetables).

Address	중구 남대문로 52-5	52-5, Namdaemun-ro, Jung-gu
Contact	02-776-0508	82-2-776-0508
Operation	11:00~21:30	11:00~21:30
Closed	둘째 · 넷째 주 일요일, 설 · 추석 연휴	2nd and 4th Sun, Holiday of Lunar New Year's Day & Chuseok

리샨

강남 삼성전자 서초 사옥 지하에 위치한 리샨은 양이 부담 없고 담백한 일품요리를 선보인다. 대표 메뉴인 와사비 크림새우는 기존의 느끼한 크림새우에 와사비 소스를 가미해 톡 쏘면서도 달착지근하다.

Lisyan

Lisyan, situated on a basement level of the Samsung Town in Seocho-dong, serves à la carte dish with plain flavor and in an appropriate portion. Its specialty is Wasabi Cream Saeu (fried shrimp in cream and wasabi sauce) added with wasabi to relieve greasy flavor of original Cream Saeu.

Address	서초구 서초대로74길 11 지하 1층(삼성타운점)	B1F, 11, Seocho-daero 74-gil, Seocho-gu
Contact	02-587-6700	82-2-587-6700
Operation	11:00~22:00(Break 15:00~17:00)	11:00~22:00(Break 15:00~17:00)
Closed	설 · 추석 연휴	Holiday of Lunar New Year's Day & Chuseok

태가원

중국 요리의 황금기인 명·청 시대 요리 전문점. 중국인 주방장이 주방을 이끌기 때문에 직원 모두 원활한 소통을 위해 중국어 교육을 받았을 정도다. 총 250석의 다양한 크기와 분위기의 테이블, 중국 황실을 재현한 화려한 인테리어는 중국 본토에 와 있는 듯한 착각을 불러일으킨다. 왕새우 칠리소스가 대표 메뉴다.

Taegawon

Taegawon is specialized in cuisines of the Ming and Qing Dynasties, the golden age in the Chinese history. To efficiently communicate with a Chinese head chef, their waiting staff learns Chinese. Their 250 tables are much various in its size and shape and the splendid interiors of the hall would make you feel as if you are at an imperial palace of China. Wangsaeu Chili sauce (jumbo shrimp with chili sauce) is truly wonderful.

Address	강남구 영동대로 325	325, Yeongdong-daero, Gangnam-gu
Contact	02-555-3003	82-2-555-3003
Web	www.taegawon.com	www.taegawon.com
Operation	11:30~22:00	11:30~22:00
Closed	연중무휴	Open all year round

경발원

"이곳을 모르고 감히 최고의 깐풍기를 먹어봤다고 말하지 마라"라는 소문이 있을 정도로 맛 하나로 승부하는 집. 명성 높은 깐풍기는 고추와 부추를 넣어 매콤하게 양념해 술안주로 그만이다. 주문 후 바로 닭을 손질해 요리하기에 인내심을 갖고 음식이 나오길 기다려야 한다. 그리 친절한 편은 아니지만 맛 하나는 최고!

Gyeongbalwon

You have not eaten the best Kkanpunggi (deep-fried chicken in hot pepper sauce) until you have visited Gyeongbalwon. That is, Kkanpunggi of this restaurant has no rival. Plus, its spicy flavor from chili peppers and Chinese chives makes this meal a good side dish to alcoholic beverage. Right after you make an order, the chef starts to prepare chicken. For this reason it would take time for you to finally eat it. Unfortunately, you cannot expect friendly service.

Address	동대문구 망우로21길 34	34, Mangu-ro 21-gil, Dongdaemun-gu
Contact	02-2244-2616	82-2-2244-2616
Operation	12:00~21:30(Break 15:00~17:00)	12:00~21:30(Break 15:00~17:00)
Closed	일요일	Sun

명화원

한창 저녁 먹을 시간인 오후 7·8시만 되면 영업을 종료하는 배짱 두둑한 곳으로 찹쌀 탕수육이 특히 유명하다. 단, 허름한 인테리어나 불친절한 서비스에 상처받지 말자. 손님이 많아 30분 이상 기다리는 것도 감수해야 한다.

Myeonghwawon

This restaurant, near the Samgakgi Station, puts the closed sign on at 7 in the evening, when people are usually in the middle of dinner. So you will have to hurry up if you want their specialty, Chapssal Tangsuyuk (sweet and sour pork whose batter is made from glutinous rice flour). But please do not expect fancy interiors or very friendly service and you would have to wait for over 30 minutes.

Address	용산구 한강대로 202	202, Hangang-daero, Yongsan-gu
Contact	02-792-2969	82-2-792-2969
Operation	월~금 Mon to Fri 11:00~20:00(Break 15:00~17:00), 토 Sat 11:00~19:00	
Closed	일요일	Sun

브루스 리(구 팔선생)

탕수육 하면 두툼한 돼지고기를 한입 크기로 썰어놓은 탕수육만 알던 시절, 넓적하게 썬 고기에 찹쌀 반죽을 입힌 새콤달콤한 베이징 탕수육으로 화제를 일으킨 곳. 2013년에 이름을 '브루스 리'라고 바꾸고 수제 딤섬, 만두, 면, 죽 등의 메뉴를 추가로 선보인다.

Bruce Lee (formerly 'Palseonsaeng')

In those days, when people thought that Tangsuyuk was simple fried pork, this restaurant started serving a new Beijing-style Tangsuyuk, by wearing glutinous rice flour batter over meat cut into thin slices. In 2013, they changed their name to 'Bruce Lee' and added some items like Suje Dim Sum (handmade dumplings), Mandu (dumplings), noodle dishes, Juk (porridge), etc. on their menu. The store is closed to the Hak-dong intersection.

Address	강남구 선릉로14길 5	5, Seolleung-ro 14-gil, Gangnam-gu
Contact	02-548-8845	82-2-548-8845
Operation	11:30~00:00	11:30~00:00
Closed	설·추석 당일	Day of Lunar New Year's Day & Chuseok

루이

서울 신라 호텔 '팔선' 출신의 중식 조리장 여경옥의 레스토랑. 식욕을 돋우는 소스의 맛과 튀긴 닭의 바삭한 식감이 유쾌한 유린기와 여름철 보양식 불도장을 추천한다.

Luii

Chef Yeo Kyung-Ok, from Palsun, a Chinese restaurant of the Shilla Seoul Hotel, is the owner cum head-chef of Luii in Gwanghwamun. With its crispy texture and savory sauce, Yuringi (fried chicken with hot and sour sauce) is considered its specialty. Buldojang (Chinese soup with chicken, seafood and medicinal ingredients), is also popular as a health food for summer.

Address	중구 세종대로21길 40(광화문점)	40, Sejong-daero 21-gil, Jung-gu
Contact	02-736-8889	82-2-736-8889
Web	www.luii.co.kr	www.luii.co.kr
Operation	11:30~21:30(Break 14:30~17:30)	11:30~21:30(Break 14:30~17:30)
Closed	설·추석 당일	Day of Lunar New Year's Day & Chuseok

송가

맛과 콘셉트 모두 중국 현지 스타일에 충실한 곳. 흔한 짜장면과 짬뽕을 찾아볼 수 없고 중국식 술안주와 가정식 요리가 주를 이룬다. 대파로 속을 채운 돼지곱창, 돼지 위 냉채 등은 색다른 중식에 도전하고 싶어 하는 이들에게 추천한다.

Songga

Its taste and concept are much closed to a local Chinese restaurant in China. Located in Yeonnam-dong, Songga does not serve Jajangmyeon and Jjambbong but its main items on the menu are Chinese-style pub grubs and home-style cuisines. Dwaeji Gopchang (pork chitterlings) crammed with spring onion and Dwaejiwi Naengchae (cold pork tripe salad) are good items for those who look for an unusual Chinese cuisine.

Address	마포구 성미산로 197	197, Seongmisan-ro, Mapo-gu
Contact	02-338-6637	82-2-338-6637
Operation	17:00~23:30	17:00~23:30
Closed	일요일	Sun

크리스탈 제이드 상하이 딜라이트

정통 상하이 요리를 선보이며, 특히 신선한 재료와 수제 만두피가 어우러진 샤오롱바오와 면 요리가 수준급이다. 샤오롱바오는 세트로 주문할 수 있으며, 만두피를 찢어 흘러나오는 탕즙을 마신 뒤 내용물을 먹는 것이 정석이다. 상하이식 일품요리가 궁금하다면 아스파라거스 가리비볶음이나 상하이식 칠리 새우, 고추 닭고기볶음, 탕수육 등의 메뉴를 주문해볼 것.

Crystal Jade Shanghai Delight

They serve authentic Shanghai-style cuisines and among them, noodles dishes and Xiaolongbao (a kind of Chinese dumplings) with fresh ingredients in handmade wrappers are excellent. The most desirable way to enjoy Xiaolongbao, served only as an item of a set menu, is sipping broth coming from a torn dumpling wrapper slowly and then eating dumpling filling. If you want to try à la carte dish cooked in the Shanghai style, Asparagus Garibi Bokkeum (sauteed scallops with asparagus) and Chili Saeu (chili shrimp), Gochu Dakgogi Bokkeum (sauteed chicken with chili peppers) and Tangsuyuk would be great.

Address	서초구 사평대로 205(센트럴시티점)	205, Sapyeong-daero, Seocho-gu
Contact	02-599-8818	82-2-599-8818
Web	www.crystaljade.co.kr	www.crystaljade.co.kr
Operation	10:00~22:00(Break 15:00~16:30)	10:00~22:00(Break 15:00~16:30)
Closed	연중무휴	Open all year round

코스 요리

다양한 재료와 조리법을 자랑하는 중국 음식의 진가는 역시 최고급 코스 요리에서 드러난다. 샥스핀과 바닷가재 등 고급 식재료를 아낌없이 사용해 미식가들에게 호응을 얻는 곳도 있고, 중식에 보르도산 와인을 매치해 갈라 디너까지 선보이는 곳도 있다. 그만큼 코스 요리야말로 중식당의 스타일과 실력을 마음껏 발휘할 수 있는 요리다. 최고급 음식과 극진한 서비스, 고풍스러운 분위기가 뛰어난 중식 코스 요리 전문점 여섯 곳을 소개한다.

COURSE MENU

A true taste of Chinese cuisines, using a diversity of ingredients with endless variations in recipes, is well proved when you taste a fine course cuisine. Using gourmet ingredients like shark's fin or lobster or presenting a gala dinner program serving Chinese cuisines with a bottle of Bordeaux wine, some upscale Chinese restaurants are attracting more and more epicures.

청

모던하고 조용해 여유롭게 코스 요리를 즐기기 좋은 집. 너무 격식 차리거나 지나치게 캐주얼하지 않은 편안한 분위기에서 식사할 수 있다. 한때 삼청동에서 인기를 끌었으나 2014년 9월 한남동으로 이전해 운영하고 있다. 해물 냉채가 입맛을 돋워 부담 없이 코스 요리를 즐길 수 있다.

Chung

Chung is a good place to enjoy a course meal in a modern, tranquil atmosphere. Not too formal, not too casual, this restaurant would make you feel comfortable while you are dining. In 2014, Chung moved to Hannam-dong from Samcheong-dong. Its Haemul Naengchae (chilled seafood salad) is an excellent appetizer of a course meal.

Address	용산구 한남대로20길 47-24 D동 2층	2F, 47-24, Hannam-daero 20-gil, Yongsan-gu
Contact	02-720-3396	82-2-720-3396
Web	www.chinesechung.com	www.chinesechung.com
Operation	11:30~22:30(Break 15:00~17:30)	11:30~22:30(Break 15:00~17:30)
Closed	설·추석 연휴	Holiday of Lunar New Year's Day & Chuseok

홍보각

한국 최고의 중식 조리장 중 한 명으로 손꼽히는 여경래 셰프가 주방을 책임지는 그랜드 앰배서더 서울 내 중식당. 수준급 서비스와 중국 본토의 맛을 재현해내는 셰프의 솜씨를 만끽할 수 있다.

Hong Bo Gak

Chef Yeo Kyung-Rae, one of the veteran chefs of Chinese cuisine in Korea, is the executive chef of Hong Bo Gak in the Grand Ambassador Seoul. In its excellent service, you would enjoy the chef's high caliber in his cuisines.

Address	중구 동호로 287	287, Dongho-ro, Jung-gu
Contact	02-2270-3141	82-2-2270-3141
Operation	12:00~22:00(Break 14:30~18:00)	12:00~22:00(Break 14:30~18:00)
Closed	연중무휴	Open all year round

팔선 / Palsun

미식가들에게 최고의 중식당으로 손꼽히는 서울 신라 호텔의 팔선. 한국인이 선호하는 베이징 요리에 기반을 두고 있으며 최근에는 웰빙 트렌드에 따라 굽고 찌는 방식을 접목해 코스 요리를 먹어도 부담이 없다. 코스 요리 마지막에 나오는 고소한 짜장면까지 정성을 다한다.

Epicures always choose Palsun of the Shilla Seoul as one of the best Chinese restaurants in Seoul. Originally based on Beijing-style cuisines preferred by Koreans, they recently introduced a well-being cooking method. You would taste its chef's skill from Jajangmyeon, the last item of a course dish.

Address	중구 동호로 249	249, Dongho-ro, Jung-gu
Contact	02-2230-3366	82-2-2230-3366
Web	www.shilla.net	www.shilla.net
Operation	12:00~22:00(Break 14:30~18:00)	12:00~22:00(Break 14:30~18:00)
Closed	연중무휴	Open all year round

홍연 / Hong Yuan

서울 웨스틴 조선 호텔에 위치하며 모던한 느낌의 룸과 붉은 톤으로 세련되게 연출한 홀의 인테리어가 매혹적이다. 합리적인 가격에 대표 메뉴를 즐길 수 있는 주말 특선 코스와 평일 오후 차이니스 티 타임을 추천한다.

The modern interiors of the hall decorated in the reddish tone look attractive as well. Hong Yuan is placed in the Westin Chosun Seoul. The weekend choice menu offered at a reasonable price and Chinese tea time on a weekday afternoon are famous.

Address	중구 소공로 106 지하 1층	B1F, 106, Sogong-ro, Jung-gu
Contact	02-317-0494	82-2-317-0494
Web	www.echosunhotel.com	www.echosunhotel.com
Operation	12:00~22:00(Break 14:30~18:00)	12:00~22:00(Break 14:30~18:00)
Closed	상황에 따라 다름	Closed date may vary, please call in advance to confirm.

타이판

밀레니엄 서울 힐튼의 중식 레스토랑으로 호텔 일대의 비즈니스맨이 많이 찾는다. 세계 밀레니엄 힐튼 체인에서 활동하는 중국 셰프뿐 아니라 싱가포르, 대만 등의 셰프를 초빙해 다양한 크로스오버 메뉴를 선보여 찾을 때마다 새롭다. 그중에서도 생선찜, 바닷가재찜 등 주로 해산물을 중심으로 한 광둥 요리는 깔끔하고 담백한 맛이 일품이다.

Taipan

Taipan, a Chinese restaurant of the Millennium Seoul Hilton is a popular place with nearby business people. They have invited Chinese chefs of other Millennium Hotel branches and other renowned chefs from Singapore and Thailand to offer a varied crossover cuisine. In particular, Cantonese cuisines using seafood as main ingredients, such as steamed fish or steamed lobster, are boasting their simple and plain flavor.

Address	중구 소월로 50 지하 1층
Contact	02-317-3237
Web	www.seoul.hilton.co.kr
Operation	11:30~22:00(Break 14:30~18:00)
Closed	연중무휴

Address	B1F, 50, Sowol-ro, Jung-gu
Contact	82-2-317-3237
Web	www.seoul.hilton.co.kr
Operation	11:30~22:00(Break 14:30~18:00)
Closed	Open all year round

가향

결혼을 앞둔 커플들 사이에서 상견례 명소로 알려진 대치동의 중식당. 소규모 모임을 할 때 주로 찾으며 남녀노소 즐길 수 있는 깔끔한 코스 요리와 서비스가 일품이다. 정통 중식에 기반을 두지만 찜 요리가 많아 어른들도 부담 없이 즐길 수 있다.

Gahyang

Gahyang, a Chinese restaurant in Daechi-dong, is popular as a meeting place between families of the bride and the bridegroom or of a small group of people. Not to mention an excellent service, a neatly prepared course dish is remarkable. While representing authentic Chinese cuisine, they serve meals in various steamed recipes, which are agreeable to old people's taste.

Address	강남구 삼성로 706
Contact	02-516-6859
Operation	09:00~22:00
Closed	설·추석 전날과 당일

Address	706, Samseong-ro, Gangnam-gu
Contact	82-2-516-6859
Operation	09:00~22:00
Closed	The eve and the day of Lunar New Year's Day & Chuseok

dining story

프랑스 요리는 어떻게

미식의 최고봉이 되었나?

"프랑스 요리는 미인과 같다. 향을 즐기려면 기다려야 한다." 프랑스의 정치가이자 미식가인 브리야 사바랭의 말이다. 음식을 예술이자 쾌락으로 생각하는 프랑스 요리는 세계 미식의 기준이라 할 수 있다. 음식 문화 전체가 유네스코 세계무형문화유산으로 등재됐을 정도다. 프랑스 요리가 세계 최고가 된 배경과 힘, 대표 음식과 특징은 과연 무엇일까?

프랑스혁명, 프렌치 퀴진의 전성기를 열다

프랑스에서 가장 부러운 것 중 하나가 천혜의 자연환경이다. 대서양, 지중해와 접한 해안 길이가 5000km에 이르고 국토의 3분의 2가 남북으로 넓게 펼쳐진 기름진 평원인 이곳에서는 다양한 먹을거리가 재배된다. 파리 중심에 있는, 수백 년 전통의 무프타르mouffetard 거리 시장에 가면 정육점에는 사냥한 꿩과 야생 토끼가 걸려 있고, 치즈 가게에는 소젖, 양젖, 염소젖으로 만든 수백 가지 치즈가 진열돼 있다. 돼지고기 전문 매장인 샤르퀴트리charcuterie에는 곰팡이가 핀 건조 소시지, 돼지 허벅지를 숙성시킨 햄, 내장으로 만든 순대 등 수십 종류의 돼지고기 가공품이 절로 군침이 돌게 한다. 베르사유 궁전을 방문하면 궁전뿐만 아니라 거대한 정원과 연못에서 벌어졌을 장대하고 화려한 연회가 연상된다. 수많은 왕과 귀족의 연회를 통해 프랑스 요리는 더욱 세련되고 정교해졌으며, 요리 기술 또한 지속해서 발전했다. 17세기부터 통일 국가를 이루고 절대왕권을 확립한 프랑스는 오랫동안 유럽의 중심이었다. 프랑스 어는 유럽 귀족의 공용어였고, 파리는 문화의 중심지였으며, 프랑스 요리는 서양 요리의 근간이었다.

프랑스혁명은 요리 발전에 결정적인 역할을 했다. 왕과 귀족이 처형되거나 망명하면서 이들이 고용한 요리사들이 거리로 나올 수밖에 없었기 때문이다. 그들이 대중을 위해 음식을 만들면서 파리를 중심으로 레스토랑이 급속도로 성행했다. 귀족 음식이 점점 대중화되고 외식 산업이 발전하면서 19세기 말에 이르러 고도로 세련된 '오트 퀴진haute cuisine'이 유럽 요리계를 지배했다. 이른바 '프랑스 요리의 제국주의' 시대가 열린 것이다. 서양 요리 용어 중 상당수가 프랑스 어이고, 오늘날 세계 많은 도시에서 프렌치 레스토랑을 가장 뛰어난 서양 요리를 맛볼 수 있는 곳으로 여기는 데는 이런 역사적 배경이 있다. 자국은 물론이고 여러 식민지에서 공수한 온갖 재료를 활용할 수 있었다는 점도 프랑스 요리가 막강해진 이유 중 하나다. 왕의 파티시에였던 앙토냉 카렘, 19세기 말까지 프랑스 고전 요리 조리법을 집대성한 오귀스트 에스코피에부터 폴 보퀴즈, 조엘 로부숑, 알랭 뒤카스까지 프렌치 퀴진의 전통과 스타일이 매끄럽게 이어진 것도 프랑스 음식 문화 발전에 큰 역할을 했다. 프랑스 셰프들은 요리사를 최고의 아티스트로 인정하고 대접하는 프랑스의 사회적 분위기를 동력 삼아 지금도 세계 곳곳에서 창작욕을 불태우고 있다.

오트 퀴진, 왕정과 귀족 문화의 아름다운 압축

고급 레스토랑에서 오트 퀴진을 맛보는 즐거움은 프랑스 요리의 역사와 문화를 압축해서 즐기는 최고의 방법이다. 입을 즐겁게 하는 아뮤즈부슈 amouse-bouche, 샴페인이나 가벼운 화이트 와인 같은 식전주인 아페리티프 aperitif, 다양한 전채 요리, 해산물과 육류로 대표되는 메인 요리, 모듬 치즈, 디저트, 차와 소화를 돕는 식후주 순서로 진행된다. 소믈리에가 추천한 와인과 함께 요리를 즐기는데 다음 코스로 넘어가는 시간이 20~30분 이상이라 보통 두세 시간 넘게 식사를 한다. 프랑스가 자랑하는 세계 3대 진미는 오트 퀴진을 구성하는 핵심 요소라 할 만하다. 먼저 캐비아. 달지 않으면서 상큼한 브뤼 brut, 프랑스 어로 '가공하지 않은'이란 뜻. 샴페인이나 스파클링 와인 맛이 드라이할 때 이 단어로 표현한다 샴페인에 곁들이면 더 맛있게 즐길 수 있다. 캐비아의 비릿하면서 짠맛이 샴페인의 산도와 어울려 풍부하고 상큼한 맛을 선사한다. 전채로 자주 나오는 푸아 그라 foie gras도 빼놓을 수 없다. 푸아 그라는 거위 간이라고 알려져 있는데, 사실 대부분 오리 간이고 거위 간은 10퍼센트 정도다. 센 불로 팬에 구워 과일과 달콤한 소스를 곁들이거나, 틀테린에 넣어 중탕으로 익힌 후 식으면 적당히 잘라 샐러드나 과일, 구운 빵과 함께 내놓는다. 마지막 진미는 식탁 위의 다이아몬드라 불리는 트러플 truffle, 송로버섯. 인공 재배할 수 없어 더 귀하다.

향토 음식에서 찾는 프렌치 퀴진의 DNA

소스를 중시하고, 생크림과 버터, 향신료를 다양한 방법으로 활용하던 프랑스 요리의 전통적 특징은 1970년대 '누벨 퀴진 nouvelle cuisine, 새로운 요리'이 등장하면서 크게 달라졌다. 모든 식재료를 주문과 함께 즉시 조리해 접시에 올리기 위해 요리 가짓수를 줄이고 단순하면서도 시각적인 아름다움을 추구하는 것이 누벨 퀴진의 특징. 고열량, 고지방 첨가물인 생크림과 버터는 점점 사용이 줄어들고, 소나 송아지 뼈를 곤 육수로 만드는 등 엄청난 공을 들이던 소스 역시 가볍게 찍어 먹는 정도로 트렌드가 바뀌었다. 그 때문에 누벨 퀴진에서 프랑스 요리의 뿌리와 DNA를 발견하기가 점점 어려워지고 있다. 진짜 프랑스 요리란 어떤 것일까, 하는 물음에 속 시원한 답을 제시할 수 있는 것은 오히려 향토 음식이다. '맛있는 집 밥'을 맛볼 수 있는 비스트로나 간단한 식사는 물론 다양한 술까지 판매하는 브라세리를 찾는 것이 진짜 프랑스 음식을 경험하는 좋은 방법이 되는 것이다.

최근에는 한층 업그레이드한 음식을 선보인다는 뜻에서 이름 붙인 '가스트로 비스트로 가스트로노미gastronomy와 비스트로bistro의 합성어' 식당도 많아지는 추세다.

프랑스 요리 하면 떠오르는 에스카르고escargot는 한 번 익힌 달팽이 살을 달팽이 껍데기에 넣고 입구를 허브와 마늘을 섞은 버터로 막아 오븐에서 익혀낸다. 오리 다리와 가슴살을 오리 기름에 서서히 익혀 저장했다가 오븐이나 팬에서 구워내는 '콩피 드 카나르confit de canard', 푸아 그라를 위해 살찌운 오리 가슴살 껍질 쪽을 바삭하게 굽고 오렌지 소스와 곁들여 내는 '마그레 드 카나르magret de canard'가 대표적 가금류 요리다. 개구리 뒷다리를 버터, 마늘, 파슬리에 볶는 '퀴스 드 그러누이 소테cuisse de grenouille sautée'도 대중적이다. 뒷다리 뼈를 발라내고 그 안을 채우다 보면 손에 쥐가 날 정도지만 별미임은 분명하다. 영국인은 이런 프랑스 식문화를 타깃 삼아 '개구리 먹는 사람들frog eaters'이라고 조롱하기도 한다.

와인의 나라답게 와인을 곁들인 향토 요리도 많다. 와인과 육수에 수탉을 익힌 찜 요리 '코코뱅coq au vin', 쇠고기 사태처럼 질긴 부위를 와인에 푹 익힌 '뵈프 부르기뇽bœuf bourguignon', 쇠고기 양지 또는 꼬리를 당근, 무, 대파 등과 함께 넣고 푹 삶은 다음 꼬마 오이 피클, 굵은 소금과 곁들이는 '포토푀pot au feu'도 즐겨 먹는다. 올리브유에 채소를 볶고 허브를 곁들이는 '라타투이ratatouille'는 니스 지방의 대표 음식이다. 군대와 학교에서 특히 자주 나오는데 대량으로 만들면 맛이 없어 맛없는 메뉴가 나오면 "오늘도 라타투이네"라고 말한다. 만화영화 <라따뚜이>에서 냉혹한 요리 평론가 안톤 이고가 먹고 눈물을 흘린 음식이 바로 라타투이. 프랑스에서는 어릴 적 어머니가 만들어주신 '집 밥'을 의미하기도 한다.

글. 정한진

dining story

French Cuisine, a Very Diamond of Gastronomy

"French cuisine is like a beautiful woman. You have to wait if you want to appreciate its or her fragrance," said Jean Anthelme Brillat-Savarin, a French politician and famous epicure. The culinary culture of France, in which food itself is regarded as an art and great pleasure, has contributed significantly to other Western culture and provided criteria to evaluate the taste of the world. In 2010, French gastronomy was added to the list of the world's intangible cultural heritage by the UNESCO. Let's take a look at the background and power of French cuisine and a variety of delicacies and their own characteristic.

FRENCH REVOLUTION, A NEW PATH TO THE GLORY OF FRENCH CUISINE

One of the biggest advantages French cuisine has is a wonderful natural environment and resulting rich resources. The length of its coastline bordering the Atlantic ocean and the Mediterranean sea is roughly 5,000 km and two-thirds of the country is covered with fertile farmland in which various food materials can be cultivated. This banquet for numerous kings and nobles continued to enhance the quality and cooking method of the French cuisine. Since Louis XIV consolidated the absolute monarchial rule in France in the 17th century, France had been central in Europe. French language was used as an official language by noblemen in many European countries in the past, Paris has remained a cultural center of the world until now and cooking skills and recipes of French cuisine provided the foundation for Western cuisines. The French Revolution was integral to the rapid development of the French cuisine. As King Louis XVI was executed by the guillotine, chefs who worked in the palace came out to a street and started to produce and sell any culinary item for the public, not for the king. In this way, the cuisine originally prepared for the king and nobles became common and popularized and restaurants were thriving around Paris, which later resulted in an emergence of highly refined 'haute cuisine' in the end of the 19th century. This meant an outset of a so-called 'culinary imperialism' of France. This historical fact explained why most of culinary terms are written in French and why French gastronomy is always considered the best Western cuisine all around the world. The use of various food materials procured from many French colonies as well as France was another important factor to consolidate the status of the French cuisine.

Many French chefs, for instance, Marie-Antoine Carême who worked as a patissier in the king's palace, Georges Auguste Escoffier who organized all the classical cooking skills of France until the 19th century, Paul Bocuse, Joël Robuchon and Alain Ducasse, can maintain and improve the culinary culture of France by handing down the tradition and style of the French cuisine. And the French society which regards an excellent chef as an artist continues to boost their abilities to the utmost.

HAUTE CUISINE, AN ESSENCE OF FRENCH COURT CULTURE

Enjoying haute cuisine is probably the best way to appreciate the culinary history and culture of France. The haute cuisine consists of amuse-bouche (literally a light dish to amuse your mouth), apéritif (alcoholic drink served before a meal), hors d'oeuvre, main course (usually seafood or meat), cheese course, dessert and digestif (alcoholic drink served after a meal). And the haute cuisine is accompanied usually by fine wine based on a sommelier's recommendation. As it takes about 20 to 30 minutes to move from one course to the next, it takes two to three hours generally to complete the entire meal. The world three delicacies take up a primary part of this haute cuisine. The first delicacy is caviar. A glass of brut champagne, not too sweet and fresh, improves the taste of the caviar more ('brut' meaning 'unprocessed' in French is used to describe a dry taste of champagne or sparkling wine), because the acids in champagne imparts richer and fresher flavor when it is combined with the fishy and salty taste of caviar. The second delicacy is foie gras, a popular dish for hors d'oeuvre. The foie gras is known to be made of a goose liver but most of them are made of a duck liver. The proportion of the goose liver is approximately 10% of the whole consumption. The foie gras is fried on the pan at high heat and then added with a sweet sauce. Or, there is a foie gras terrine served with salad, fruits or baked bread and it is made by packing the whole raw liver into a terrine mold and then boiling at low temperature in a double boiler. The third and last is truffes ('truffle' in English), also called "the diamond of the kitchen." As it is not possible yet to cultivate truffles in an artificial way, truffles are much rare and scarce and highly expensive.

LOCAL CUISINE, A TRUE SUCCESSOR OF FRENCH CUISINE

The traditional characteristic of the French cuisine, that is, putting an emphasis on sauce and using fresh cream, butter and spice in a number of ways, experienced the greatest change, when nouvelle cuisine ("new cuisine") emerged in the 1970s as a new approach to cooking and food presentation in French cuisine. To cook all the ingredients right after an order is made, this approach reduces the number of dishes and focuses on simple, delicate food presentation. In this approach, also, there are tendencies to reduce the use of fresh cream and butter with high calorie and high fat and avoid the use of sauce made in existing complex way. This being so, it became difficult to find the root and essence of the French cuisine from the nouvelle cuisine. Rather, a local dish would come up with an answer to the question, 'What is the French cuisine?' A bistro serving up a delicious home-style dish or a brasserie offering various alcoholic beverages as well as a light meal would be a good place to experience a true taste of the French cuisine. Recently there are more and more gastro-bistros, a bistro serving up a gastronomic food.

The first cuisine that comes to our mind when we think of French cuisine is Escargot. For this dish, the snails, removed from their shells and cooked once, are placed back into the shells with the butter mixed with herbs and garlics and then cooked again in the oven. Confit de Canard and Magret de Canard are also typical French dishes using fowl as main materials. Confit de Canard is made by grilling the slow-cooked duck breast and legs on the pan or in the oven and Magret de Canard means a grilled duck breast with an orange sauce. Cuisse de Grenouille Sautées, frog's hind legs sautéed with butter, garlic and parsley, is one of the most traditional and popular French cuisines. Though it is not easy to remove a bone from the leg and put a filling into it, this dish is a definitely excellent delicacy. Some English people call those who enjoy this food 'frog eaters' with a sneer. There are a variety of local cuisines using wine as an ingredient, for example, Coq au Vin (rooster braised in wine and broth), Bœuf Bourguignon (beef braised in wine for a long time), Pot-au-feu (beef cooked with carrots, white radish and scallion and then served with pickled gherkins and coarse salt). Ratatouille, vegetables sautéed in olive oil and added with herbs, is a traditional French dish, originating in Nice. But as this dish is also commonly served in schools and military camps, it somehow became a pronoun of an unpopular, tasteless food. In the film Ratatouille, however, you can see Anton Ego, a discriminating restaurant critic, eating Ratatouille with tears in his eyes. In France, Ratatouille means a dish that a mom makes at home in a nostalgic aspect.

Contributor Chung Han-Jin

dining story
:
Basic
Ingredients
for
French Gastronomy

프랑스
미식을
완성하는

기본
식재료

해양성·지중해성·대륙성 기후가 공존해 유럽 기후의 축소판이라 할 수 있는 프랑스. 전 국토에서 나는 채소와 과일 등의 신선 식품은 물론 치즈와 버터 등의 유제품, 푸아 그라와 송로버섯 등 특별하고 고급스러운 식재료는 프랑스 미식을 지탱하는 원천이 되었다.

Geographically, the oceanic, continental and Mediterranean climates are all found in France. Owing to this diverse climate, it has become possible to procure a wide variety of food materials within France, from fresh vegetables, fruits and dairy products including cheese and butter to rare and expensive ingredients such as foie gras and truffles, which in turn provide and support the foundation of the French cuisine.

치즈

매년 150만 톤에 이르는 1000여 종의 치즈를 생산하는 치즈 왕국 프랑스. 넓고 비옥한 목초지에서 키운 소젖, 양젖, 염소젖으로 양질의 치즈를 만드는 유럽 최대 치즈 생산국이다. 프랑스 치즈를 구입할 때는 프랑스 국립 원산지 명칭 연구소 INAO가 통제하는 AOC와 유럽연합이 관장하는 AOP 인증 마크를 획득했는지 확인할 것. 국내에도 잘 알려진 노르망디의 부드럽고 촉촉한 카망베르, 아키텐-미디피레네의 양젖 치즈 로크포르가 대표적이다.

밀가루

프랑스는 주식이 빵이니만큼 밀가루 역시 발달했다. 프랑스의 밀가루 분류법은 구체적이며, 봉투에 적힌 숫자로 종류를 확인할 수 있다. 디저트를 만들 때 쓰는 밀가루는 Type 45, 빵을 만드는 데 쓰는 밀가루는 Type 55로 표기한다. 숫자가 높아질수록 단백질 함량이 높다.

푸아 그라

기원전 이집트 인은 철새인 야생 거위가 대이동하기 직전, 미리 먹이를 먹고 에너지를 축적한다는 것을 알고 있었다. 이렇게 비대해진 간은 훨씬 더 기름지고 부드러워 미식가들이 탐내는 고급 식재료로 사랑받았다. 프랑스에 알려진 것은 북동부 알자스Alsace로 이주한 유대 인들이 돼지 대신 오리나 거위를 키우면서 푸아 그라 조리법을 전파한 이후부터. 거위에게 억지로 사료를 먹이는 가혹한 사육 방식 때문에 유럽 대다수 국가에서 생산과 판매를 금지했지만, 프랑스는 여전히 전 세계 푸아 그라 생산량의 80퍼센트를 차지한다.

송로버섯

푸아 그라, 캐비아와 더불어 세계 3대 진미로 꼽히는 송로버섯. 못생긴 감자처럼 투박하고, 퀴퀴하며 독특한 향을 풍긴다. 대표적인 생산 지역은 페리고르다. 버섯을 캐는 전문 업자들이 암퇘지 또는 개를 데리고 다니며 땅속에 숨어 있는 송로버섯을 찾는다.

달걀

프랑스인이 달걀 코너에서 꼭 확인하는 것은 '달걀 코드'. 자연 방사 유정란은 0, 항생제를 쓰지 않은 무항생제 유정란은 2, 공장형 양계장에서 나온 일반란은 3으로 코드 첫 번째 숫자를 표기한다. 그다음은 나라 이름의 약자인 FR, 마지막 숫자는 양계장 이름을 코드화해 쓴다.

버터

버터는 프랑스 요리에서 가장 많이 쓰이는 기본 식재료 중 하나다. 프랑스에 버터가 전해진 것은 스칸디나비아 게르만 지역의 바이킹이 노르망디를 정복한 11세기경. 프랑스에서 AOC 인증을 받은 버터 중 가장 유명한 이지니Isigny 버터는 오랜 시간 숙성해 부드럽고 진한 헤이즐넛 향이 난다. 루아르Loire 지방에서 생산하는 에시레Échiré는 살균을 하지 않고 티크 나무통에서 숙성하는 전통 방식을 고수한다. 타닌 맛이 과하게 배지 않아 풍미가 진하고 부드럽다.

머스터드

프랑스의 고급 소스 머스터드는 겨자씨를 분쇄한 뒤 와인과 소금, 향신료 등의 재료를 넣어 알싸한 맛이 나도록 가공한 것으로 1850년대 부르고뉴의 디종Dijon에서 처음 탄생했다. 갓 간 페이스트는 눈물이 찔끔 나올 만큼 매운맛이 나지만, 여기에 식초나 포도즙, 와인 원액을 첨가한 뒤 레몬이나 라즈베리 같은 과일, 절인 생선, 케이퍼 등 부재료를 더해 각기 다른 맛을 만든다.

소금

북서부의 게랑드Guerande 마을과 남부의 카마르그Camargue 마을은 프랑스의 프리미엄 소금 산지다. 이곳의 흙바닥에서 만든 토판염은 바다와 갯벌의 미네랄을 흡수해 영양분이 풍부하고 맛이 좋아 세계적으로 사랑받는 소금이다. 그중에서도 회색을 띠는 토판염을 더 고급으로 친다. 천일염보다 입자가 곱고 바닷물이 증발하기 전 얇은 소금막을 걷어내 뽀얀 흰색을 띠는 플뢰르 드 셀fleur de sel은 '소금의 꽃'이라는 이름처럼 짠맛과 단맛, 감칠맛의 균형이 완벽하다.

달팽이

포도잎을 즐겨 먹는 달팽이는 프랑스 최고 와인 산지 중 하나인 부르고뉴의 특산물이다. 원래는 고대 로마 인이 즐겨 먹던 식재료인데 부르고뉴산 달팽이가 인기를 끌면서 약 20가지 이상의 조리법이 생겨났다.

와인 식초

식초는 곡물, 과일, 허브, 술 등을 발효해서 만드는 일종의 조미료다. 곡물을 발효해 만든 아시아의 흑초, 스페인 헤레스 지역의 셰리 식초 등이 유명하며 이탈리아의 발사믹 식초, 프랑스의 보르도나 부르고뉴에서 나오는 화이트 & 레드 비니거 등 포도주로 만든 식초도 있다. 와인 식초는 톡 쏘는 특유의 향과 새콤달콤한 끝 맛이 매력적이며 주로 샐러드 등의 드레싱과 소스로 활용한다.

CHEESE

France is the largest cheese producer in Europe, producing over 1.5 million tons of cheese every year. Their 1,000 different types of a good-quality cheese are made from cow milks, sheep milk and goat milk and these animals are raised in the large, fertile grassland. When you buy French cheese, you should check whether it is obtained the French AOC logo from INAO and the AOP certification mark protected by the EU. Camembert, soft and moist cheese of Normandy, and Roquefort, a sheep milk cheese of Aquitaine and Midi-Pyrénées are the most typical cheeses of France.

WHEAT FLOUR

In France where bread is consumed as a staple food, the type of wheat flour is classified according to more detailed criteria. The number on the package indicates the type of flour. Type 45 is usually used for desserts and Type 55 is for baking. The higher number means the flour has the higher protein content.

FOIE GRAS

Around 2500 BC, the ancient Egyptians learned that wild geese used to be fattened by overfeeding in advance before their migration. And their fattened livers came to be preferred by many gourmets because of the more greasy and soft texture. After Jewish people who raised duck or goose instead of pig settled down in Alsace, the northeastern region of France, the recipe of foie gras was widely spread. The force-feeding or sale of foie gras has been banned in most of the European countries because of a practice of fattening geese or ducks by force-feeding but France is still the largest producer of foie gras, accounting for 80% of world production.

TRUFFLE

Truffle is one of the world's three delicacies along with foie gras and caviar. It looks like an ugly potato or bumpy rock and smells fusty. The major truffle producing region is Périgord. Truffle hunters tend to employ truffle hog or truffle dog to locate and extract truffles from underground.

EGG

If you want to buy some eggs in France you should check the egg code first. The first number of the egg code indicates four levels of production quality, for example, '0' for an organic egg production, '2' for fertile egg from deep-litter indoor housing system and '3' for ordinary egg from battery cage farming. Then the country code 'FR', an abbreviation of France follows it. The last number means egg production facilities.

BUTTER

Butter is one of the most common and basic ingredients for the French cuisine. The butter was first introduced in France around the 11th century when the Vikings who came from the German part of Scandinavia conquered Normandy. Beurre d'Isigny, the most famous butter that obtained the AOC logo, is very soft because it is aged for a long time. It also gives off a strong scent of hazelnut. Beurre Échiré is made in a traditional way that the butter is not pasteurized but is aged in a teak-wood barrel. In this fashion, the butter has deep and soft flavor, with not strong tannin taste.

MUSTARD

A high-quality mustard of France was created in Dijon, Burgundy in the 1850s. The ground mustard seeds are mixed with wine, salt and other spices to bring out spicy flavor. The first taste of the mustard is very tangy but when mustard mixed with vinegar, grape juice or crude wine meets fruits (lemon or raspberry) and other ingredients (pickled fish or caper), the taste varies in different ways.

SALT

Guérande, the northwest region of France, and Camargue, the southern region of France, are the biggest producers of the premium French salt. The grey salt collected from these regions is very popular around the world because it absorbs more mineral from sea and mud flat, resulting in rich nutrition and excellent taste. Fleur de sel, "flower of salt" in French, has white color because its thin top layer of salt is removed right before seawater is evaporated. As its name suggests, its salty and sweet taste is wonderfully balanced.

LAND SNAILS (ESCARGOT)

Land snails living on grape leaves are the principal product of Burgundy, which is also one of the largest wine producers in France. Land snails were originally popular with the ancient Romans as a food material. Later, however, snails from Burgundy became popular for its excellent flavor and this popularity led to creation of over 20 recipes using land snails.

WINE VINEGAR

Vinegar is a kind of condiment made with fermented grains, fruits, herbs and liquors. Both of Asian black vinegar made from rice, wheat, millet or sorghum, and Sherry vinegar from Jerez, Spain, are especially well known. And Italy's Balsamic vinegar and France's red or white wine vinegar are also famous. Wine vinegar is usually used as dressing or sauce for salad because of its distinctive acidic scent and sweet and sour aftertaste.

dining scene
:
Course
of
French
Table

식사
매너부터
코스 요리까지,

프렌치
테이블

The French cuisine, according to its fastidious principle, should always be served with the fittest wine and the table for it should be set depending on a situation and atmosphere. And each course should follow its order, from aperitif, appetizer, starter, main dish and cheese to dessert and coffee. Let's take a look at the way of table setting and manner suitable for a French course meal. *By Continental of the Shilla Seoul*

까다로운 원칙을 지키는 프랑스 요리는 반드시 적절한 와인과 함께 내고, 격식에 맞게 테이블을 세팅하며, 아페리티프부터 애피타이저, 스타터, 메인 디시, 치즈와 디저트, 커피 순으로 내는 것이 정석이다. 프랑스식 코스에 따른 테이블 세팅과 매너를 배워보자.

요리 / 서울 신라 호텔 콘티넨탈

테이블 세팅 & 매너

테이블 위에 올려둔 냅킨은 코스를 시작할 때 반으로 접어 무릎 위에 올리며, 커틀러리는 코스가 시작되면 메인 접시 양쪽 끝부터 중앙을 향해 놓인 순서대로 사용한다. 포크는 왼손으로 잡되 날이 아래로 향하도록 하고, 대화 중 포크와 나이프로 상대방을 가리키지 않도록 주의할 것. 복잡해 보이는 프랑스 요리 이름은 대부분 '조리법+소스+재료' 순서이며, 마지막에 지역 이름이 붙을 수도 있다. 식사 중 양손 모두 테이블 위에 올리되 팔꿈치는 테이블에 닿지 않게 하는 것이 정석이다. 식사 중 잠시 쉴 때는 포크와 나이프를 X자로 엇갈려 놓으며, 식사를 마치면 각각 4시 20분 방향으로 나란히 놓되 포크의 날이 아래로 향하게 한다.

TABLE SETTING & MANNER

Napkins, folded in half, should be placed on the lap before a meal is started. The general cutlery etiquette is to use the cutlery from outside in. The fork should be held in the left hand, with the prongs facing downwards. Be careful not to gesticulate with the fork or knife during a conversation. The name of French food sounds complex but most of them are a combination of a cooking method, sauce and ingredients and sometimes a name of a region. While having a meal, both hands should be on the table but putting elbows on the table should be avoided. In the middle of a meal, the knife and fork is set in a crossed position on a plate. After the meal is finished, the knife and fork should be placed in parallel, with tines of the fork pointing down.

오르되브르

프랑스 정찬 코스 요리는 일반적으로 9~10가지에 이른다. 많은 코스를 모두 맛보기에 앞서 식욕을 돋우도록 준비하는 것이 바로 '오르되브르'다. 영어로는 애피타이저로, 다른 음식에 비해 양이 적어 배가 부르지 않는 것이어야 한다. 오찬에서는 여러 종류의 오르되브르를 내지만 디너인 만찬에서는 1~2품의 진미만 대접한다. 석화, 캐비아, 푸아 그라, 훈제 연어 등으로 만든 차가운 음식이 주를 이룬다.

HORS D'OEUVRE

In France, a full course meal generally consists of nine to ten courses. Hors d'oeuvre is usually served prior to a main course, for the purpose of arousing an appetite. It is also called an appetizer or starter and typically smaller than a main dish. Several hors d'oeuvres are served for lunch but less than a couple of delicacies are served as hors d'oeuvres for dinner. Usually, most of hors d'oeuvres are cold dishes such as oysters, caviar, foie gras or smoked salmon.

수프와 빵

프랑스 요리는 오르되브르에서 디저트까지 재료, 컬러, 맛에 변화를 주면서 전체적으로 균형을 이루는 것이 특징이다. 오르되브르와 아페리티프로 식욕을 돋운 뒤 그다음 이어지는 코스는 수프다. 정찬인 경우에는 반드시 맑은 수프인 콩소메를 내는데 부용보다 국물이 맑고 맛이 담백한 콩소메는 향이 강한 양파, 셀러리, 파슬리, 월계수잎, 마늘 등 채소와 두 가지 이상의 고기를 사용한다. 다 끓인 다음 접시에 담고 당근, 마카로니, 토마토 등을 잘라 넣는데, 이때 무엇을 넣었는가에 따라 이름이 달라진다.

SOUP & BREAD

From hors d'oeuvres to dessert, the French cuisine is well balanced, with variations in ingredients, colors and tastes. Hors d'oeuvres and apéritif are followed by soup. Consommé, of more clear liquid and more plain flavor than Bouillon, is made with two or more kinds of meat and several vegetables including onion, celery, parsley, bay leaf and garlic and it is usually served for a lunch course meal. After a stock is simmered, cut vegetables such as carrots and tomatoes or macaroni are added into the bowl.

메인 요리

메인 요리는 크게 생선과 고기로 나뉜다. 프랑스는 지중해와 대서양을 끼고 있어 연어, 송어, 새우, 바닷가재, 굴, 홍합 등 풍부한 해산물 요리가 발달했는데, 만찬에서는 단백질과 지방이 풍부한 생선 요리가 주를 이룬다. 고기 요리는 소·닭·돼지·오리·토끼·양·송아지·비둘기 고기 등 종류가 다양하다. 메인 요리에는 입맛을 돋우는 가니시를 함께 내는데, 데친 채소나 시럽에 조린 채소를 곁들이는 경우가 많다.

MAIN DISH

The primary ingredient of the main dish is meat or fish. France, bordering the Atlantic ocean and the Meciterranean sea, is highly rich in seafood such as salmon, trout, shrimp, lobster, oyster, mussel, etc. and fish of rich protein and fat is especially preferred for a dinner course meal. Meat dishes are also varied from beef, chicken, pork, duck, rabbit, lamb and veal to pigeon. The main dish is usually accompanied by a garnish, for example, blanched vegetables or boiled vegetables in syrup.

디저트

요리의 진가를 음미하기 위해 식사 맨 마지막에 내는 디저트는 식사의 여운을 감미롭게 마무리하는 의미를 지녔다. 화려하게 장식하는 디저트는 프랑스 정찬의 꽃이다. 커다란 접시에 케이크, 타르트, 과일, 아이스 크림 등 달콤한 음식을 그림처럼 담아내며 차나 커피를 곁들인다. 이때 한입에 먹는 과자나 초콜릿인 '프티 푸르petits-four'를 함께 제공하기도 한다.

DESSERT

The dessert, served at the end of the meal, has a meaning to finish the meal with a mellow flavor and thus is generally considered a 'flower of the dinner.' An assortment of desserts including cakes, tarts, fruits and ice cream could be enjoyed with a cup of tea or coffee. Sometimes Petits-four, a bite-sized cookie or chocolate, is served with the dessert.

place
:
24
Best
French Restaurants

프랑스인도
인정한

프렌치
레스토랑
24

What French people in Korea are missing most is probably French cuisine they enjoyed in their country. If they recommend any French restaurant relieving their nostalgia for home cuisine, it sounds much reliable.

한국 생활을 하고 있는 프랑스인들에겐 제대로 된 프랑스 요리야말로 가장 큰 힘일 것이다. 그들이 직접 추천한 곳이라면 믿을 만하지 않을까? 프랑스인에게 고향에 대한 그리움도 잠시 잊게 하는 서울 속 프렌치 레스토랑을 공개한다.

프랑스인의 단골 레스토랑	서래마을의 프렌치 레스토랑	호텔 프렌치 레스토랑
르 꽁뜨와	제로 콤플렉스	콘티넨탈
아 따블르	더 그린테이블	시즌스
라 쎌틱	스와니예	더 비스트로 & 더 델리
앙 드 뜨와	라 싸브어	테이블 34
라메르 풀라르	쉬떼르	피에르 가니에르 서울
줄라이		
가스트로 통		
퀴송 82		
루이 쌍끄		
레스쁘아 뒤 이부		
메종 드 라 카테고리		
비스트로 드 욘트빌		
르 빠니에 블루		
팔레 드 고몽		

French Restaurants French People Loves Most	French Restaurants in Seorae Village	French Restaurants in Hotels
Le Comptoir	Zero Complex	Continental
A Table	The Green Table	Seasons
La Celtique	Soigné	The Bistro & The Deli
Un Deux Trois	La Saveur	Table 34
La Mère Poulard Seoul	Sur Terre	Pierre Gagnaire à Séoul
July		
Gasto Tong		
Cuisson 82		
Louis Cinq		
L'Espoir du Hibou		
Maison de la Catégorie		
Bistro de Yountville		
Le Panier Bleu		
Palais de Gaumont		

프랑스인의 단골 레스토랑

서울에 사는 프랑스인 25명이 각종 비즈니스 미팅이나 가족 간 외식을 위해 자주 찾는 최고의 레스토랑을 추천했다. 프랑스 향토 음식을 맛볼 수 있는 편안한 분위기의 비스트로부터 최고의 정찬인 오트 퀴진을 제공하는 정통 레스토랑까지!

FRENCH RESTAURANTS FRENCH PEOPLE LOVES MOST

25 French people living in Seoul have recommended French Restaurants they love for a formal business meeting or eating out with family. This list varies from a small bistro serving native French dishes in a friendly atmosphere to a fine restaurant with haute cuisine.

르 꽁뜨와

프랑스 미슐랭 3 스타 레스토랑 등 현지 경력 10여 년의 서문용욱 오너 셰프가 직접 경영하고 요리하는 캐주얼 레스토랑. 프랑스 가정식을 모티브로 다양한 요리를 선보이는데 양이 푸짐한 것이 특징. 호주산 와규 등심구이에 구운 감자와 샐러드를 곁들이는 식이다.

Le Comptoir

Chef Seomun Yong-Uk, a skillful chef with more than 10 years of experience in France including a three Michelin starred restaurant, is the owner and chef of Le Comptoir. Based on home-style French recipes, they serve various kinds of fabulous meals in a hearty size. For example, you can enjoy grilled Australian wagyu sirloin accompanied with a plate of grilled potatoes and salad at the same time.

Address	용산구 이태원로27길 7	7, Itaewon-ro 27-gil, Yongsan-gu
Contact	02-792-8506	82-2-792-8506
Web	blog.naver.com/lecomptoir	blog.naver.com/lecomptoir
Operation	화~목·일 Tue to Thur & Sun 12:00~22:30(Break 15:00~18:00), 금·토 Fri & Sat 12:30~00:00(Break 15:00~18:00)	
Closed	월요일	Mon

아 따블르

삼청동 한옥을 개조해 만든 아담한 레스토랑. 프레젠테이션과 인테리어가 훌륭하며 제철 식재료에 맞춰 '오늘의 요리'를 선보인다. 메뉴가 코스 요리 한 종류라 프랑스 요리에 익숙하지 않은 이도 무얼 시킬까 고민할 필요 없이 편하게 즐길 수 있다. 자리에 앉으면 스태프가 작은 칠판을 들고 와 메뉴를 설명해준다. 오렌지와 당근, 가리비를 넣어 만든 앙트레, 아스파라거스와 비트를 곁들인 훈제 연어 타르타르 등 눈과 입을 즐겁게 하는 메뉴가 많다. 다양한 채소와 과일로 만든 소스를 요리에 접목하는 것도 인상적이다.

A Table

Placed in a remodeled traditional Korean house of Samcheong-dong, A Table offers 'Today's special' based on seasonal ingredients. As today's special is simple one-course menu, all you have to do is just enjoy what they serve, sitting in a comfortable and beautiful hall. Once you sit down at the table, staff comes to you with a small board to explain their meals. Entrée made with orange, carrot and scallop, Smoked Salmon Tartare added with asparagus and beet and other distinctive dishes would catch your eye and taste. Their sauce made from different kinds of fruits and vegetables are impressive.

Address	종로구 팔판길 29	29, Palpan-gil, Jongno-gu
Contact	02-736-1048	82-2-736-1048
Operation	12:00~22:00(Break 15:00~18:00)	12:00~22:00(Break 15:00~18:00)
Closed	일요일, 설 · 추석 연휴	Sun, Holiday of Lunar New Year's Day & Chuseok

라 쎌틱

프랑스 브르타뉴식 크레페 전문점. 크레페는 프랑스 브르타뉴 지방에서 발달한 음식으로 감자나 밤으로 만든 크림, 아이스크림 등 다채로운 토핑을 얹어 먹는다. 라 쎌틱의 크레페는 큼지막한 메밀 전병 위에 햄과 달걀 프라이, 양파와 감자 등을 올려 든든한 한 끼 식사로도 부족함이 없다. 고소한 메밀과 채소 등이 어우러져 깔끔하면서도 담백한 맛을 낸다. 라 쎌틱은 프랑스 어로 '켈트 족 문화'란 뜻. 브르타뉴 지방에 켈트 족 문화가 많이 남아 있어 이런 이름을 붙였다고 한다.

La Celtique

La Celtique's specialty is Brittany crêpes. Made by putting ham, fried egg, onion, potato, etc. on a large buckwheat pancake, a crêpe is enough as a single meal. The taste of buckwheat is well kept even after it is mixed with vegetables. Crêpes, especially popular throughout France but mainly developed in Brittany, are enjoyed with various toppings on it, such as cream made from potato or chestnut, ice cream, etc.

Address	서대문구 명물길 72	72, Myeongmul-gil, Seodaemun-gu
Contact	02-312-7774	82-2-312-7774
Operation	12:00~22:00	12:00~22:00
Closed	월요일	Mon

앙 드 뜨와

프랑스 어로 1, 2, 3을 뜻하는 브라세리 앙 드 뜨와는 프랑스 출신의 셰프가 50여 가지 메뉴를 총괄한다. 아늑한 홀과 바가 있어 정찬은 물론 가볍게 들러 와인 한잔하기에 좋다. 스테이크 위에 달걀노른자를 올리고 감자튀김을 더한 '클래식 프렌치 타르타르 스테이크'와 바닐라 아이스크림과 베리 무스를 쌓고 머랭을 듬뿍 올린 디저트 '베이크 알래스카', 다양한 종류의 홍합 요리가 인기 있다.

Un Deux Trois

A brasserie with the name meaning 'one, two, three' in French serves around 50 kinds of items made by a French chef. With a casual hall and bar, this place is worth the visit for dining or a glass of wine. Steak Tartare De Boeuf (classic French-style seasoned raw beef) with an egg yolk and a various kinds of mussel dishes are the best menus.

Address	용산구 이태원로 189	189, Itaewon-ro, Yongsan-gu
Contact	02-796-1244	82-2-796-1244
Web	brasserie123.com	brasserie123.com
Operation	월~토 12:00~다음 날 03:00, 일 11:00~20:00	Mon to Sat 12:00~The next day 03:00, Sun 11:00~20:00
Closed	연중무휴	Open all year round

라메르 풀라르

1888년, 요리사 아네트 풀라르가 프랑스 몽생미셸에서 처음 시작한 라메르 풀라르 서울점. 선명하고 경쾌한 빨간색으로 의자와 테이블클로스, 창문 난간과 프레임에 포인트를 줬으며 테라스 공간을 두어 이국적인 분위기를 연출했다. 주요 메뉴는 애피타이저와 캐서롤, 육류 코코트와 파스타, 디저트와 코스 요리로 구성됐다. 꼭 맛봐야 하는 오믈렛은 수작업으로 반죽해 거품을 낸 달걀을 화덕에 구워 낸다. 채소, 버섯, 양념 새우, 감자와 베이컨 등 다양한 종류의 오믈렛이 있으며 크림처럼 부드러운 질감과 담백한 끝 맛이 일품이다. 둥근 캐서롤 냄비에 찌는 프랑스식 찜 요리도 훌륭하다. 돼지고기, 새끼 양고기, 오렌지 소스를 곁들인 오리고기가 주물 캐서롤 냄비에 담겨 나온다. 마무리로는 캐러멜 애플 크레페와 크렘 브륄레, 사과 조림 파이 등 가정식 디저트를 추천한다.

La Mère Poulard Seoul

La Mère Poulard is a Seoul branch of La Mère Poulard which first opened by Madame Annette Poulard at Mont Saint Michel in 1888. This restaurant in Seoul is of so much similar atmosphere to its head store in France that you could feel as if you are at Mont Saint Michel. Its decorations of a clean and light red color displayed on chairs, tablecloths, windowsill and frame look distinctive and its indoor terrace creates an exotic ambiance. Its main menu consists of appetizers, casseroles, pastas, desserts and course meals.

Address	서초구 사평대로 205	205, Sapyeong-daero, Seocho-gu
Contact	1644-5769	82-2-1644-5769
Operation	11:00~23:00	11:00~23:00
Closed	연중무휴	Open all year round

줄라이 / July

매일 스쿠터를 타고 장을 보는 오세득 오너 셰프의 레스토랑. 영동 호두, 진주 우엉, 상주 곶감, 횡성 더덕, 예산 사과, 고흥 유자 등 국내산 제철 식재료를 프렌치 레시피와 접목해 새로운 맛과 세련된 스타일링을 선보인다. 셰프 테이스팅 코스는 아홉 가지 요리로 구성되는데 음식은 식재료에 따라 그때그때 달라지며 1등급 쇠고기를 사용한 와규 안심 스테이크, 토마토 수프와 게살 샐러드를 함께 담아낸 킹크랩 샐러드 등이 특히 인기 있다.

Chef Oh Se-Deuk, who goes to market everyday on a scooter, is the owner and chef of July. He offers a new taste and refined style of food using native seasonal ingredients of Korea based on French recipes. The Chef Tasting Course consists of nine dishes, varied depending on available ingredients. Wagyu Tenderloin Steak made of prime beef and King Crab Meat Salad served with tomato soup are especially popular.

Address	서초구 동광로 164	164, Donggwang-ro, Seocho-gu
Contact	02-534-9544	82-2-534-9544
Web	www.julyrestaurant.org	www.julyrestaurant.org
Operation	월~토 Mon to Sat 12:00~22:30(Break 15:00~18:30),	일 Sun 12:00~21:00(Break 15:00~18:00)
Closed	설·추석 당일	Day of Lunar New Year's Day & Chuseok

가스트로 통

국내 특급 호텔 총주방장으로 일한 롤랑 히니 Roland Hinni 셰프와 와인업체에서 마케터로 일한 김영심 부부가 함께 운영하는 통의동의 맛집. 레스토랑 이름은 미식을 뜻하는 '가스트로'와 마을 이름이기도 한 한자어 '통할 통通'의 합성어다. 프랑스 음식에 기초를 둔 다양한 유러피언 음식을 선보인다. 송아지 정강이나 오리 가슴살을 저온 조리한 부르고뉴식 찜 요리가 시그너처 메뉴. 감자와 육두구 가루로 감싼 광어 등 계절 식재료를 활용한 요리도 선보인다.

Gasto Tong

Chef Roland Hinni, who has worked in several five-star hotels, runs Gastro Tong in Tongui-dong with his wife, Yeongshim Kim, an experienced wine expert. 'Gastro' comes from the word 'Gastronomy' and 'Tong' means a communication. They serve a variety of European cuisine including French cuisine. The signature dish is a slow-braised Burgundian cuisine using veal shank or duck breast cooked in a low temperature. This restaurant also serves some dishes based on seasonal ingredients.

Address	종로구 자하문로6길 11-36	11-36, Jahamun-ro 6-gil, Jongno-gu
Contact	02-730-4162	82-2-730-4162
Web	www.gastrotong.co.kr	www.gastrotong.co.kr
Operation	12:00~21:00(Break 15:00~18:00)	12:00~21:00(Break 15:00~18:00)
Closed	연중무휴	Open all year round

퀴쏭 82

양재천 길가에 있는 퀴쏭 82는 '정식당', '봉에보', '더 그린테이블' 등에서 일한 김영원 셰프가 오픈한 프렌치 레스토랑이다. 레스토랑 이름은 식재료가 적절하게 익은 온도를 뜻하는 'cuisson'과 파리가 연상되는 숫자 82의 합성어. 비스트로를 표방하는 곳으로 코스 메뉴보다 단품 메뉴에 집중한다고. 어니언 수프, 버터 풍미가 가득한 감자 그라탱, 렌틸콩과 감자 퓌레를 곁들인 삼겹살 스테이크 등을 선보인다.

Cuisson 82

'Cuisson' is a word indicating a temperature at which ingredients are properly cooked and '82', when it is pronounced in Korean, sounds similar to the pronunciation of 'Paris.' This restaurant, as a kind of bistro, mainly serves one-dish meal. Their main dishes include Onion Soup, Potato Gratin with flavored butter, Pork Belly Steak served with lentils and potato purée, etc.

Address	강남구 양재천로 167		167, Yangjaecheon-ro, Gangnam-gu
Contact	02-529-3582		82-2-529-3582
Operation	화~토 Tue to Sat 12:00~22:00(Break 15:00~18:00), 일 Sun 11:30~21:30		
Closed	월요일		Mon

루이 쌍끄

《맛있는 위로》의 저자로 잘 알려진 이유석 셰프가 운영하는 프렌치 비스트로. 프랑스 요리를 안주 삼아 새벽 1시까지 와인을 마실 수 있는 편안한 분위기다. 프랑스, 스페인 등의 파인 다이닝 레스토랑에서 경력을 쌓은 이유석 셰프는 프랑스와 한국의 식재료를 절묘하게 조합해 늘 새로운 메뉴를 개발한다. 시그너처 메뉴도 여러 가지인데 그중 가장 사랑받는 메뉴는 '메추리구이'. 뼈를 발라낸 뒤 푸아 그라로 속을 채우는 게 정통이지만, 푸아 그라 대신 보리 리소토를 넣어 꿰맨 뒤 오븐에 구워 식감을 살렸다.

Address	강남구 선릉로157길 33 2층
Contact	02-547-1259
Web	www.louiscinq.com
Operation	18:00~다음 날 01:00
Closed	일요일

Louis Cinq

In a nice ambiance of Louis Cinq you could sip a glass of wine with French side dishes until 1 a.m. Chef Lee Yoo-Seok, who worked at numerous fine dining restaurants in France and Spain, has always tried to develop a new menu by combining various food materials from France and Korea. This being so, he has several signature dishes that show his own characteristics very well. The most popular menu among them is Grilled Quail. Its original recipe is filling it with foie gras after removing bones but he instead puts barley risotto before grilling the quail in the oven for a better texture of it.

2F, 33, Seolleung-ro 157-gil, Gangnam-gu
82-2-547-1259
www.louiscinq.com
18:00~The next day 01:00
Sun

레스쁘아 뒤 이부

미슐랭 3 스타에 빛나는 뉴욕의 프렌치 레스토랑 '대니얼 Daniel'에서 경력을 쌓은 임기학 셰프가 청담동에 개업한 정통 비스트로. 한국에서는 맛보기 힘든 프랑스 남서부 지방의 전통 요리를 선보인다. 우리나라 〈블루 리본 서베이〉에도 이름을 올리며 실력을 인정받았다. 수란과 캐비아를 얹은 샐러드, 오렌지 콩피를 곁들인 '부챗살 스테이크' 등 다양한 요리를 맛볼 수 있다.

Address	강남구 선릉로152길 33
Contact	02-517-6034
Operation	12:00~22:30(Break 15:00~18:00)
Closed	설·추석 연휴

L'Espoir du Hibou

L'Espoir du Hibou is a French bistro serving traditional cuisines of the southwest France. Chef Im Gi-Hak, who is now the owner and chef of this restaurant, worked as a chef at Daniel, a three Michelin starred restaurant located in New York. He was also acknowledged by Blue Ribbon Survey, a kind of guide for restaurants and cuisines in Korea. Various dishes such as Salad garnished with poached eggs and caviar and Top Blade Steak added with orange confit are available.

33, Seolleung-ro 152-gil, Gangnam-gu
82-2-517-6034
12:00~22:30(Break 15:00~18:00)
Holiday of Lunar New Year's Day & Chuseok

메종 드 라 카테고리

프렌치 레스토랑 '라 카테고리'를 이끈 이형준 셰프가 좀 더 캐주얼한 분위기로 2013년에 오픈한 곳. 코스보다 단품 메뉴, 차와 디저트에 집중한 브라세리다. 버섯과 파르메산 치즈로 맛을 낸 리소토, 레몬 오일에 로브스터와 새우, 루콜라를 넣은 파스타, 팬프라이한 양갈비 등을 맛볼 수 있다. 식사 전에는 다양한 종류의 샴페인을 글라스로 즐길 수 있는 샴페인 카트를, 식후에는 위스키를 샷으로 고를 수 있는 위스키 카트를 제공한다.

Maison de la Catégorie

Chef Lee Hyung-Jun, the executive chef of a French restaurant 'La Catégorie,' newly opened this place with a more casual concept in 2013. Maison de la Catégorie is a kind of brasserie, more focusing on one-dish meal, tea and dessert, rather than a course meal. Risotto flavored with mushrooms and parmesan cheese, Pasta cooked with lobster, prawn, arugula and lemon oil, Pan-fried Lamb Chops and other dishes are served. Before meal they provide a champagne cart to try each glass of different kinds of champagne and then after meal you would be served with a whiskey cart, from which you can pick out a shot of whiskey.

Address	강남구 선릉로 826	826, Seolleung-ro, Gangnam-gu
Contact	02-545-6640	82-2-545-6640
Web	www.lacategorie.com	www.lacategorie.com
Operation	월~토 Mon to Sat 11:30~23:30(Break 14:00~18:00), 일 Sun 11:30~22:00	
Closed	연중무휴	Open all year round

비스트로 드 욘트빌

오너 셰프인 토미 리가 캘리포니아의 '프렌치 런드리 French Laundry' 등에서 닦은 실력을 무기 삼아 청담동에 오픈한 곳. 프랑스 어로 '진공 저온 요리'라는 뜻의 수비드 sous vide 등 다양한 조리법으로 만든 요리를 선보인다. 각 식재료의 질감과 향, 영양소가 최적인 상태에서 조리하는 것이 특징. 그만큼 신선하고 맛있게 즐길 수 있다. 오렌지 소스로 맛을 낸 오리구이가 특히 맛있다.

Bistro de Yountville

Bistro de Yountville was started in Cheongdam-dong by the owner cum chef, Tommie Lee, who has experienced in several restaurants including the French Laundry located in California. For his cuisine he uses various cooking methods such as 'Sous-vide,' a French word which indicates a vacuum-sealing and low-temperature cooking. The characteristic of this method is to cook the food by keeping its texture, smell and nutrition in the most optimal state, resulting in much fresh and flavored food. Grilled Duck flavored with orange sauce is especially wonderful.

Address	강남구 선릉로158길 13-7	13-7, Seolleung-ro 158-gil, Gangnam-gu
Contact	02-541-1550	82-2-541-1550
Operation	12:00~22:30(Break 15:00~18:00)	12:00~22:30(Break 15:00~18:00)
Closed	연중무휴	Open all year round

르 빠니에 블루

르 코르동 블뢰를 졸업한 뒤 미슐랭이 선정한 프렌치 레스토랑에서 경력을 쌓은 권기문 셰프가 13년간의 파리 생활을 정리하고 돌아와 2010년에 오픈한 곳. 완두콩, 느타리버섯을 곁들인 닭 가슴살 스테이크가 인기 메뉴. 프랑스에서 직접 공수한 수제 버터와 크림으로 소스 맛을 냈다. 포도주가 아닌 코냑을 넣은 코코뱅도 유명하다.

Le Panier Bleu

Le Panier Bleu was started in 2010 by Chef Kwon Ki-Moon, who worked at a French restaurant appointed by Michelin Guide after graduating from Le Cordon Bleu. Its specialty, Chicken Breast Steak added with oyster mushrooms, is flavored with homemade butter and cream brought directly from France. Also, Coq au Vin using cognac instead of wine is very popular.

Address	광진구 능동로 149-1	149-1, Neungdong-ro, Gwangjin-gu	
Contact	02-468-1358	82-2-468-1358	
Operation	12:00~23:00(Break 15:00~18:00)	12:00~23:00(Break 15:00~18:00)	
Closed	연중무휴	Open all year round	

팔레 드 고몽

영화를 전공한 서현민 대표가 프랑스 영화 기술 발전에 선구자적 역할을 한 레옹 고몽의 이름을 따서 만든 정통 프렌치 레스토랑이다. 1999년 오픈할 당시 "100년이 지나도 살아남는 진짜 프렌치 레스토랑을 운영하고 싶다"라고 말했던 대표의 철학을 담아 최고의 식재료만 고집한다. 프랑스산 푸아 그라와 달팽이 등을 공수해 제공한다. 요리는 '뚜또베네'에서 자리를 옮긴 이재훈 셰프가 총괄한다.

Palais de Gaumont

Owner Seo Hyeon-min, who majored in film, named this authentic French restaurant after Léon Gaumont who was a French pioneer of a motion picture industry. In 1999, when he first opened Palais de Gaumont, he wished it would remain as a top-notch restaurant even after a century. To reach this goal, this restaurant only uses foie gras and snails directly procured from local markets in France. Chef Lee Jae-Hun, from the Italian restaurant, Tutto Bene, is the executive chef of Palais de Gaumont as well.

Address	강남구 도산대로81길 21		21, Dosan-daero 81-gil, Gangnam-gu
Contact	02-546-8877		82-2-546-8877
Operation	18:00~23:00		18:00~23:00
Closed	설·추석 전날과 당일		Day of Lunar New Year's Day & Chuseok

서래마을의 프렌치 레스토랑

서래마을은 1985년 프랑스 학교가 옮겨 오면서 프랑스인이 가장 많이 거주하는 곳이 됐다. 프랑스 어 방송이 나오는 버스, 프랑스 어를 하는 직원이 있는 가게 등 곳곳에 프랑스 문화가 자리 잡았고 레스토랑과 바도 프랑스인의 입맛에 맞춰 발전했다. 서울 속의 작은 프랑스, 서래마을에서 손꼽히는 프렌치 레스토랑을 소개한다.

FRENCH RESTAURANTS IN SEORAE VILLAGE

Since a French school moved into Seorae Village in 1985, this village has become the biggest French enclave in Korea. As you can see from a bus announcement in French, a French-speaking staff in a store, French people have settled with the culture of France in this area and in the meantime, the culinary taste of restaurants and bars in this village has been evolved, paced with such a change.

제로 콤플렉스

이충후 오너 셰프가 운영하는 제로 콤플렉스는 아트 디렉터인 셰프의 누나가 좋아하는 숫자에서 이름을 땄다. 모던하고 미래 지향적인 인테리어와 창의적이고 혁신적인 메뉴 아이디어를 결합한 네오 비스트로를 표방한다.

Zero Complex

The owner and chef Lee Chung-Hu got an idea for the name of his restaurant from the favorite number of his sister, working as an art director. The concept of this restaurant is a neo-bistro matching modern and future-oriented decorations well with creative, innovative recipes.

Address	서초구 동광로 113	113, Donggwang-ro, Seocho-gu
Contact	02-532-0876	82-2-532-0876
Web	www.facebook.com/Zerocomplexby00000000000000	
Operation	12:00~23:00(Break 15:00~18:00)	12:00~23:00(Break 15:00~18:00)
Closed	일 · 월요일	Sun & Mon

더 그린테이블

미국 CIA 요리학교에서 공부한 김은희 셰프가 총괄하는 곳. 이름에서 느껴지듯 신선한 제철 식재료를 활용해 모던하고 세련된 감각으로 완성한 파인 다이닝을 선보인다. 1층에서는 파인 다이닝을, 2층에서는 단품을 선보이며 메뉴는 재료 상태에 따라 그때그때 달라진다.

The Green Table

The Green Table is run by Chef Kim Eun-hui, who graduated from the Culinary Institute of America. Like its name, this restaurant serves a fine dining using fresh seasonal ingredients based on a modern and refined culinary art. A fine dining is served on the first floor and you can enjoy one-dish meals on the second floor. The menu varies depending on food availability.

Address	서초구 동광로 91	91, Donggwang-ro, Seocho-gu	
Contact	02-591-2672	82-2-591-2672	
Web	thegreentable.co.kr	thegreentable.co.kr	
Operation	11:30~22:00(Break 15:00~18:00)	11:30~22:00(Break 15:00~18:00)	
Closed	월요일	Mon	

스와니예

이준 오너 셰프가 운영하는 스와니예는 '잘 만든', 혹은 '정돈된'이라는 뜻으로 컨템퍼러리 퀴진을 표방한다. 두 가지 점심 코스와 한 가지 저녁 테이스팅 코스를 판매하며 3~8가지에 이르는 가지각색 아뮤즈부슈가 오감을 사로잡는다.

Soigné

Soigné, meaning 'well-made' or 'orderly' in French, embodies contemporary cuisine. This restaurant, owned by Chef Lee Jun, serves two courses for lunch and one tasting course for dinner. There are three to eight items on the amuse-bouche menu.

Address	서초구 반포대로39길 46	46, Banpo-daero 39-gil, Seocho-gu
Contact	02-3477-9386	82-2-3477-9386
Web	soigneseoul.com	soigneseoul.com
Operation	12:00~23:00(Break 15:00~18:00)	12:00~23:00(Break 15:00~18:00)
Closed	설·추석 연휴	Holiday of Lunar New Year's Day & Chuseok

라 싸브어

2002년 오픈한 서래마을의 최장수 프렌치 레스토랑. 이곳을 지휘하는 진경수 오너 셰프는 매달 새로운 메뉴를 준비하고, 12월에 그해 가장 좋은 반응을 얻은 음식을 다시 한 번 선보인다. 지나치게 모던하지도, 전통적이지도 않은 자연 친화적인 요리를 추구한다.

La Saveur

Since it was opened in 2002, La Saveur has become the oldest French restaurant of Seorae Village. Its owner and chef, Jin Kyung-Soo has served a new dish each month and then the most popular dish of the year again in December. An eco-friendly cuisine is what La Saveur is pursuing.

Address	서초구 서래로 24 5층	5F, 24, Seorae-ro, Seocho-gu
Contact	02-591-6713	82-2-591-6713
Operation	11:30~23:00(Break 15:00~18:00)	11:30~23:00(Break 15:00~18:00)
Closed	설·추석 연휴	Holiday of Lunar New Year's Day & Chuseok

쉬떼르

'땅 위'라는 뜻의 쉬떼르에는 땅에서 난 식재료를 정직하고 좋은 방법으로 요리하겠다는 최승광 오너 셰프의 철학이 담겨 있는 레스토랑이다. 점심은 단품 위주로, 저녁은 5~6가지로 구성한 두 가지 코스 요리와 단품 메뉴로 구성했다.

Sur Terre

Sur Terre, with the meaning of 'on the ground,' embodies the culinary philosophy of the owner and chef, Choi Seung-Gwang, that is, cooking with ingredients gained from the ground in an honest and desirable way. Sur Terre serves mainly one-dish meal for lunch and two dinner course menus consisting of five and six dishes each along with one-dish meal.

Address	서초구 사평대로26길 24	24, Sapyeong-daero 26-gil, Seocho-gu
Contact	02-532-1021	82-2-532-1021
Operation	12:00~22:00(Break 15:00~18:00)	12:00~22:00(Break 15:00~18:00)
Closed	월요일, 설·추석 연휴	Mon, Holiday of Lunar New Year's Day & Chuseok

호텔 프렌치 레스토랑

우리나라에서 프렌치 레스토랑은 호텔을 중심으로 발전했다. 국내 최초의 프렌치 레스토랑은 '나인스 게이트 그릴 The Ninth Gate Grille'로 이름을 바꾼 서울 웨스틴 조선 호텔의 '팜 코트 Palm Court'. 1914년 문을 열었다. 그 후 1979년에 개장한 서울 신라 호텔 '콘티넨탈'부터 2008년 롯데 호텔 서울에 입성한 '피에르 가니에르 서울'까지, 세계 미식의 정점인 프랑스 요리를 제대로 맛볼 수 있는 다섯 곳의 호텔 레스토랑을 소개한다.

FRENCH RESTAURANTS IN HOTELS

French Restaurants in Korea have been developed mainly around hotels. The first French restaurant opened in Korea was Palm Court of the Westin Chosun Seoul, which later changed its name to the Ninth Gate Grille. Then it has been followed by many French restaurants including Continental of the Shilla Seoul opened in 1979 and Pierre Gagnaire à Séoul which came in the Lotte Hotel Seoul in 2008.

서울 신라 호텔
콘티넨탈

호텔 최고 층인 23층에 위치하며 윤준식 책임 주방장이 총괄한다. 2013년 호텔 재개관과 레스토랑 리뉴얼을 통해 품격 있는 프렌치 정찬을 선보이는 최고의 레스토랑으로 재정비했다. 프랑스 푸아 그라, 미국 메인 주의 가리비, 호주 순종 와규 등 최고급 식재료를 고집한다. 채식주의자를 위한 메뉴도 있으며 테이스팅 메뉴를 추천한다.

The Shilla Seoul
Continental

Continental, situated on the 23rd floor, the highest level of the building, is a French restaurant managed by its executive chef Yun Jun-Sik. When the Shilla Seoul Hotel was refurbished and its restaurants were remodeled in 2013, Continental has also been transformed into an utmost restaurant serving a refined French dining. This restaurant insists on using local food ingredients of the highest quality, for example, foie gras from France, scallops from the U.S., wagyu to Australia. Meals for vegetarians are available as well and its tasting menu is very recommendable.

Address	중구 동호로 249	249, Dongho-ro, Jung-gu
Contact	02-2230-3369	82-2-2230-3369
Web	www.shilla.net	www.shilla.net
Operation	12:00~22:00(Break 14:30~18:00)	12:00~22:00(Break 14:30~18:00)
Closed	연중무휴	Open all year round

밀레니엄 서울 힐튼
시즌스

박효남 총주방장이 지휘하는 이곳에서는 프랑스 각 지역의 정통 요리와 식재료를 활용한 음식을 선보인다. 단골이 많아 총주방장이 고객의 입맛과 취향을 미리 체크해 별도의 음식을 준비하기도 하고, 입맛에 맞춰 소금량이나 소스 농도를 조절하기도 한다. 고객이 요청하면 메뉴판에 없는 요리도 만들어준다. 계절마다 메뉴가 바뀌며 개편 전 테이스팅 이벤트도 연다.

Millennium Seoul Hilton
Seasons

Seasons, serving exquisite cuisine based on authentic recipes and ingredients of each region of France, has been run by its executive chef Park Hyo-Nam. He sometimes offers extra dishes or adjusts the quantity of salt and the consistency of sauce for regular customers after checking their taste in advance. And if there's a customer's request he also cooks and serves a meal, even if it is not on the menu. Seasons changes its menu each season and has a tasting event before the change.

Address	중구 소월로 50	50, Sowol-ro, Jung-gu	
Contact	02-317-3060	82-2-317-3060	
Web	www.seoul.hilton.co.kr	www.seoul.hilton.co.kr	
Operation	11:30~22:00(Break 14:30~18:00)	11:30~22:00(Break 14:30~18:00)	
Closed	주말, 공휴일	Sat & Sun, Public Holidays	

노보텔 앰배서더 강남
더 비스트로 & 더 델리

묵직하고 칼로리 높은 프랑스 요리에서 탈피해 담백하고 심플한 메뉴를 선보이는 곳. 프랑스적인 감성을 담은 비스트로노미를 지향하며 2015년 봄 리뉴얼 오픈했다. 비스트로노미란 편안한 분위기의 식당을 뜻하는 '비스트로 bistro'와 미식이란 뜻의 '가스트로노미 gastronomy'를 합친 신조어. 프랑스와 한국의 식재료를 접목한 모던하고 세련된 스타일링을 경험할 수 있다.

Novotel Ambassador Gangnam
The Bistro & The Deli

The Bistro & the Deli prefers plain and simple French dishes over greasy and high calorie French cuisine. Embodying a 'bistronomy' in a French style, they opened its remodeled restaurant in the spring of 2015. Their modern and fresh style is well proved by an excellent combination of ingredients from France and Korea.

Address	강남구 봉은사로 130	130, Bongeunsa-ro, Gangnam-gu
Contact	02-531-6604	82-2-531-6604
Web	novotel.ambatel.com/gangnam	novotel.ambatel.com/gangnam
Operation	12:00~23:00	12:00~23:00
Closed	연중무휴	Open all year round

그랜드 인터컨티넨탈 서울 파르나스
테이블 34

지난 2011년 〈미슐랭 그린 가이드〉에 선정됐고, 〈자갓〉에 이어 〈밀레 가이드〉에도 소개된 테이블 34. 뉴욕의 알랭 뒤카스 Alain Ducasse 레스토랑, 만다린 오리엔탈 제네바와 마닐라 출신의 레미 버셀리 Remy Vercelli 셰프가 총괄한다. 프랑스 남부 정통 요리를 모던하게 재해석해 섬세한 장식으로 마무리하는 것이 특징이며, 다채로운 와인 리스트를 보유했다.

Grand Intercontinental Seoul Parnas
Table 34

Table 34 is managed by Michelin Star Chef Remy Vercelli, who worked at the Alain Ducasse in New York and at the Mandarin Oriental in Geneva before. It was chosen by the Michelin Green Guide in 2011 and introduced on the Zagat and then the Miele Guide as well. His modern twist of authentic southern French cuisines is especially distinguishing. On top of this, Table 34 also has an extensive wine list.

Address	강남구 테헤란로 521	521, Teheran-ro, Gangnam-gu
Contact	02-559-7631	82-2-559-7631
Web	grandicparnas.com	grandicparnas.com
Operation	월~금 Mon to Fri 12:00~22:00(Break 14:30~18:00), 토·일 Sat & Sun 11:00~22:00	
Closed	연중무휴	Open all year round

롯데 호텔 서울
피에르 가니에르 서울

세계적인 요리 거장 피에르 가니에르가 문을 연 피에르 가니에르 서울. 단품 메뉴에도 4~6가지 실험적인 요리를 다양하게 담는다. 5~6가지 디저트가 연속 등장하는 등 코스 구성이 파격적이고 불규칙한 것이 특징. 혁신적이고 다양한 조리법으로 요리하며 270여 종의 와인 컬렉션을 갖추고 있다.

Lotte Hotel Seoul
Pierre Gagnaire à Séoul

An eponymous restaurant of Pierre Gagnaire, the world renowned chef, was opened in Seoul in 2008. He is always trying to put four to six kinds of experimental food on a single plate based on innovative and diverse recipes. A selection of diverse wine is also ready to serve.

Address	중구 을지로 30	30, Eulji-ro, Jung-gu
Contact	02-317-7181	82-2-317-7181
Web	www.lottehotel.com/seoul	www.lottehotel.com/seoul
Operation	12:00~22:00(Break 15:00~18:00)	12:00~22:00(Break 15:00~18:00)
Closed	설·추석 당일	Day of Lunar New Year's Day & Chuseok

이탈리아 요리

dining story
:
History of
Italian Cuisine,
or the Story
of Western Cuisine

이탈리아 음식의 역사는

서양 음식의 역사다

지역마다 고유한 특색이 있고, 재료의 가짓수가 적고 레시피가 간결해 원재료의 맛을 그대로 살리는 이탈리아 요리는 2013년 CNN에서 세계 최고의 요리로 선정된 바 있다. 세계 최고의 미식으로 칭송받는 프랑스 요리조차 사실은 이탈리아 음식의 영향을 받았다는 사실을 알고 나면 고개가 끄덕여진다. 이탈리아 음식의 역사는 서양 음식의 역사이기도 하다. 르네상스의 문화적 유산과 재정적 뒷받침 덕에 번성한 이탈리아의 메디치가는 15세기 프랑스 왕실에 미식을 전파했고, 이는 곧 유럽 식문화의 전형이 되었다.

밀라노를 중심으로 한 북부 지역은 옥수수로 만든 수프 폴렌타와 리소토를 주식으로 하면서 아드리아 해에서 잡은 게와 정어리로 만든 해산물 요리, 와인으로 졸인 송아지찜과 소 내장 요리 등 풍부한 식재료로 만든 요리로 미각을 유혹한다. 나폴리를 중심으로 한 남부 지역은 피자, 파스타 등 소박한 요리가 발달했다. 저녁 식사를 중시하는 이탈리아 사람들은 보통 8시부터 밤늦게까지 정찬을 즐긴다. 식전 음식인 스투치키니 stuzzichini 부터 간단한 채소 요리나 어패류 등으로 입맛을 돋우는 안티파스티 antipasti, 파스타나 리소토, 피자 등의 프리미 피아티 primi piatti, 해산물과 육류를 이용한 메인 요리인 세콘디 피아티 secondi piatti 와 이 메인 요리에 곁들이는 채소 요리 콘토르니 contorni, 여러 가지 치즈를 맛보는 포르마지 formaggi, 식사 후 치즈 다음으로 맛보는 디저트를 의미하는 돌체 dolce, 식후주나 커피까지 마셔야 정찬이 마무리된다.

다양한 요리가 발달한 미식 국가답게 음식점 종류도 다채롭다. 어떤 곳을 선택해야 할지 망설여진다면 이름 앞에 붙은 수식어로 특성을 파악하는 게 좋다. 레스토랑을 의미하는 리스토란테 ristorante, 가정요리를 중심으로 한 대중적인 음식점 트라토리아 trattoria, 옷차림에 구애받지 않고 가볍게 즐길 수 있는 오스테리아 osteria, 피자 전문점 피제리아 pizzeria, 카페테리아 형식의 타볼라 칼다 tavola calda 중에서 고를 수 있다.

오늘날 새삼스럽지만 서울에서 가장 '핫'한 미식도 이탈리아 요리다. 1970~1980년대 '외식' 하면 중식을 떠올렸듯, '서양 요리' 하면 이탈리아 음식을 떠올리곤 했다. 다채로운 면 메뉴와 토마토소스는 한국인의 입맛에도 딱 맞아 1970년대 이후 지금까지 가장 사랑받는 서양 요리가 되었다. 1970년대 국내 호텔 레스토랑에 처음 등장한 이탈리아 요리는 1980년대 파스타 전문점으로 확대되었으며, 1990년대부터 이탈리아 요리 전문점이 생기면서 한국인의 입맛을 사로잡았다.

2000년대 들어서는 국내에서도 오너 셰프의 정찬을 맛볼 수 있는 리스토란테, 캐주얼하게 즐기기 좋은 피제리아까지 다양한 형태의 이탤리언 레스토랑을 볼 수 있게 되었다. 레스토랑마다 이탈리아 본토의 다양한 식재료를 적극적으로 사용하고 셰프들의 시그너처 메뉴를 선보이면서 기껏해야 토마토소스를 넣은 스파게티, 피자 정도로만 알고 있던 이탈리아 음식에 대한 인식도 많이 달라졌다. 바야흐로 지금 서울은 이탈리아 요리 황금기다. 오늘 저녁 약속을 앞두고 있다면, 당신이 떠올릴 가장 쉬운 선택이자 믿음직한 메뉴 역시 바로 이탈리아 음식일 것이다.

Italian cuisine, which was designated as 'the world's best cuisine' by CNN in 2013, is well known that each regional characteristic is well reflected into its dishes and that simple ingredients and recipes keep an original taste of ingredients well. This reputability of the Italian cuisine is much acceptable on account of the fact that French cuisine on the apex of gastronomy was in fact affected by the Italian cuisine. The development of the Western cuisine has been in parallel with the history of the Italian cuisine. The Medici family, an Italian banking family who flourished based on the Renaissance culture and its financial background, spread a culinary culture of Italy to the French court in the 15th century and this contributed to form a prototype of the culinary culture of the whole Europe.

In Northern Italy, Polenta, a kind of cornmeal soup, and Risotto are popular as a main dish. And a seafood dish made with crab and sardine caught in the Adriatic sea, a wine-braised veal and a dish made with beef intestines are well known too. In Southern Italy including Naples, a rather modest dish such as pizza or pasta is served as a main dish. Dinner is the most important meal of a day for most Italians and they usually start dinner around 8 p.m. finish late at night. They start their meal with Stuzzichini served before a meal and move to Antipasti, a kind of hors d'oeuvre such as a vegetable or seafood dish, and then enjoy Primi Piatti served with pasta, risotto or pizza and Secondi Piatti, a main dish made of fish or meat. Then this main dish is followed by Contorni, a kind of vegetable garnish, Formaggi served with several cheeses and then Dolce, the dessert. All these courses are finished with a digestif or coffee.

In Italy, the type of eatery is quite varied depending on its size and form. A ristorante is similar to a general restaurant and a trattoria is a kind of bistro serving a home-style meal. An osteria is a rather casual place serving a simple food and a pizzeria is a store specializing in pizza. There is also a tavola calda, a sort of cafeteria.

Still and again, Italian cuisine is considered the best gastronomy in Seoul. In the 1970s and 1980s 'eating out' meant 'going out to a Chinese restaurant,' and 'Western food' implied the 'Italian food.' As a variety of noodles and a tomato sauce are quite agreeable to Korean's taste, the Italian cuisine has become one of the most popular Western foods since the 1970s. The Italian food which was first served at a restaurant of a domestic hotel in the 1970s was expanded widely with appearance of pasta houses in the 1980s. And in the 1990s, an authentic Italian restaurant was introduced in Korea and then became more popular.

In the 2000s, as an Italian restaurant in Seoul was sub-divided and became varied from a ristorante offering a fine dining prepared by an expert chef to a pizzeria with a rather casual ambiance. Along with a variety of ingredients procured from Italy and a chef's own signature dish, the understanding of the Italian cuisine has been improved. The Italian cuisine is briskly booming in Seoul now more than ever. If you have an appointment this evening, the first and reliable food that you can think as dinner would be the Italian cuisine.

place
:
18
Most Reliable
Italian Restaurants

5년이 흘러도
건재하다,

믿고 가는
이탤리언
레스토랑
18

In Seoul where you can witness the fast-paced trend of food service and food retailing industry, it is not easy for a restaurant to stand firm and be loved more than a couple of years. Some restaurants, however, have been passed the test of the ever-changing culinary trend at least over 5 years, or up to more than 40 years. One of them began the history of Italian cuisine in Korea and there are various forms of other Italian restaurants, featuring a formal fine dining, casual home-style meal, authentic Neapolitan pizza, etc.

서울의 레스토랑업계는 1~2년을 버티는 것조차 쉽지 않을 만큼 빠르게 변화한다. 그런데 짧게는 5년, 길게는 무려 40년 이상 꾸준히 사랑받고 있는 레스토랑이 있다. 한국식 이탤리언 레스토랑의 전신이라 할 만한 곳부터 격식 있는 파인 다이닝, 편안한 가정식, 정통 나폴리 피자까지 다양한 형태로 자신들이 추구하는 이탈리아 음식을 묵묵히 선보이는, 믿음직한 이탤리언 레스토랑 18곳을 소개한다.

라 칸티나	까사 안토니오	빌라 오띠모
보나세라	블루밍 가든	톰볼라
베라짜노	부자 피자	볼라레
리스토란테 에오	미 피아체	더 키친 살바토레 쿠오모
그란 삐아띠	그랑 씨엘	알라또레
파올로 데 마리아	두에꼬제	스파소

La Cantina	Casa Antonio	Villa Ottimo
Buona Sera	Blooming Garden	Tombola
Verrazzano	Pizzaria D'buzza	Volare
Ristorante EO	Mi Piace	The Kitchen Salvatore Cuomo
Gran Piatti	Grand Ciel	Allatorre
Paolo de Maria	Duecose	Spasso

라 칸티나

1967년 경양식집으로 문을 연 라 칸티나가 이탤리언 레스토랑으로 바뀐 것은 1980년대 초반의 일이다. 현재 라 칸티나를 운영하는 이태훈 대표의 아버지가 이탈리아계 미국인 벨라르디 셰프를 영입하면서 이탤리언 메뉴를 선보인 것이 시초였다고. 2012년 개조해 최신 설비를 갖췄지만 묵직하고 고풍스러운 인테리어는 오픈할 때부터 한결같다. 가구나 소품 대부분이 레스토랑과 수십 년의 세월을 함께했다. 임승환 지배인은 "향수를 불러일으키는 요리와 공간이 이곳의 매력"이라고 말한다. 20년 넘게 근무한 셰프를 비롯해 스태프 대부분 40대 이상이며, 요리 역시 1980년대 선보인 메뉴에서 크게 달라진 것이 없다. 이탈리아의 특정 지역이나 재료보다 한국인의 입맛에 맞는 메뉴 구성에 주력하며, 가장 인기 있는 메뉴는 '링귀네 라 칸티나'다. 조개와 새우로 우려낸 맑은 소스와 버터에 볶은 면이 어우러져 개운하면서 담백하다. 토마토소스에 새우와 홍합, 오징어를 넣은 스파게티 '탈리아텔레 페스카토레'와 조개탕 느낌이 나는 '봉골레 스파게티' 역시 사랑받는 메뉴. 스테이크나 파스타 세트 메뉴를 고르면 갓 구운 마늘빵과 수프, 샐러드, 커피까지 합리적인 가격으로 맛볼 수 있다.

La Cantina

Originally opened in 1967 as a restaurant featuring à la carte dishes served in a simple way, La Cantina was transformed into an Italian restaurant in the early 1980s. Even after it was refurbished with the up-to-date cooking facilities, its grand, antique interiors have remained intact and most of furniture and decorations have been kept well for several decades. "It is nostalgic food and place that our customers love most." said Im Seung-Hwan, a manager of La Cantina. La Cantina is focusing on developing a new recipe to satisfy the Korean's taste. Its most popular dish is Linguine La Cantina. Spaghetti cooked with shrimps, mussels, squid and tomato sauce and Spaghetti alle Vongole with the taste of Clam Soup are also customer's favorite. If you order Steak or Pasta Set Menu, you can enjoy new baked garlic bread, soup, salad and coffee at a reasonable price.

Address	중구 을지로 19 지하 1층	B1F, 19, Eulji-ro, Jung-gu
Contact	02-777-2580	82-2-777-2580
Operation	월~토 Mon to Sat 11:30~22:00(Break 14:00~17:30), 일 Sun 17:30~22:00	
Closed	연중무휴	Open all year round

보나세라

1층에는 넓은 홀과 잘 가꾼 정원, 2층에는 프라이빗한 룸이 있으며 품격 있는 식사를 하기에 좋은 장소다. 2002년 오픈 당시에는 이탈리아에서 온 파올로 데 마리아 셰프가, 지금은 샘 킴 셰프가 주방을 책임지고 있다. 총괄 셰프 샘 킴은 매달 새로운 메뉴를 내놓는다. "정통 이탈리아 요리의 틀에서 벗어나지 않고 제철 식재료로 신선한 맛을 내는 것이 원칙입니다. 1~2주 동안 스태프와 함께 여러 가지 시도를 하고, 3주차에 확정한 다음 그달의 메뉴를 정하지요." 매장에서 허브를, 서울 근교 농장에서 채소를 재배하는 샘 킴 셰프는 재료를 직접 얻는 즐거움이 크다고 말한다. 토마토, 루콜라, 로메인 등을 키우면서 다시 한 번 식재료의 매력에 빠졌다고. 그가 추천하는 요리는 '브리타 치즈를 곁들인 대저 토마토'와 '새우와 미나리가 들어간 생면 키타라 파스타'. 직접 뽑은 얇은 생면인 키타라는 이탈리아 중남부에서 즐겨 먹는데 해산물 소스와 궁합이 좋다. 속이 꽉 찬 찰토마토인 대저 토마토는 식욕을 돋우는 애피타이저로 안성맞춤. 디저트 트롤리, 다양한 와인 리스트, 세련된 서비스까지 보나세라의 매력은 무궁무진하다.

Buona Sera

A large and nice hall is harmonized with a well-trimmed garden on the first floor and private dining rooms on the second floor are the best place to have a formal and elegant dining. Sam Kim, a celebrity chef, is the head chef in charge of the kitchen of Buona Sera. Growing herbs in his store and vegetables in a farm near Seoul he found great pleasure of harvesting them from his farm and learned again about charming features of food materials like tomato, arugula, romaine, etc. He especially recommends 'Daejeo Tomato with Burrata Cheese' and Chitarra Pasta with shrimp and Chinese celery. On top of these exquisite cuisines, you would also be fascinated by Buona Sera's dessert trolley, a wine list filled with a wide range of wine and attentive service.

Address	강남구 도산대로45길 18-2	18-2, Dosan-daero 45-gil, Gangnam-gu
Contact	02-543-8373	82-2-543-8373
Web	www.buonasera.co.kr	www.buonasera.co.kr
Operation	12:00~23:00(Break 15:00~18:00)	12:00~23:00(Break 15:00~18:00)
Closed	연중무휴	Open all year round

베라짜노

2002년 오픈한 이후 청담동 와인 골목을 책임져온 레스토랑으로 이탈리아 키안티 지방에 있는 '카스텔로 베라짜노'에서 이름을 따왔다. 작은 정원을 마주한 테라스와 클래식한 분위기의 룸에서 와인 한잔 마시며 식사를 하기에 그만이다. 지하에 별도의 와인셀러를 두고 400여 종의 와인 리스트를 갖췄다. 이탈리아 와인을 비롯해 프랑스, 미국, 칠레 등 여러 산지와 다양한 빈티지 와인을 구비했으며 쉽게 접하기 어려운 고급 와인 위주로 구성돼 있다. 8년 동안 근무한 이정희 지배인은 "와인을 즐기기 위해 오는 사람이 많고, 대부분 단골이라 취향, 선호하는 메뉴 등에 대해 미리 짐작할 수 있다"라고 말한다. 이곳의 시그너처 메뉴로는 '한우 등심과 양갈비, 왕새우, 관자 모둠 플래터'를 꼽을 수 있다. 레드, 화이트, 스파클링 등 어떤 와인과도 두루 잘 어울린다. 투 플러스 등급의 한우 안심으로 만든 '카르파치오'도 풍미가 깊은 이탈리아 레드 와인과 잘 어울리는 요리다.

Verrazzano

Since it was opened in 2002, Verrazzano, named after Castello di Verrazano, a restaurant in Italy, has now become one of the oldest restaurants at the wine alley of Cheongdam-dong. Its terrace facing a small garden or classical private room would be a great place to enjoy dining with a glass of wine. In the basement, they have a wine cellar housing 400 kinds of wine. Hanu Sirloin, Lamb Chop, King Prawn and Assorted Scallop Platter are referred to as Verrazzano's signature dishes and are good accompaniments to any kinds of wine.

Address	강남구 도산대로57길 13-4	13-4, Dosan-daero 57-gil, Gangnam-gu	
Contact	02-517-3274	82-2-517-3274	
Operation	월~금 Mon to Fri 18:00~다음 날 The next day 02:00, 토·일 Sat & Sun 18:00~00:00		
Closed	연중무휴	Open all year round	

리스토란테 에오

어윤권 셰프는 품격 있는 파인 다이닝을 내놓으며 새로운 이탈리아 요리를 제안한 인물. 특히 2006년 청담동에 오픈한 리스토란테 에오는 매일 달라지는 테이스팅 메뉴로 미식가들을 사로잡았다. "파인 다이닝은 조화로운 재료에 크리에이티브한 디자인을 더합니다. 접시에 아름답게 담고, 향을 음미하고, 맛을 보는 즐거움으로 파인 다이닝을 완성합니다." 리스토란테 에오는 간판도 없이 아는 사람만 입소문으로 찾아온다. 품격 있는 모던한 인테리어와 잘 정리된 와인 셀러가 눈에 띄며 룸 두 개와 작은 홀로 나뉘어 있다. 단품 없이 매일 다른 코스 요리를 선보이며 사전 예약이 필수다. "그날 가장 신선한 식재료를 고르고, 손님의 취향에 따라 코스를 구상합니다. 같은 요리라도 조금씩 달라지고 코스의 조합에도 변화를 줍니다." 그가 추천하는 요리는 '지중해식 해산물 요리'와 '한우 데미그라스 소스가 어우러진 빠게리 요리'. 클래식한 이탈리아 요리에 한국적인 터치를 가미하는 어윤권 셰프의 장기대로 그림처럼 아름다운 요리를 선보인다.

Ristorante EO

The owner and chef, Eo Yun-Gwon suggests a new type of Italian cuisine through a high-class fine dining. His restaurant Ristorante EO, opened in Cheongdam-dong in 2006, has captured numerous gourmets with its ever-changing tasting menus. As it has not any sign outside it is not possible to find the restaurant if you have never heard of it. Its modern and refined interiors and well-arranged wine cellar are outstanding. This place consists of two private dining rooms and one small hall. It does not serve à la carte but a new course meal every day. Since it has only five or six tables, you would have to make reservation in advance. Mediterranean Seafood and Paccheri Pasta Dish with Hanu demi-glace sauce are considered its specialty.

Address	강남구 도산대로75길 15	15, Dosan-daero 75-gil, Gangnam-gu
Contact	02-3445-1926	82-2-3445-1926
Operation	12:00~22:30(Break 15:00~18:00)	12:00~22:30(Break 15:00~18:00)
Closed	일요일	Sun

그란 삐아띠

피렌체에서 18년간 생활한 김병희 오너 셰프가 현지 경험을 바탕으로 만드는 그란 삐아띠의 요리는 소박한 편이다. 대표 메뉴는 파스타와 스테이크. 피자를 만들지 않는 대신 파스타의 종류가 16종에 이른다. 가장 인기 있는 메뉴는 감베리 파스타. 생새우를 갈아 올리브유에 볶아 넣고 안초비와 해물 국물로 간을 맞춰 담백하고 고소하다. 파스타 면을 먹는 중간중간 새우가 씹혀 독특한 식감을 낸다. 애피타이저 역시 다양한데 이탈리아식 버섯만두라 불리는 '풍기리 삐에네'가 인기 메뉴다. 새송이버섯을 반으로 갈라 가운데를 사각형으로 자른 다음 피망과 새송이버섯, 파르미자노 치즈를 다져 넣고 그 위에 모차렐라 치즈를 올려 구운 후 토마토소스를 얹는다. 코키지 차지는 1병당 3만 원이며, 격식을 차리지 않는 편안한 분위기에서 푸짐한 이탈리언 음식을 즐기기에 가장 좋은 장소다.

Gran Piatti

Gran Piatti, run by Chef Kim Byeong-Hui, serves a rather simple dish based on his 18 years' experiences in Florence, Italy. Its best menu is Pasta and Steak. Unfortunately, Pizza is not available but instead Gran Piatti offers 16 kinds of Pasta. Amongst those pastas, the most popular is Pasta con Gamberoni. He sautés ground fresh shrimp with olive oil and then seasons it with anchovy and seafood broth for plain and savory flavor. Ground shrimp mixed with pasta creates distinctive texture. Its corkage fee is \30,000 per bottle. This restaurant is one of the best Italian restaurants you could enjoy hearty Italian cuisine in casual ambiance.

Address	서초구 서래로7길 15	15, Seorae-ro 7-gil, Seocho-gu
Contact	02-595-5767	82-2-595-5767
Operation	런치는 예약제 Lunch Reservations required, 디너 Dinner 17:30~22:00, 토 Sat 17:30~22:00	
Closed	일요일	Sun

파올로 데 마리아

이탈리아 북서부 피에몬테 출신의 파올로 데 마리아 셰프가 자신의 이름을 걸고 문을 연 이 레스토랑은 2009년 서래마을에 오픈한 후 2013년에 한남동으로 이사했다. 레스토랑보다 격식을 덜 차리는 '트라토리아'에 '파인'을 덧붙여 정통 이탤리언 음식을 편안하게 맛볼 수 있는 트라토리아를 지향한다. 가장 단순한 조리법으로 요리하고 한 가지 음식에 세 가지 이상의 재료를 사용하지 않는 것이 이곳의 원칙이다. 파올로 데 마리아의 시그너처 메뉴이자 손님들이 가장 많이 찾는 메뉴는 생면 파스타. 매일 아침 직접 링귀네와 스파게티를 만들어 쫄깃함이 뛰어나다. 직접 만든 이탈리아 햄의 일종인 살시차로 속을 채운 라비올리도 인기 메뉴다. 살시차 특유의 진한 맛이 묵직한 레드와인과 잘 어울린다. 디저트로는 홈메이드 타르트와 케이크, 비스코티, 초콜릿, 크림 등 여덟 가지 디저트가 담긴 디저트 트롤리를 맛보자. 이탈리아 전통 가정식을 배울 수 있는 요리 학교도 함께 운영하고 있다.

Paolo de Maria

The eponymous restaurant of Chef Paolo de Maria who came from Piedmont, the northwest region of Italy, was first opened in Seorae Village in 2009 and then moved to Hannam-dong in 2013. They style themselves as a 'fine-dining trattoria,' which means a casual place serving authentic Italian cuisine, by combining the term 'trattoria' meaning 'casual' with the word 'fine.' They stick to their principle to cook food based on the simplest recipe and not to use more than three food materials for one meal. Their signature dish, Fresh Pasta, is the most popular dish as well. Their linguine and spaghetti, being handmade every morning, boast an amazing texture. Ravioli filled with homemade salsiccia, a sort of Italian sausage, is one of the best-selling dishes as well. In addition, anyone who wants to learn Italian home-style cooking could take a cooking class in his culinary school.

Address	용산구 대사관로31길 13	13, Daesagwan-ro 31-gil, Yongsan-gu
Contact	02-599-9936	82-2-599-9936
Web	www.paolodemaria.net	www.paolodemaria.net
Operation	11:30~22:30(Break 15:00~17:30)	11:30~22:30(Break 15:00~17:30)
Closed	연중무휴	Open all year round

까사 안토니오

이탈리아인인 안토니오 파텔라Antonio Patella 대표가 운영하는 곳인 까사 안토니오는 '안토니오의 집'이라는 뜻이다. 이탈리아 남부 해안 지역 플리아 출신인 안토니오 대표는 해산물의 선도를 중요하게 여겨 제철 재료만 사용하고 매일 아침 직접 시장에 가 장을 본다. "한국의 다양한 해산물을 사용해 고향의 요리를 만듭니다. 봄에는 도다리로 찜이나 구이를 하는 식이죠." 안토니오 대표가 추천하는 메뉴는 안초비를 식초와 올리브유에 절인 후 화이트 와인 소스와 함께 내는 '안초비 마리네이드'와 '갯가재 로제 링귀니'다. 또 이탈리아 현지인들이 즐겨 마시는 와인을 다양하게 구비했다. 이탈리아 사람들도 고향이 그리울 때 찾아와 먹을 정도로 요리도, 와인 리스트도 인정받은 곳이다.

Casa Antonio

Casa Antonio means 'Antonio's house.' Its owner, Antonio Patella, whose was born in Apulia, a region of Southern Italy bordering the sea, uses only seasonal ingredients and goes to markets every morning as he puts the greatest importance on freshness of fish and seafood. Anchovy Marinade (pickled anchovy in vinegar and olive oil with white wine sauce) and Rose Linguine with Mantis Shrimp are excellent. Casa Antonio also has an extensive list of wine popular in Italy.

Address	용산구 이태원로27길 6 2층	2F, 6, Itaewon-ro 27-gil, Yongsan-gu
Contact	02-794-8803	82-2-794-8803
Web	www.casantonio.co.kr	www.casantonio.co.kr
Operation	월~목 Mon to Thur 12:00~23:00, 금 · 토 Fri & Sat 12:00~23:30, 일 Sun 12:00~22:00	
Closed	연중무휴	Open all year round

블루밍 가든

2008년 오픈한 이래 '활짝 핀 정원'을 뜻하는 이름처럼 친근한 이탈리언 퀴진을 선보여온 곳. 블루밍 가든의 메뉴는 SG다인힐의 현정 총괄 셰프가 담당한다. 이탈리아 남부의 영향을 받아 해산물을 많이 활용하고 아시아식 조리 노하우를 적용해 특별한 요리를 만든다. 인기 메뉴인 '보따르가 스파게티니'는 숭어알, 날치알에 일식에 쓰는 백명란과 청주를 가미해 담백함을 강조했다. 식전 빵과 '성게알 로제 스파게티니', '꽃게 로제 스파게티니'가 이곳의 시그너처 메뉴이며 성게알과 꽃게를 넣은 스파게티는 비리지 않고 고소한 맛이 일품이다. 현정 총괄 셰프는 이탈리아 남부 바실리카타의 채소 요리, 시칠리아의 맵고 자극적인 맛을 블루밍 가든 스타일로 재현하는 것이 목표라고 말한다. "이탈리아 요리와 제 고향인 강원도 음식이 비슷해요. 감자, 옥수수 등과 이탈리아 요리의 조화를 새롭게 시도하고 싶습니다."

Blooming Garden

Blooming Garden has served friendly, casual Italian cuisine since 2008. They use a wide variety of seafood for their cuisines based on recipes of Southern Italy and apply Asian-style culinary arts to create its own special cuisine. Sea Urchin Rose Spaghettini and Blue Crab Rose Spaghettini are recognized as their signature dishes, along with bread appetizer. People say that their spaghettini with sea urchin roe or blue crab doesn't taste fishy rather than savory. According to the executive chef Hyeon Jeong of Blooming Garden, their ultimate goal is to embody vegetable meals of Basilicata, a region in the south of Italy and spicy and piquant taste of Sicily into their own style.

Address	강남구 강남대로 358 지하 1층(강남역점)		B1F, 358, Gangnam-daero, Gangnam-gu
Contact	02-3466-1962		82-2-3466-1962
Web	www.dinehill.co.kr		www.dinehill.co.kr
Operation	11:30~22:00		11:30~22:00
Closed	연중무휴		Open all year round

부자 피자

2011년 한남동에 둥지를 튼 부자 피자는 레스토랑의 외관에서부터 자유분방한 느낌을 물씬 풍긴다. 이탈리아 ICIF 요리학교를 졸업한 이일주 셰프는 피자를 생각하는 것을 그대로 담을 수 있는 캔버스라 여겨 다양한 형태로 만들어낸다. 이 레스토랑을 유명하게 만든 피자는 '콰트로 풍기' 피자로 네 종류의 버섯을 토핑으로 얹고 화이트 트뤼플 오일로 풍미를 더한 후 100퍼센트 참나무 장작으로 전용 화덕에서 굽는다. 피자 외에도 샐러드와 튀김, 수프와 디저트까지 다양한 이탈리아 요리를 선보이며, 모차렐라 치즈는 원유를 수입해 직접 만든다. 메뉴에 맞게 점성을 조절하며 매일 그날 쓸 분량만 만들어 사용하므로 항상 신선한 치즈를 맛볼 수 있다. 바질과 루콜라 역시 직영 농장에서 가져온다고. 곁들여 먹는 음료로는 생라즈베리를 듬뿍 올린 '라즈베리 상그리아'가 제격이다. 달지 않고 상큼해 피자와 함께 즐기기 좋다.

Pizzaria D'buzza

Located in Hannam-dong since 2011, Pizzaria D'buzza gives off its animated and welcoming ambiance from its exteriors. Chef Lee Il-Ju, who graduated from ICIF (Italian Culinary Institute for Foreigners), thinks of a disk of pizza dough as a kind of canvas, on which he can put everything he imagines and tries to made different kinds of pizza. Quattro Funghi Pizza that makes this restaurant famous has four kinds of mushrooms as toppings and is flavored with white truffle oil. They bake pizza in a special oven using oak firewood only. A variety of Italian foods from salad, fried dish, soup to desserts are also available as well as pizza. They import raw milk to make Mozzarella cheese and bring basil and arugula directly from its farm.

Address	용산구 이태원로55가길 28	28, Itaewon-ro 55ga-gil, Yongsan-gu
Contact	02-794-9474	82-2-794-9474
Web	www.buzzapizza.com	www.buzzapizza.com
Operation	11:30~22:30	11:30~22:30
Closed	설·추석 당일	Day of Lunar New Year's Day & Chuseok

미 피아체

2003년 오픈해 10년 넘게 청담동을 지키고 있다. 이탈리아 어로 '나의 기쁨, 즐거움'을 의미하는 이름처럼 편안한 분위기에서 음식을 맛볼 수 있는 곳이다. 파스텔 톤의 벽, 화사한 꽃 장식, 우아한 테이블웨어가 이탈리아 가정집에 온 듯한 느낌을 준다. 10여 년 동안 이곳을 운영해온 김혜령 대표는 미 피아체의 매력을 '언제 찾아도 균일한 맛'으로 꼽았다. 이탈리아 가정식을 선보이는 이곳의 가장 큰 특징은 2~3인이 나눠 먹기 좋은 애피타이저가 많다는 것. 문어를 넣은 라타투이, 한치튀김, 조개찜 등 따뜻한 음식과 다채로운 샐러드가 균형을 이룬다. '성게알 토마토 크림소스 링귀니'와 '가리비, 양배추, 안초비 소스 스파게티'는 이곳의 베스트 메뉴. 볶은 양배추의 단맛과 안초비의 짭조름한 맛이 조화를 이루는 스파게티는 그야말로 명불허전이다. 미 피아체에서는 매달 새로운 메뉴를 개발해 런치 세트로 선보여 반응을 본 뒤 정규 메뉴로 추가한다. 올여름에는 새우, 관자, 한치 등의 해산물을 넣은 '해물 볼 튀김'이 주인공이라고. 한입 깨물면 입안 가득 고소함을 만끽할 수 있다.

Mi Piace

It has been more than 10 years that Mi Piace has settled in Cheongdam-dong. Mi Piace, meaning 'my pleasure,' gives a comfortable and casual impression as their name does. This Italian home-style restaurant features various appetizers enough for two or three people to share. Warm dishes and diverse salads including Octopus Ratatouille, Fried Dried Cuttlefish and Steamed Clam are well balanced on their menu. Linguine al riccio di mare (tomato cream sauce linguine with fresh sea urchin roe) and Spaghetti with Scallop, Cabbage and Anchovy' are amazingly wonderful. Mi Piace develops a new dish every month, which is then included on the lunch course meals. If the new dish wins fans, it is finally put on the regular menu.

Address	강남구 압구정로80길 19-2		19-2, Apgujeong-ro 80-gil, Gangnam-gu
Contact	02-516-6317		82-2-516-6317
Operation	12:00~22:00(Break 15:00~18:00)		12:00~22:00(Break 15:00~18:00)
Closed	연중무휴		Open all year round

그랑 씨엘

2005년 도산공원 앞에 오픈한 그랑 씨엘은 높은 천장, 노란색 벽과 네이비 컬러 차양을 내린 테라스로 이국적인 분위기가 물씬 풍긴다. 박근호, 이송희 부부 셰프가 함께 운영하는 이곳은 원 테이블 레스토랑 '인 뉴욕' 이후 두 사람이 오픈한 두 번째 레스토랑이다. 재료의 맛에 충실하게 기본 요리를 구성하고 트렌드에 맞춰 메뉴를 조금씩 업그레이드해왔다. 초창기에 단출했던 메뉴가 벌써 품목에 따라 10여 가지로 늘어났다고. 이탈리아 정통 토마토 수프, 리코타 치즈를 넣은 가지롤, 샐러드, 파스타, 리소토, 스테이크, 디저트까지 메뉴 종류도 다양해졌다. 박근호 셰프는 주변 레스토랑에 신경 쓰지 않는다고 말한다. "트렌드보다 나만의 스타일을 유지하는 것이 중요합니다. 핫 플레이스만 찾다가도 편하게 올 수 있는 곳이 필요하잖아요. 그런 역할을 저희가 하는 것이지요." 한편 두 사람은 지난해 식재료와 도구를 판매하는 '팩토리 마이쏭'을 론칭했다. 증도 갯벌에서 생산한 천일염을 3·5·8년 동안 숙성시킨 마이쏭 솔트에 이어 2015년 하반기에는 식재료 패키지를 내놓을 예정이다.

Grand Ciel

In 2005, Grand Ciel, full of exotic ambiance from its yellow wall and terrace with a navy canopy, was opened in front of Dosan Park. This restaurant, run by a married couple, Chef Park Geun-Ho and Chef Lee Song-Hui together, is their second restaurant following In New York, the one-table restaurant. Grand Ciel develops a simple basic dish focusing on specific flavor of each ingredient and upgrades it depending on a recent trend. First they started only with a few items on the menu but now have more than 10 dishes for each category. Their menu from Salad, Pasta, Risotto and Steak to Dessert presents more detailed items such as Authentic Italian Tomato Soup, Eggplant Rolls with Ricotta cheese. Last year, two chefs also launched Factory My Ssong, a store for food materials cookware.

Address	강남구 도산대로45길 16-6	16-6, Dosan-daero 45-gil, Gangnam-gu
Contact	02-548-0283	82-2-548-0283
Operation	월~토 11:00~23:00, 일 10:00~22:00	Mon to Sat 11:00~23:00, Sun 10:00~22:00
Closed	연중무휴	Open all year round

두에꼬제

두에꼬제는 이탈리아 어로 '두 가지'란 뜻으로 이곳의 두 가지는 '피자와 파스타', 혹은 '맛과 서비스'를 의미한다. 우선 2002년부터 한결같은 맛과 서비스를 지켜온 덕분에 단골손님이 많다. 10년이 넘는 세월 동안 두에꼬제를 이끌어온 안옥경 사장의 말에 따르면 손님들이 가장 많이 주문하는 메뉴는 피자와 파스타. 특히 인기 메뉴인 '할라피뇨 파스타'는 할라피뇨를 잘게 다진 후 올리브유에 마늘과 안초비를 넣어 같이 볶아낸다. 올리브유의 고소함과 할라피뇨의 매콤한 맛이 잘 어울려 느끼하지 않다. 두 가지 피자를 동시에 먹고 싶다면 '하프 앤 하프'를 주문하면 된다. 블루치즈를 넣어 만든 고르곤졸라와 마르게리타 피자 위에 루콜라를 얹은 '마르게리타에 루콜라'의 조합이 베스트셀러. 곁들일 만한 맥주 라인업도 훌륭하다. 생맥주로는 필스너 스타일의 스크림쇼가 마련돼 있다. 이외에도 페로니 같은 라거 맥주와 스컬핀 등의 에일 맥주를 판매한다.

Duecose

Duecose means 'two things' in Italian. For Duecose, two things here indicate 'Pizza and Pasta' or 'Taste and Service.' Their taste and service well kept in a consistent way since 2002 are the main factor that makes their customers come back again and again. An Ok-Gyeong, the owner of Duecose, says that Pizza and Pasta are always their best menu. Spaghetti al Jalapeno which is especially popular dish is cooked by frying well-chopped jalapeno, garlic and anchovy with olive oil. The specific flavor of olive oil and spicy jalapeno are well harmonized. If you try two kinds of pizza at the same time, you can order 'Half and Half.' Half Margherita and half Arugula, combining Gorgonzola Pizza added with blue cheese and Margherita Pizza with arugula on it, are the best-seller.

Address	용산구 한남대로60(한남점)	60, Hannam-daero, Yongsan-gu
Contact	02-795-1405	82-2-795-1405
Operation	11:30~22:00(Break 15:00~17:00)	11:30~22:00(Break 15:00~17:00)
Closed	설 · 추석 연휴	Holiday of Lunar New Year's Day & Chuseok

빌라 오띠모

서래마을의 가정집을 개조해 만들어 넓은 정원이 특징인 빌라 오띠모는 이탈리아 남부 가정식을 표방한다. 이곳의 시그너처 메뉴는 캐주얼 파스타와 팬프라이 스테이크. 팬프라이 스테이크는 꽃등심, 안심, 양갈비 세 가지가 준비돼 있다. 3주 이상 숙성시킨 고기를 특별 제작한 주물 팬에 서브하는데 갓 구운 스테이크의 지글거리는 소리가 식욕을 돋운다. 이탈리아 시칠리아 스타일의 '부라타 치즈 샐러드'는 손님들이 가장 많이 찾는 애피타이저다. 직접 만든 생부라타 치즈 위에 라타투이와 바질 페스토, 루콜라를 얹어 상큼하면서도 고소하다. 라자냐에 배춧잎을 얹은 후 오징어 먹물 소스를 곁들이는 '배추 라자냐', 안심과 견과류를 넣은 '고르곤졸라 크림소스 페투치네' 등 한국 식재료를 결합해 만든 메뉴도 다양하다. 점심시간에는 합리적인 가격으로 애피타이저와 피자, 파스타, 커피를 즐길 수 있는 세트 메뉴를 제공한다. 시즌별로 메뉴가 바뀌는데 여름에는 '이탈리아 파르마 닭백숙' 같은 이색적인 요리를 선보인다. 이탈리아, 프랑스 등지에서 수입한 120종의 와인을 함께 즐길 수 있다.

Villa Ottimo

Seorae Village's Villa Ottimo, placed in a remodeled family house with a large garden, styles themselves as a home-style cuisine of southern Italy. Casual Pasta and Pan-Fried Steak are well known as their signature dishes. And Burrata Cheese Salad in Sicily-style is the most popular appetizer. Some dishes are cooked with Korean food ingredients. For example, for Cabbage Lasagna they put Korean cabbage leaves on the lasagna in squid ink sauce and for Fettuccine with Gorgonzola Cream Sauce, they use tenderloin and nuts. Pan Fried Steak, one of their main dishes, is served at your choice of meat among rib eye, tenderloin and lamb chop. Meat aged more than 3 weeks is served on a customized cast-iron pan. Its sizzling would do not fail to capture your taste buds.

Address	서초구 서래로3길 17-13	17-13, Seorae-ro 3-gil, Seocho-gu	
Contact	02-518-1947	82-2-518-1947	
Operation	11:00~22:00(Break 15:00~17:30)	11:00~22:00(Break 15:00~17:30)	
Closed	연중무휴	Open all year round	

톰볼라 / Tombola

이탈리아 피렌체풍 가정식 요리를 선보이는 곳. 이탈리아에서 10년간 유학한 김주환 대표가 자주 다니던 현지 식당에서 영감을 받아 탄생했다. 2003년 오픈할 당시에는 흔치 않았던 화덕 피자로 유명해졌다. 이틀 정도 숙성시킨 도 위에 루콜라와 두툼한 파르미자노 치즈를 얹은 피자는 톰볼라의 상징이자 인기 메뉴. 도는 10퍼센트 우리 밀로 반죽해 씹으면 씹을수록 고소한 향이 난다. 개점 14주년을 맞은 2015년에는 해산물을 이용한 메뉴를 새롭게 선보였다. 캐나다에서 직접 수입한 생바닷가재를 통째로 넣어 만든 '로브스터 파스타'가 대표 메뉴. 바닷가재의 살을 발라 파스타에 넣고, 껍데기를 이용해 소스를 만드는데 독특한 감칠맛 덕분에 누구나 좋아한다. 이외에도 키조개, 연어, 새우 등 제철 해산물로 만든 해산물 모둠구이는 저녁에만 맛볼 수 있는 별미다. 한우 스테이크는 그릴에 구운 후 구운 소금을 뿌려 맛을 내는데, 센 불에서 순식간에 구워 육즙이 입안 가득 퍼진다. 피에몬테, 베네토, 몬탈치노, 토스카나 등 이탈리아 지역별 와인을 다양하게 구비하고 있으니 함께 곁들여보자.

Tombola serves home-style cuisine in Florence style. Its owner Kim Ju-Hwan got inspiration for Tombola from a local restaurant he frequently visited while staying in Italy. Tombola's pizza cooking by putting arugula and thick parmigiano-reggiano cheese on the dough aged 2 days is their symbolic and most popular dish. They present a new dish using seafood to celebrate their 14th anniversary in 2015. Lobster Pasta using a whole lobster procured directly from Canada is their specialty as well. Plus, there is Grilled Assorted Seafood with pen shell clam, salmon, shrimp, etc. available only for dinner. Their various kinds of Italian wine would go well with these dishes.

Address	서초구 서래로7길 16	16, Seorae-ro 7-gil, Seocho-gu
Contact	02-593-4660	82-2-593-4660
Web	www.tombola.co.kr	www.tombola.co.kr
Operation	월~토 Mon to Sat 11:30~23:00(Break 15:30~18:00), 일 Sun 11:30~22:30(Break 14:30~17:30)	
Closed	설·추석 연휴	Holiday of Lunar New Year's Day & Chuseok

볼라레

2010년 서래마을에 문을 연 볼라레는 나폴리 피자 전문점이다. 정두원 오너 셰프는 이탈리아 ICIF 요리학교를 졸업하고 나폴리의 피자 레스토랑에서 경력을 쌓았다. 그는 볼라레를 연 지 일 년 만에 한국인 최초로 나폴리 피자 협회에서 피자 장인 혹은 피자 셰프를 뜻하는 '피자이올로 pizzaiolo'로 인증받았으며, 전 세계에서 386번째 나폴리 피자 인증 마크인 '베라 피자 Vera Pizza'를 받았다. 볼라레의 메뉴는 단출하다. 피자는 여섯 가지, 파스타는 다섯 가지. 가장 대표적인 메뉴이자 인기 있는 메뉴는 마르게리타다. 토마토소스를 베이스로 모차렐라 치즈와 바질을 얹고 올리브유를 뿌린 이 피자는 투박한 모양이 먹음직스러워 보인다. 피자 도우는 비린내 없이 고소하고 부드럽다. 피자와 함께 곁들이는 파스타로는 카르보나라 스파게티를 추천한다. 정 셰프가 이탈리아 현지의 레스토랑에서 일할 때 먹던 직원 식사의 레시피를 그대로 재현한다고. 달걀노른자를 넣어 밀도가 높지만 깔끔한 맛을 낸다. 이탤리언 클래식 칵테일인 아메리카노와 네그로니도 맛볼 수 있다.

Volare

Volare, opened at Seorae Village in 2010, specializes in Neapolitan Pizza. Its owner and chef Jeong Du-Won worked as a chef at a pizza restaurant in Naples after graduating from ICIF (Italian Culinary Institute for Foreigners). A year after he opened Volare, he became the first Korean who becomes a certified Neapolitan Pizzaiolo (professional pizza maker) and then got the 386th Vera Pizza Napoletana (a certification of Neapolitan pizza) in the world. Volare has a simple menu including 6 kinds of pizza and 5 kinds of pasta. Their specialty and most popular dish is Margherita Pizza. They put mozzarella cheese and basil on the dough with tomato sauce and then sprinkle olive oil over the pizza. Its unsophisticated shape makes it look amazingly delicious. The pizza dough is luscious and savory.

Address	서초구 사평대로20길 8
Contact	02-537-1100
Operation	11:30~00:00
Closed	연중무휴

	8, Sapyeong-daero 20-gil, Seocho-gu
	82-2-537-1100
	11:30~00:00
	Open all year round

더 키친 살바토레 쿠오모

일본의 스타 셰프이자 레스토랑 프로듀서인 살바토레 쿠오모Salvatore Cuomo의 레스토랑. '세계 피자 대회Pizza Fest'에서 최우수상을 수상했으며, 국내 최초로 '나폴리 피자 협회Associazione Verace Pizza Napoletana'의 인증을 받은 레스토랑이다. 나폴리의 장인이 현지의 재료로 만든 화덕을 사용하고, 모든 피자에 이탈리아산 부팔라 모차렐라 치즈를 넣는다. 피자는 크게 토마토소스 베이스와 치즈 베이스로 나뉘며, 체리 토마토와 바질, 부팔라 모차렐라 치즈를 넣은 'D.O.C 피자'가 인기 메뉴다. 재료를 아끼지 않고 풍성하게 사용해 피자의 어디를 베어 물든 신선한 재료의 맛이 그대로 느껴진다. 피자 외에도 파스타, 해산물, 육류 요리 등을 맛볼 수 있는데 제철 해산물 요리가 특히 인기가 많다. 시즌별로 메뉴가 바뀌지만 해산물 파스타인 '링귀네 페스카토레'는 더 키친 살바토레 쿠오모가 오픈한 이래 6년간 바뀌지 않은 스테디셀러다. 페로니 생맥주, 이탈리아산 레드·화이트 와인 등이 준비돼 있다. 소믈리에와 전문 바텐더가 추천하는 다양한 주류와 칵테일도 맛볼 수 있다.

The Kitchen Salvatore Cuomo

Salvatore Cuomo, an Italian-born Japanese celebrity chef cum restaurant producer, opened his restaurant, the Kitchen Salvatore Cuomo in Sinsa-dong. He won the first prize at the International Pizza Festival and the Kitchen Salvatore Cuomo is the first restaurant obtaining a certification of Associazione Verace Pizza Napoletana. They use a Neapolitan style oven manufactured by an Italian professional maker and add Italy's buffalo mozzarella cheese on every pizza. Pizza is mainly classified into tomato sauce base and cheese base and D.O.C Pizza with cherry tomato, basil and buffalo mozzarella cheese are most popular. Rich ingredients make every part of pizza worth the bite. Pasta, seafood and meat dishes are also available and seasonal seafood cuisine is highly excellent.

Address	강남구 언주로164길 29	29, Eonju-ro 164-gil, Gangnam-gu
Contact	02-3447-0071	82-2-3447-0071
Web	www.kitchensalvatore.kr	www.kitchensalvatore.kr
Operation	일~목 Sun to Thur 11:30~23:00(Break 14:30~18:00, Café ~17:00), 금·토 Fri & Sat 11:30~00:00	
Closed	설·추석 연휴	Holiday of Lunar New Year's Day & Chuseok

알라또레

알라또레는 이탈리아 어로 '탑에서'란 뜻이다. 음식은 물론 서비스와 인테리어 모두 최고를 추구한다는 의미다. 2001년 홍대 앞에 오픈했고, 2013년 잠시 휴업했다가 2015년 4월, 새로운 건물에서 새로운 메뉴로 다시 문을 열었다. 이진석 셰프가 이끄는 이 레스토랑은 이탈리아 전역의 요리를 선보인다. 이 셰프가 추천하는 요리는 전복과 완두콩, 아스파라거스로 맛을 낸 전복 리소토와 이탈리아식 육회라 불리는 비프 타르타르. 비프 타르타르는 다진 쇠고기를 트뤼플 오일에 재워 만드는데 쇠고기 사이사이 파르미자노 치즈로 만든 젤라토를 채운 후 달걀 푸딩을 깔아 고소하고 촉촉하다. 제철 재료만 사용하기에 메뉴는 2주에 한 번씩 개편된다.

Allatorre

Allatorre means 'on a tower' in Italian. It also means that they try to be the best in its food, service and interiors. Allatorre run by Chef Lee Jin-Seok, serves a wide range of Italian cuisine. Chef Lee especially recommends Risotto flavored with abalone, green peas and asparagus and Beef Tartare, an Italian raw beef. As they insist seasonal ingredients only, their menu is changed every 2 weeks.

Address	마포구 와우산로23길 8	8, Wausan-ro 23-gil, Mapo-gu
Contact	02-324-0978	82-2-324-0978
Operation	11:30~22:00(Break 15:00~17:00)	11:30~22:00(Break 15:00~17:00)
Closed	연중무휴	Open all year round

스파소

호텔 못지않은 서비스로 최고급 스테이크를 선보이겠다는 것이 이곳의 모토. 이탈리아 어로 '즐거운, 유쾌한'이라는 뜻을 지닌 스파소는 지하 동굴처럼 아늑한 분위기를 자랑한다. 안쪽에는 이탈리아에서 직접 가져온 접시, 그림, 꽃병 등으로 꾸민 프라이빗 룸이 있는데 마치 이탈리아 시골 마을에 와 있는 듯한 기분이 든다. 스파소의 시그너처 메뉴는 상위 2퍼센트 쇠고기에서만 얻을 수 있는 US 프라임 등급의 꽃등심 스테이크. 이탈리아 어로 사이드 디시를 의미하는 콘토르니Contorni를 곁들이면 좋다. 파스타로는 담백하고 쫄깃한 생면으로 만든 오징어 먹물 치타레가 인기 있다. 고객의 시식과 평가를 반영해 다양한 메뉴 개발에 힘쓰는 것도 스파소의 매력. 이탈리아식 빙수 등 계절에 어울리는 독특한 디저트도 선보인다. 이탈리아 와인을 포함해 약 100 종의 와인 리스트도 갖췄다.

Spasso

Spasso, meaning 'pleasant' or 'amusing' in Italian, always tries to serve up the best steak and also boasts its cozy and relaxed ambiance. A private room decorated with plates, vases and paintings brought directly from Italy would give you an impression as if you are in a peaceful village of Italy. Spasso's signature menu is Rib-Eye Steak made with US prime beef, which can be obtained only from the finest beef. A contorni, a kind of side dish, would be well harmonized with this steak. Squid Ink Chitarra, a kind of pasta made with fresh noodles, is also a popular dish. They always carefully listen to their customer's opinions and try to apply them when they create a new dish. They serve specific seasonal desserts such as Italian-style shave ice and have an extensive wine list including Italian wine.

Address	강남구 도산대로61길 14	14, Dosan-daero 61-gil, Gangnam-gu
Contact	02-3445-8422	82-2-3445-8422
Web	thespasso.com	thespasso.com
Operation	11:00~22:00	11:00~22:00
Closed	설·추석 당일	Day of Lunar New Year's Day & Chuseok

세계 요리

place
:
12
Global Cuisine
Restaurants

기분 전환을
위한

세계 요리
레스토랑
12

You don't necessarily have to hit the road to enjoy all the local cuisines around the world. Now you are exposed to more opportunities to try all sorts of global food through chefs who studied cooking at a local culinary school overseas, foreign residents, media and so on. Here is a list of excellent global cuisine restaurants you can enjoy right now in Seoul. When you want to taste some unusual food on an important day, when you participate in a casual gathering with a glass of beer, when you need to refresh yourself but can't go on a trip right now, this list would help you.

이제 서울에서도 한결 쉽게 세계 곳곳의 요리를 맛볼 수 있다. 본토에서 요리를 배운 셰프나 외국인 거주자, 각종 미디어를 통해 다양한 나라의 먹을거리를 접할 기회가 많아졌기 때문이다. 인터내셔널 미식 도시 서울에서 지금 맛볼 수 있는 세계 요리를 꼽아본다. 특별한 날 특별한 요리를 맛보고 싶을 때, 맥주 한잔 곁들이는 가벼운 모임을 할 때, 여행은 가지 못하더라도 기분은 내고 싶을 때, 기분 전환을 하기에 좋은 그곳 & 그 요리.

일식
갓포 요코모리
하카타 셉템버
오젠

태국 요리
디 안다만
반 피차이
부아

스페인 요리
타페오
타파스 구르메
모멘토스

멕시코 요리
온더보더
시릴로
그릴 파이브 타코

Japanese Cuisine
Kappo Yokomori
Hakata September
Ojen

Thai Cuisine
The Andaman
Ban Pichai
Bua

Spanish Cuisine
Tapeo
Tapas Gourmet
Momentos

Mexican Cuisine
On the Border
Cirilo
Grill 5 Taco

일식

캐주얼한 이자카야와 스시집 일색이던 서울 시내에 새로운 다이닝 바람이 불고 있다. 전통 일식 레시피에 셰프의 창의적인 아이디어를 더한 메뉴를 선보이는 '요릿집'이 등장한 것. 매번 다른 요리를 기대하게 되는 일식 셰프의 레스토랑 세 곳을 소개한다.

JAPANESE CUISINE

An izakaya or sushi house was the only place you could taste Japanese food in Seoul. Now, however, a new type of 'Japanese restaurant' starts to spring out. You would experience a new dish combining creative ideas with traditional Japanese cuisine recipes in the following restaurants.

갓포 요코모리

가이세키보다는 캐주얼하고, 이자카야보다는 고급스러운 갓포 레스토랑이 이곳의 콘셉트. 'ㄷ' 자 모양 바에 둘러싸인 널찍한 오픈 키친과 테이블 세 개가 있는 아담한 홀이 눈에 들어온다. 장식적인 요소는 배제해 색감을 절제한 인테리어가 돋보인다. 요리는 기본적으로 제공하는 그랜드 메뉴와 식재료 공급에 따라 매일 달라지는 메뉴로 나뉜다. 그랜드 메뉴는 전채와 숯불구이, 튀김, 찜, 조림, 회 등 조리법에 따라 나뉜다. 전문 셰프가 따로 있는 숯불구이 스테이션에서는 일본에서 수입한 화로와 비장탄을 사용한다. 비장탄은 여느 숯과는 달리 열기가 식재료에 직접 닿지 않고 재료 전체를 골고루 감싸 고르게 굽는 것이 특징. 훈연 향이 은은히 감도는 이곳의 구이 메뉴를 꼭 맛보기 바란다.

Kappo Yokomori

The concept of Kappo Yokomori is 'more casual than kaiseki (a traditional multi-course Japanese dinner)' and more luxurious than izakaya.' It has a large open kitchen surrounded by U-shaped bar table and a small hall with three tables. A less decorated and modest interiors make this place rather attractive. They provide a basic menu called 'Grand Menu' and seasonal menu. At a charcoal grill station controlled by an expert chef, a brazier and white charcoal imported from Japan are used. Their smoke flavored grilled dish is really great.

Address	강남구 언주로152길 4	4, Eonju-ro 152-gil, Gangnam-gu
Contact	02-545-6811	82-2-545-6811
Operation	18:00~다음 날 01:00	18:00~The next day 01:00
Closed	일요일	Sun

하카타 셉템버

서영민 오너 셰프가 요리를 배운 일본 후쿠오카의 옛 지명 '하카타'와 자신이 가장 좋아하는 계절인 9월을 결합한 하카타 셉템버. 벽 한쪽을 낮은 통유리창으로 마감해 낮에는 아늑하면서도 밝은 분위기다. 바와 테이블, 한 개의 룸으로 구성했으며 흰색 벽과 나무 테이블로 심플하게 꾸몄다. 메뉴는 매일 달라지는 점심 가정식과 매달 한 번씩 교체하는 저녁 요리가 있다. 점심은 30그릇만 한정 판매하는데 생선구이와 고기 요리 반찬이 딸려 나온다. 밥은 솥밥을 고집하며 고시히카리 쌀로 지어 밥알에 윤기가 흐르고 씹을수록 단맛이 난다. 예약하는 사람이 많으니 참고할 것. 저녁 메뉴는 코스 요리 한 가지만 제공한다.

Hakata September

Hakata is an old name of Fukuoka in Japan, a city where the owner and chef, Seo Yeong-Min, learned Japanese cuisine, and September is his favorite month. The one side of the walls, made up of half wall (upper) and half glass (lower), gives off cozy yet bright ambiance. The restaurant is of a bar and tables along with one private dining room and decorated in a simple way with white wall and wood dining tables. They serve different home-style lunch every day and course dinner is changed each month. For lunch that only 30 plates can be served, grilled fish and meat side dish are available. For dinner, only course meal is available. Note that majority of customer makes reservations in advance.

Address	강남구 압구정로34길 24	24, Apgujeong-ro 34-gil, Gangnam-gu
Contact	02-549-6139	82-2-549-6139
Operation	월~금 Mon to Fri 12:00~20:00(Break 13:30~18:00), 토 Sat 18:00~20:00	
Closed	일요일	Sun

오젠

일본어로 '밥상'을 뜻하는 오젠은 2011년 2월 오픈했다. 벽과 천장을 나무와 벽돌로 마감해 일본 가정집에 온 듯 편안한 분위기가 느껴진다. 입구에 들어서면 바뒤쪽 장식장이 눈에 띈다. 김도영 오너 셰프가 수집한 일본의 식기를 예술 작품처럼 전시한 곳이다. 오젠의 메뉴는 두 달마다 바뀌는데 여섯 가지 코스로 구성한 점심과 여덟 가지 코스로 구성한 저녁 메뉴로 나뉜다. 저녁 코스는 네 가지의 전채 요리와 회, 구이, 튀김을 내며 여기에 식사도 포함된다.

Ojen

Ojen, meaning a 'dining table' in Japanese, was opened in February 2011. Its wall and ceiling made of bricks is of a comfortable feeling like an ordinary family house in Japan. At the entrance, you can see a cabinet behind its bar, in which the owner and chef Kim Do-Yeong displayed his collection of Japanese tableware. Ojen's menu, changed every two months, consists of a 6 course lunch and an 8 course dinner. For dinner, 4 kinds of appetizer, sashimi, grilled dish and fried dish are served with a main meal.

Address	강남구 봉은사로68길 6-5	6-5, Bongeunsa-ro 68-gil, Gangnam-gu
Contact	02-564-7066	82-2-564-7066
Operation	12:00~22:30(Break 14:30~18:00)	12:00~22:30(Break 14:30~18:00)
Closed	일요일	Sun

태국 요리

일 년 내내 무더워 자극적인 맛과 향신료로 승부하는 태국 요리는 길거리 음식부터 왕실 음식까지 다양한 조리법이 발달했다. 매콤하고 새콤한 맛과 독특한 향이 조화로운 태국 음식을 맛보기 좋은 레스토랑 세 곳.

THAI CUISINE

Thai cuisine features pungent flavor and spices, a characteristic which is influenced by a hot weather throughout the year, and has developed recipes with wide variations from street food to royal cuisine. Here are three Thai restaurants to serve this authentic Thai cuisine.

디 안다만

태국 푸껫의 유명 레스토랑 '타이난Thainan' 오너의 아들인 아마릿 셰프가 스위스 호텔 학교에서 공부하며 만난 차성제 대표와 의기투합해 문을 연 곳. 2015년 8월 양재동으로 이전해 재개업했다. 디 안다만 주방에는 타이난 레스토랑에서 오랫동안 일한 태국인 셰프 세 명이 음식을 만들어 현지와 거의 비슷한 맛을 재현한다. 음식은 애피타이저, 수프, 메인 요리, 면과 쌀 요리, 디저트로 구성했다. 특히 메인 요리가 다양한데 가장 추천할 만한 메뉴는 레드 카레 소스로 맛을 낸 해산물 찜 요리 '호목'. 그린 칠리로 매운맛을 내고 코코넛 밀크를 뿌린 새우와 오징어를 배춧잎에 싸 먹는다. 카레 리스트도 흥미롭다. 인도네시아산 소프트 크랩에 옐로 카레와 함께 먹는 '푸님 팟 퐁 카레'가 인기 있다.

The Andaman

Chef Ammarit Aikwanich, a son of the owner of Thainaan restaurant, famous in Phuket, Thailand, met Cha Seong-Jae, the co-owner of the Andaman now, at a hotel school in Switzerland. Their menu consists of appetizer, soup, main dish, noodle and rice and dessert. The main dish has an extensive list and amongst them, Hor Mok (steamed seafood) flavored with red curry sauce is the best. They also have an interesting list of curry. Poo Nim Pad Pong Ka Ree (Indonesian soft shell crab with yellow curry) is one of their popular dishes.

Address 서초구 남부순환로 2636
Contact 02-537-1997
Operation 11:00~23:00(Break 15:00~17:30)
Closed 토요일

2636, Nambusunhawan-ro, Seocho-gu
82-2-537-1997
11:00~23:00(Break 15:00~17:30)
Sat

반 피차이

국내 외식 기업의 타이 레스토랑에서 일하다 태국 음식과 사랑에 빠진 허혁구 셰프가 약 1년 6개월 동안의 태국 미식 여행을 끝내고 논현동에 차린 레스토랑. 약 60가지에 이르는 메뉴는 샐러드와 애피타이저, 볶음밥과 면 요리, 국물 요리, 볶음 요리, 카레, 튀김 요리로 구성했다. 파파야, 라임잎, 태국 셜롯 등 태국 요리에 꼭 필요한 식재료는 전국 곳곳에서 수소문해 공수하는 것이라고. 메뉴를 고를 때는 지역적 특색이 강한 요리를 시도해봐도 좋다. 태국의 전라남도라 여겨지는 이싼 지역의 전통 샐러드 '랍 루엄 밋'은 쌀을 굽거나 볶아서 간 뒤 고춧가루, 육류, 채소를 곁들여 먹는 매운 요리다. 방콕의 대표 음식인 '팟 키마오'도 추천한다. 매운맛이 강한 볶음 쌀국수인데 해장용으로 그만이다.

Ban Pichai

Chef Heo Hyeok-Gu, who fell in love with Thai food while working at a Thai restaurant run by a Korean food service corporation, finally opened his own restaurant in Nonhyeon-dong, after gourmet trip in Thailand for 1.6 years. Ban Pichai serves around 60 kinds of menu, consisting of salad & appetizer, sautéed rice & noodle, soup, sautéed dish, curry and fried dish. They procure fundamental local food ingredients like papaya, lime leaves and Thai shallot from all over the country. Pad Kee Mao (also known as pad ki mao or drunken noodles) is the most representative of Bangkok cuisine. It is a kind of stir fried rice noodle whose strongly pungent flavor is helpful to cure hangovers.

Address	강남구 강남대로124길 23
Contact	02-3444-9920
Web	blog.naver.com/banpichai
Operation	월~금 11:30~00:00, 토·일 12:00~00:00
Closed	연중무휴

23, Gangnam-daero 124-gil, Gangnam-gu
82-2-3444-9920
blog.naver.com/banpicha
Mon to Fri 11:30~00:00, Sat & Sun 12:00~00:00
Open all year round

부아

액세서리 디자이너 출신 김유아 셰프는 태국 왕실에서 인증한 요리학교 완디 컬리너리 스쿨에서 요리를 배웠다. 진짜 태국인이 즐겨 먹는 요리를 선보이기 위해 이태원에 부아를 오픈했다고. 레스토랑은 그녀가 좋아하는 방콕의 '그레이하운드' 레스토랑에서 영감을 얻어 태국 도자기와 새장, 이국적인 쿠션으로 현지 분위기를 살렸으며, 향신료 같은 주요 식재료는 셰프가 방콕을 주기적으로 방문해 직접 사 온다고. 추천 메뉴는 꽃게 철에만 내는 게 요리 '쏨땀 뿌'다. 대나무 통에 내는 찹쌀밥, 파파야 샐러드 '쏨땀'과 함께 먹으면 맛있다. 카레는 그린, 옐로, 레드 등 세 가지가 있는데 직접 만든 홈메이드 카레 페이스트라 향이 진하고 복합적인 맛이 일품. 함께 내는 화덕에 구운 로띠와 곁들이면 된다. 톰얌꿍은 인공감미료나 코코넛 밀크를 넣지 않고 최대한 현지의 맛을 살려 만든다.

Bua

Chef Kim Yu-a, who used to be an accessory designer before, learned culinary arts of Thai cooking in Wandee Culinary School acknowledged by Grand Palace. Then she opened Bua in Itaewon, featuring authentic Thai food loved by Thais. She got an idea from Greyhound Café in Bangkok, one of her favorite restaurants, and decorated Bua with Thai ceramics, cage and exotic cushions in a Thai style. She regularly visits Bangkok to purchase local ingredients like spices. Its specialty is Som Tam Poo, a kind of crab dish available only in blue crab season. It would taste better if you enjoy together with Steamed Sticky Rice in Bamboo and Papaya Salad Som Tam. They also serve Tom Yum Kung which does not include artificial additives or coconut milk.

Address	용산구 보광로59길 9
Contact	02-792-3340
Operation	11:30~22:00
Closed	월요일

	9, Bogwang-ro 59-gil, Yongsan-gu
	82-2-792-3340
	11:30~22:00
	Mon

스페인 요리

와인 잔에 벌레가 들어가지 않도록 빵을 덮고 갖은 재료를 얹어 먹은 데서 유래한 타파스는 대표적인 스페인 요리다. 서울에서 현지의 맛과 분위기를 느끼고 싶다면 셰프 3인이 요리하는 타파스 식당을 방문해볼 것!

SPANISH CUISINE

One of the most well-known Spanish dishes is Tapas, derived from a habit of covering a glass of wine with bread to prevent insects. How about visiting the following restaurants to try the tapas with authentic Spanish flavor in Seoul?

타페오

스페인 어로 '먹는 행위'를 뜻하는 타페오. 녹사평역 근처 언덕에 위치한 타페오에 들어서면 곳곳에 걸린 그림과 사진이 먼저 눈에 들어온다. 스페인 마드리드와 바르셀로나에서 요리를 배운 유호성 셰프가 현지에 있는 아트 디렉터에게 부탁해 3~4개월마다 테마가 다른 전시를 하고 있는 것. 요리 메뉴는 브런치, 파에야, 타파스로 구성했다. 브런치는 생토마토소스와 마늘 바게트, 하몬 등 칼로리는 낮고 영양은 풍부한 메뉴 위주다. 파에야는 세 가지 스타일 중 고를 수 있으며 아이올리 소스를 듬뿍 뿌려주는 오징어 먹물 파에야가 가장 인기라고. 타파스는 올리브나 하몬 샐러드 등 한입에 먹기 좋은 간편한 음식도 있고, 생선 요리, 등심 스테이크 등 육류를 곁들인 메뉴까지 선택의 폭이 넓다. 스페인 맥주도 갖추고 있다.

Tapeo

Tapeo means the 'act of eating' in Spanish. In this restaurant located on a hill near Noksapyeong Station, you would see paintings and pictures of a young artist on its walls and this place looks like a gallery somehow. It displays art works with a different theme every three or four months with the help of an art direct. Chef Yu Ho-Seong makes up the menu of Tapeo with brunch, paella and tapas. For brunch low-calorie and nutritious meals such as raw tomato sauce, garlic baguette and jamon are available and for paella they provide three kinds of it. On the tapas menu are a light meal, fish dishes with variations in its recipe and ingredients and sirloin steak. They also serve Spanish beer to whet your appetite for these dishes.

Address	용산구 녹사평대로40길 51		51, Noksapyeong-daero 40-gil, Yongsan-gu
Contact	02-794-2848		82-2-794-2848
Operation	화~금 Tue to Fri 17:00~23:00, 토 Sat 12:00~다음 날 01:00, 일 Sun 12:00~22:00		
Closed	월요일		Mon

타파스 구르메

한옥의 기와지붕과 모던한 인테리어가 독특한 조화를 이루는 레스토랑. 오너 셰프의 건축가 남편이 설계를 담당했다. 식당을 운영하는 김문정 셰프는 바르셀로나에 거주하면서 원 테이블 레스토랑 '까사 구르메'를 운영했던 인물. 서촌 타파스 구르메는 현지에서 요리하던 실력을 그대로 재현한다. 메뉴는 타파스와 2인분부터 주문 가능한 두 가지 가격대의 세트 메뉴. 구운 가지와 피망으로 만든 샐러드와 브리 치즈, 파와 발사믹 크림을 빵에 얹은 두 가지 스타일 몬타디토, 스페인식 오믈렛, 반숙으로 익힌 달걀을 올린 버섯과 꿀뚜기 튀김 등 어떤 타파스를 선택해도 후회가 없다. 맥주와 와인도 판매하지만 오렌지, 레몬 등 갖은 과일을 듬뿍 넣어 숙성한 상그리아 한 잔을 곁들여도 좋다.

Tapas Gourmet

Chef Kim Mun-Jeong ran Casa Gourmet, a one-table restaurant, while she stayed in Barcelona. Having come back to Korea she opened Tapas Gourmet based on her experiences in Spain. The exteriors with the tiled roof of a traditional Korean house and the modern interiors, as designed by her husband who is an architect, are very distinctive yet well-harmonized at the same time. As well as tapas, they serve a set menu at the price of two dishes but this set menu is available only for more than two people. They also serve beer and wine but a glass of sangria made with orange, lemon and various fruits is a good accompaniment.

Address	종로구 자하문로 9길 7		7, Jahamun-ro 9-gil, Jongno-gu
Contact	02-6014-2369		82-2-6014-2369
Web	www.tapasgourmet.co.kr		www.tapasgourmet.co.kr
Operation	18:00~22:00		18:00~22:00
Closed	일요일		Sun

모멘토스

모멘토스는 '음식을 맛보는 짧지만 강렬한 순간'을 뜻한다. 여행 관련 업계에서 일하다 요리를 하고 싶어 스페인으로 떠났던 김정민 셰프가 총괄한다. 메뉴 중에서는 오징어 먹물 파에야가 인기다. 갑오징어와 돼지 목살이 주재료로, 닭 육수에 토마토, 양파를 넣고 오랫동안 조리한 소스와 기막힌 궁합을 이룬다. 스페인식 오믈렛 토르티야는 올리브유에 감자와 갖은 채소를 고루 넣고 푹 익혀 부드럽다. 올리브유와 간장을 1 대 1 비율로 섞어 만든 소스에 재운 연어 요리도 추천할 만하다. 감자튀김은 스페인의 에스트렐라 생맥주에 곁들여볼 것. 톡 쏘는 청량한 맛이 일품이다.

Momentos

Momentos means a 'short but intense moment of tasting.' Chef Kim Jeong-Min is the executive chef of Momentos, who studied Spanish cuisine in Spain for about 3 years only with the passion for cooking. Of their main dishes, Squid Ink Paella is most popular. It is made by boiling squid and pork neck with tomato and onion in a chicken broth for a long time. Spanish Omelette Tortilla, as it is boiled with potatoes, other vegetables and olive oil for a long time, would melt in your mouth. Its fish dish with salmon soaked in olive oil and soy sauce of the same ratio is also excellent.

Address	용산구 회나무로13가길 19	19, Hoenamu-ro 13ga-gil, Yongsan-gu
Contact	02-6205-9302	82-2-6205-9302
Operation	화~일 Tue to Sun 11:30~23:00(Break 15:30~17:00), 월 Mon 17:00~23:00	
Closed	설 · 추석 연휴	Holiday of Lunar New Year's Day & Chuseok

멕시코 요리

뉴욕, 런던 등 세계의 대도시에 불었던 멕시코 음식 열풍이 서울에도 불고 있다. 한국인의 입맛에 맞는 타코, 멕시코인 셰프가 만든 정통 멕시칸 타코 등 다양한 모습으로 서울의 미식가들을 사로잡은 멕시칸 레스토랑을 소개한다.

MEXICAN CUISINE

A fad for Mexican food which was witnessed in several big cities including New York and London has now landed in Seoul. Mexican foods are fascinating numerous epicures in Seoul sometimes with its Korean-friendly ingredients and sometimes with authentic Mexican materials.

온더보더

전 세계에 1000개가 넘는 매장이 있는 멕시칸 레스토랑으로 주메뉴는 파히타, 타코, 케사디야 등 멕시코에서 맛볼 수 있는 정통 음식. 주요 식재료인 스테이크와 치킨, 해산물은 멕시코 정통 그릴 방식인 메스키트 mesquite 방식으로 굽는다. 참나무의 일종인 메스키트 칩과 함께 식재료를 굽는데, 은은한 훈연 향이 육질의 고소한 맛을 배가한다. 온더보더의 메뉴는 애피타이저와 샐러드, 파히타와 타코, 케사디야 등 메인 메뉴와 디저트로 나뉜다. 옥수숫가루나 밀가루로 만드는 얇은 팬케이크 같은 토르티야에 각종 재료를 싸 먹는 파히타 요리로는 '몬트레이 랜치 치킨 파히타', '스무더드 스테이크 파히타' 등이 인기 있다. 취향에 따라 속 재료를 골라 주문할 수도 있다. 살짝 튀긴 토르티야에 꿀을 찍어 먹는 '소파피야'는 이곳에만 있는 멕시코 정통 디저트다.

On the Border

On the Border Mexican Grill & Cantina is a food chain serving authentic Mexican food including fajita, taco and quesadilla and there are over 1,000 restaurants all around the world. They grill the main ingredients like steak, chicken and seafood on a mesquite grill using the original Mexican method. In this method food materials are grilled with mesquite wood chips, which add delicate smoke flavor and enhance natural taste of food. You can find appetizer, salad, main dish including fajita, taco and quesadilla and dessert. In this restaurant, you can also enjoy Sopapillas, a kind of Mexican dessert, by dipping lightly fried tortillas in honey sauce.

Address	영등포구 국제금융로 10 지하 3층(IFC몰점)		B3F, 10, Gukjegeumyung-ro, Yeongdeungpo-gu
Contact	02-6137-5682		82-2-6137-5682
Web	www.ontheborder.co.kr		www.ontheborder.co.kr
Operation	11:00~22:00		11:00~22:00
Closed	연중무휴		Open all year round

시릴로

오랫동안 외식 사업에 몸담았던 구교환 대표가 멕시코계 미국인 셰프 시릴로 로드리게스와 함께 오픈한 곳. 서커스에서 모티브를 얻어 색색의 타이포그래피와 전구, 극장이 연상되는 화이트와 블랙 메뉴판으로 레스토랑을 꾸몄다. 주메뉴는 타코와 케사디야, 부리토. 특히 타코용 토르티야는 매일매일 반죽해 즉석에서 굽는데, 시중에 판매되는 인스턴트 토르티야와 달리 촉촉하고 더 노란 빛깔을 띤다. 타르타르 소스가 들어간 '크리스피 피쉬 타코'는 고소한 맛이 일품이다. 부리토 중에는 두툼하게 썬 목심 스테이크를 넣은 '아사다 부리토'를 추천한다. 짭짜름하면서도 고소한 치즈 맛을 살린 치즈 케사디야도 놓칠 수 없다.

Cirilo

Gu Gyo-hwan who has worked in food service industry long time opened Cirilo with a Mexican-American chef in Dongbinggo-dong. The interiors, as inspired by circus, are decorated with colorful typography, closely spaced light bulbs and white-and-black menu board associated with a theater sign. Taco, Quesadilla and Burrito are their main dish. A tortilla for taco is baked on the table and its dough is made every day. In this way, their tortilla has more moisture and more beautiful brown color compared to store-brought tortillas.

Their Crispy Fish Taco with tartare sauce is also excellent with its savory taste.

Address	용산구 장문로 12	12, Jangmun-ro, Yongsan-gu
Contact	02-793-3358	82-2-793-3358
Operation	11:00~23:00	11:00~23:00
Closed	연중무휴	Open all year round

그릴 파이브 타코

타코 전문점 그릴 파이브 타코는 트럭에서 타코를 팔던 김현철 사장의 열정으로 탄생했다. 음식은 트럭에서 판매할 때 가장 인기 있던 메뉴를 중심으로 심플하게 구성했다. 타코가 기본 메뉴로 '쇼트립 타코', '스파이시 포크 타코', '코코넛 시림프 타코' 등이 있다. 부리토는 볶음밥 한 그릇을 먹는 것처럼 푸짐하다. '김치 케사디야'는 그릴 파이브 타코 최고의 인기 메뉴. 김치에 볶은 돼지고기를 섞고 모차렐라 치즈를 넣어 쫄깃한 식감과 고소함을 살렸다. 매콤하면서도 살짝 단맛이 느껴지는 김치 소스는 그릴 파이브 타코에서 개발한 비법 소스로 케사디야의 감칠맛을 배가한다. 생맥주도 준비되어 있으니 술 생각이 간절해진다면 주문할 것.

Grill 5 Taco

Grill 5 Taco was born by passion and effort of a young man, Kim Hyeon-Cheol, who used to make tacos on a food truck. He composed the menu with just several dishes which was most popular on the truck. The basic menu of Grill 5 Taco is Short Rib Taco, Spicy Pork Taco, Coconut Shrimp Taco and so on. Their substantial burrito is served in roll or bowl. Kimchi Quesadilla has been the best dish since the days of the food truck. It is made by mixing stir-fried pork with kimchi and then adding mozzarella cheese, in this way which its texture and flavor are enhanced.

Address	마포구 와우산로17길 19-15	19-15, Wausan-ro 17-gil, Mapo-gu
Contact	02-3114-2549	82-2-3114-2549
Operation	11:00~00:00	11:00~00:00
Closed	연중무휴	Open all year round

dining story
:
Asian
Dessert
Culture

아시아

디저트
문화

식사 후 달콤한 한입 거리로 입가심을 하는 서양의 디저트 문화가 아시아 국가로 넘어와 근대화를 거치며 다양한 형태로 발전했다. 기후와 환경, 메인 요리의 맛, 선호하는 당도에 따라 각양각색으로 발달한 아시아 디저트를 살펴본다.

A custom of enjoying dessert after a meal was introduced and localized in many Asian countries. Let's take a look at how the Asian dessert has been varied based on different climate and environment from Europe and how it has been adjusted to the flavor of a local main dish and to the taste of local people.

동남아시아

날씨가 무더워 입맛을 자극하는 맵고 짠 음식이 발달한 동남아시아. 식후에 즐기는 디저트도 화끈거리는 입안을 정리하는 달콤하고 시원한 종류가 많다. 가장 사랑받는 간식은 과육의 당도가 높고 즙이 많은 망고나 람부탄, 리치 같은 열대 과일. 거리의 노점에서는 과일을 그대로 즐기거나 스무디 또는 주스 형태로 마시는 모습을 쉽게 볼 수 있다. 레스토랑에서는 과일을 조려 푸딩 형태로 만들거나 코코넛, 요구르트, 얼음 알갱이를 넣어 떠먹는 수프 같은 형태로 제공하기도 한다. 곱게 간 얼음 위에 시럽과 젤리 등 원하는 토핑을 얹어 먹는 태국식 빙수 '남 깽 사이', 단팥 같은 곡물이나 과일에 얼음을 넣은 베트남식 디저트 음료 '쩨', 싱가포르의 과일 화채나 망고 빙수 등이 대표적이다.

SOUTHEAST ASIA

The taste of Southeast Asian dishes has become pungent and salty with an impact of an extremely hot weather of this region. For this reason, people in this area prefer sweet and cool desserts to appease the spicy taste left in a mouth. And their most favorite refreshment is succulent tropical fruits such as mango, rambutan and lychee. You can taste those raw fruits or enjoy its juice or smoothie on the street. In a restaurant, fruits are served in a form of pudding or soup made of coconut, yogurt and ice pellets. The typical desserts of Southeast Asia are Nam Keng Sai (a Thai-style shave ice topped with syrup or jellies), Chè (a traditional Vietnamese sweet beverage made from grains or fruits) and Singapore's fruit punch and mango shave ice.

한국

'이가 시리도록' 달콤한 디저트를 선호하는 유럽이나 미국과 달리, 아시아 국가에는 별도의 디저트 문화가 존재하지 않았다. 한국은 조선 시대까지 다과상을 내던 문화가 현대에 이르러 식후 디저트 형태로 발전했으며 떡, 과일을 말린 정과류, 식혜나 수정과가 한식 디저트를 대표하는 메뉴가 됐다. 곡식을 빻아 가루로 만든 다음 콩이나 팥 등 갖은 곡물을 더해 찌는 떡은 반죽의 종류와 묽기, 더하는 부재료에 따라 맛과 질감이 다채로워 가장 먼저 디저트의 형태로 발전한 간식이다. 과일이나 식물 열매에 꿀을 넣어 조리는 정과는 살구, 사과, 유자 등 과일은 물론 연근이나 도라지, 생강 등 채소로도 만들 수 있다. 식혜는 엿기름의 고소한 풍미를, 수정과는 생강과 계피의 알싸한 풍미와 달콤한 끝 맛을 음미할 수 있는 우리나라 전통 음료다.

SOUTH KOREA

While 'painfully sweet' desserts were preferred in Europe or the U.S., there was no such a thing that we can call a dessert in Asia. The custom in which a cup of tea and some refreshments were served between meals until the Joseon Dynasty was evolved into a kind of dessert culture these days. Tteok (rice cake), Jeonggwa (honey-preserved fruits), Sikhye (sweet drink made from fermented rice) and Sujeonggwa (cinnamon punch with dried persimmon) have become the typical items of traditional Korean desserts now. Tteok that is made by steaming finely ground grains with various beans was transformed into a kind of dessert first, as its taste and mouthfeel can be varied depending on the proportion of water and flour and additional ingredients. Jeonggwa is made by simmering in honey various fruits and herbs, from apricot, apple and citron to lotus root, dried balloon flower root and ginger. Both of Sikhye, flavorful because of malt powder inside, and Sujeonggwa, with piquant flavor of ginger and cinnamon and sweet aftertaste, are excellent traditional Korean beverages.

일본

일본의 디저트 문화는 한국과 비슷한 부분이 있다. 고급 코스 요리인 가이세키 요리의 마지막에 과일 한 점으로 입가심하거나, 차를 즐길 때 어울리는 양갱, 화과자를 곁들이는 정도가 전부였는데 메이지 유신 이후 서양식 레시피가 유입되면서 본격적인 디저트 시대가 열렸다. 현재 일본은 특유의 장인 정신과 종주국을 뛰어넘는 섬세한 기술, 장식미가 결합해 아시아 최고의 디저트 강국으로 자리 잡았다. 현대의 디저트로 발전한 대표적인 간식을 꼽자면 에도 시대에 등장한 화과자를 들 수 있다. 당시에는 왕족과 귀족만 즐겨 먹던 고급 과자였으며, 천연 색소를 넣은 반죽으로 꽃, 식물, 나비 등을 절묘하게 표현해 '눈으로 즐기는 디저트'라고도 불린다. 반죽에 앙금을 넣고 찌거나 구워 갈색이 감도는 것은 '만주'라고 부르고, 동그란 떡처럼 구운 두 장의 빵 사이에 소를 끼운 것은 '도라야키'라고 부른다. 양갱은 삶은 팥을 걸러 설탕이나 밀가루를 섞어 단단한 젤리처럼 굳힌 것. 18세기 이후에는 나가사키 지역에서 일본인이 새롭게 만든 카스텔라가 유행했다. 달걀노른자에 설탕을 넣어 오랫동안 저은 뒤, 거품을 낸 달걀흰자와 밀가루를 섞어 굽는 빵으로 질감이 폭신하다.

JAPAN

A dessert culture of Japan has some similarities with that of Korea. It used to be that while having Kaiseki, a traditional Japanese course meal, Japanese finished the course with a piece of fruit or that they accompanied sweet red bean jelly or Wagashi to a cup of tea. The recipes of Western desserts which were introduced after the Meiji Restoration helped diversify dessert of Japan. Owing to a combination of its own craftsmanship, delicate skills and decorative art, desserts of Japan became remarkably outstanding in Asia. Wagashi shows a good example that a traditional dessert was transformed into a modern confectionery. It was first created during the Edo period in Japan and a high-class dessert enjoyed by kings and noblemen. Wagashi was also called a 'dessert for enjoying with eyes' because of its luxurious shapes of flower, plant or butterfly and its exquisite natural colors. There are a great deal of types of Wagashi, for example, Manjū, Dorayaki and Yōkan. After the 18th century, a Japanese-style castella became popular in Nagasaki. This castella, which is made by adding egg white and flour into long-stirred egg yolk and sugar and then baking it in the oven, has a soft, puffy texture.

중국

베이징, 상하이, 광둥, 쓰촨 등 4대 미식 수도를 포함해 광활한 전 대륙에 걸쳐 다채로운 식문화가 발달한 중국. 갖은 재료를 넣어 만든 구움 과자의 역사는 남송 시대까지 거슬러 올라간다. 당시에는 디저트가 아닌 중추절에 먹는 명절 간식이었는데, 지금은 상시 즐겨 먹는 월병이 대표적이다. 둥근 달의 모양을 본뜬 월병은 밀가루, 설탕, 달걀 등이 주재료이며 말린 과일이나 견과류를 넣어 둥그런 나무틀에 찍어내 완성한다. 호두와 땅콩, 호박씨 등 16가지 재료를 넣은 십경월병, 팥과 대추고를 넣어 쫀득한 장원병, 겉을 통참깨로 장식한 지마병 등 여러 종류가 있다. 홍콩은 모던하게 해석한 중국식 간식을 맛볼 수 있는 디저트 전문점이 즐비한 도시다. 수프처럼 즐기는 단팥죽, 연두부에 시럽, 팥죽, 코코넛 밀크를 곁들인 두부 푸딩, 찹쌀가루로 빚어 팥이나 깨를 넣어 빚은 경단 모양의 탕위안, 두리안으로 만든 월병이나 아이스크림 등을 다양하게 판매한다.

CHINA

In China, a diversified culinary culture has been developed evenly across the whole country. The baked-cookies of China, which is made from varied ingredients, date back to the Southern Song Dynasty. At that time, baked cookies were served not as an ordinary dessert but as special refreshment during a holiday or festival. Mooncakes are a typical example of it. Mooncakes are made by steaming paste made of flour, sugar and eggs with dried fruits or nuts in a mold but there are many varieties. In Hong Kong, you can taste a modern variation on traditional Chinese desserts, for example, Sweet red bean porridge, Tofu pudding added with syrup, red bean paste and coconut milk, Tangyuan made from glutinous rice flour filled with red bean paste or ground black sesame and Mooncakes made from durian or ice cream, etc.

dining scene
:
**Dessert Table
for
Special Days**

일상의

디저트
테이블

인생에서 가장 행복한 순간에는 늘 달콤한 디저트가 함께한다. 사랑의 결실을 맺는 결혼식, 프러포즈를 받은 밸런타인데이, 로맨틱한 성년의 날, 내 아이의 첫 번째 생일에 함께한 네 가지 디저트 테이블.

The happiest moment of our life always comes together with a sweet and beautiful dessert. There are four proposals for a dessert table of our special days.

결혼식 + 슈거 크래프트 케이크

성대한 결혼식에는 웨딩 케이크를 빼놓을 수 없다. 설탕 가루에 달걀흰자, 젤라틴 등을 섞어 반죽을 만들고 그 위에 꽃이나 리본, 레이스, 아이싱 등으로 장식한 슈거 크래프트 케이크는 화려한 장식과 컬러 덕분에 더욱 사랑받는 웨딩 케이크의 대명사다.

Wedding Day + Sugar Craft Cake

A wedding cake is probably the most important, indispensable item for a beautiful wedding. A sugar craft cake whose batter is made from powdered sugar, egg white and gelatins and which is topped with flowers, ribbons and laces, icings, etc. has been considered the most typical and most favorite wedding cake so far.

밸런타인데이 + 초콜릿

밸런타인데이 하면 초콜릿이다. 클래식한 박스에 담긴 밀크·다크 초콜릿 가나슈와 부드러운 크림이나 캐러멜, 가나슈 등으로 속을 채운 프랄린 초콜릿을 선물하면 사랑하는 마음이 그대로 전해질 것이다.

Valentine's Day + Chocolate

Chocolate and Valentine's Day are a match made in heaven. A chocolate selection made up of milk and dark chocolate ganache and praline assortment, would be a perfect Valentine's Days present for your loved one.

성년의 날 + 마카롱

매년 5월 셋째 주 월요일, 만 19세가 되는 이들이 성년이 되었음을 축하하는 날에는 달콤한 마카롱과 향수가 제격이다. 다쿠아즈와 함께 대표적인 머랭 과자의 하나인 마카롱은 겉은 바삭바삭하고, 속은 매끄러우면서 부드러운 것이 특징.

Coming-of-Age Day + Macaron

The Monday of the third week of May is "coming-of-age day" in Korea. To celebrate this day, people give a gift to those who enter adulthood. Along with a perfume, the all-the-time-favorite present, sweet macarons would be well matched too for this lovely day. A macaron, one of the typical meringue cookies, is always popular with its crispy outside and soft inside mouthfeel.

첫돌 + 컵케이크

아이의 첫 번째 생일에는 알록달록한 크림 토핑과 과일로 포인트를 준 컵케이크를 추천한다. 패턴이 아기자기한 종이컵에 컵케이크를 담고 숫자 '1' 모양의 초, 깃발 장식 등을 꽂으면 파티 분위기를 돋우기에 그만이다.

First Birthday + Cupcake

How about decorating a baby's first birthday with cupcakes topped with colorful and pretty toppings and fruits? A cupcake in a lovely paper cup and a first birthday candle or a pretty flag on it would be very nice as a dessert as well as decorations for the party.

place
:
33
Fine Dessert Shops
&
Bars in Seoul

서울의 고급
디저트 숍
&
바
33

"Eat with your eyes first before your tongue taste it." As this sentence expresses well, lovely and sophisticated dessert on a table almost looks like an art of work and please us even before taking a bite. We have listed dessert shops serving gourmet desserts, along with terrific bars to share nice liquors with someone you like.

"눈으로 먼저 먹고 입으로 그 맛을 느낀다"라는 말이 있을 만큼 테이블 위의 예술 작품이라 일컫는 디저트. 후식으로 분류하기에 아까울 만큼 그 자체로 훌륭한 미식이 되는 고급 디저트와 디저트 숍을 소개한다. 좋은 사람과 함께 술 마시기 좋은 공간도 담았다.

오너 셰프의 파티세리
카카오봄
타르틴
마농 트로포
마카롱
오뗄두스
플랜트
디저트리
비위치
빠따슈
에클레어 by 가이하루
디시룸 by 도레도레
줄리에뜨
마망 갸또
르와지르
에이미 초코
에딸프
삐아프
글래머러스 펭귄
듀자미

전통 디저트 가게
동병상련
비원떡집
도수향
미정당

수제 맥주 펍
라일리스 탭하우스
맥파이
크래프트웍스 탭하우스

주점 & 바
드슈
커피 바 K
페타테
르쁘엥
로칸타 몽로
루
가스트로 591

Expert Chef's Pâtisserie
Cacaoboom
Tartine
Ma Non Troppo
Macaron
Hôtel Douce
Plant
DesserTree
Be Witch
Pâte à Choux
Éclair by Garuharu
Dishroom by Doré Doré
Juliette
Maman Gâteau
Loisir
Amy Choco
Étalp La Patiserie
Piaf
Glamorous Penguin
Deux Amis

Traditional Korean Desserts
Dong Byeong Sang-Ryeon
Bi Won
Do Su Hyang
Mi Jeong Dang

Craft Beer House
Reilly's Taphouse
Magpie
Craftworks Taphouse

Bar & Pub
De Chou
Coffee Bar K
Petate
Le Point
Locanda Mongro
Lu:
Gastro 591

오너 셰프의 파티세리

서울이 이제 디저트에 집중하고 있다. 가로수길, 청담동, 한남동, 서교동까지 케이크, 마카롱, 초콜릿, 과자의 달콤한 향이 이어지는 것. 그중에서도 자신이 직접 디저트를 만들고 가게도 운영하는 오너 셰프의 가게가 많다. 본토에서 유학한 사람도 있고 TV 프로그램을 통해 이름을 알린 사람도 있다. 2015년 서울의 새로운 디저트 신을 만드는 오너 셰프와 그들이 운영하는 디저트 전문점을 소개한다.

EXPERT CHEF'S PÂTISSERIE

Desserts have been gaining more and more attention of Seoulite. Cake, macaron, chocolate, cookies, biscuits, etc., now you can find a wide variety of charming desserts at dessert shcps in Garosu-gil, Cheongdam-dong, Hannam-dong and Seogyo-dong. Many professional pastry chefs have opened their own stores recently and formed a kind of dessert scene in Seoul.

카카오봄

초콜릿 전문 교육과정이 있는 벨기에 PIVA 호텔학교를 수료하고 한국으로 돌아와 부산 파라다이스 호텔 베이커리에서 초콜릿 전문가로 일한 고영주 셰프는 2003년 서교동에 수제 초콜릿 숍 카카오봄을 열었다. "초콜릿은 과학적이고 아주 예민한 재료입니다. 주성분인 카카오 버터가 온도에 민감하므로 섬세하면서도 빠른 손놀림이 필수지요. 벨기에, 스위스, 프랑스에서 들여온 재료를 사용하고 방부제와 색소 등 인공 첨가물을 넣지 않아 깔끔한 뒷맛이 돋보입니다." 카카오봄에서는 정통 벨기에 초콜릿부터 그녀만의 레시피로 완성한 메뉴까지 다채로운 초콜릿을 맛볼 수 있다. 부드럽고 깊은 풍미가 일품인 '실키봄', 문배술과 유정란을 넣은 '뜨거운 밤', 와인을 담았던 오크통에서 숙성시킨 아란 위스키를 사용한 '위스키봄' 등이 시그너처 메뉴다.

Cacaoboom

Chocolatier Go Young-Joo, who completed courses in PIVA Hotel School in Belgium, worked as a chocolatier at the bakery of the Paradise Hotel Busan, before she opened her own hand-made chocolate shop 'Cacaoboom' in Seogyo-dong in 2003. In Cacaoboom, you can taste a wide range of exquisite chocolates from authentic Belgian chocolate to chef's own chocolate based on her self-developed recipe. Her signature item is deep and flavorful 'Silkyboom,' 'Warm Night' with fertile eggs and Munbaeju (traditional Korean liquor) and 'Whisky Boom' using the Arran whisky aged in oak wine barrel.

Address	마포구 와우산로27길 6(서교점)	6, Wausan-ro 27-gil, Mapo-gu
Contact	02-3141-4663	82-2-3141-4663
Web	www.cacaoboom.com	www.cacaoboom.com
Operation	11:00~22:00	11:00~22:00
Closed	연중무휴	Open all year round

타르틴

2008년 타르틴을 오픈하며 이태원에 첫 번째 디저트숍을 연 가레트 에드워즈 Garrett Edwards 셰프는 어머니와 할머니, 할머니의 할머니에게 이어받은 레시피를 고수한다. 그가 국내 처음 선보인 오리건식 루바브 파이가 이곳의 시그너처 메뉴. 셀러리와 비슷한 생김새에 색이 붉고 새콤하며 섬유질이 풍부한 루바브 줄기를 잘라 레몬주스, 설탕을 넣고 조려 만든다. 오픈 초기 테이블 몇 개에 불과했던 것이 앞 건물에 '타르틴 투'를 열고, 2015년 초에는 그 옆으로 키시와 식빵, 베이글 등을 판매하는 '올드 타운 베이커리'를 오픈할 만큼 성장했다. 하지만 노란색 벽과 앤티크 소품, '다음 사람을 위해 1시간 8분 후에는 자리를 비워달라'는 문구는 여전하다. '미국식 파이 하면 타르틴'이라는 공식이 생길 만큼 확고하게 자리매김했지만 그는 여전히 손수 레시피를 테스트하고, 한결같은 맛과 새로운 맛의 조화를 중시한다.

Tartine

Chef Garret Edwards, who cpened Tartine in 2008, sticks to recipes handed down from his mother, grandmother and great grandmother. Oregon-style Rhubarb Pie first offered by him in Korea is his signature pie. It is made by boiling cut rhubarb stems with lemon juice and sugar. At first it started as a small bakery with a few tables but now has the second store 'Tartine Two' in the opposite building and 'Old Town Bakery' next to it. The fact that Tartine is now a symbol of American pie is unquestionable. Even after hiring more chef and staff, Chef Edwards still tests his recipes and puts much value on balance between consistent and novel tastes.

Address	용산구 이태원로23길 4(이태원 본점)		4, Itaewon-ro 23-gil, Yongsan-gu
Contact	02-3785-3400		82-2-3785-3400
Web	www.tartine.co.kr		www.tartine.co.kr
Operation	10:00~22:30		10:00~22:30
Closed	연중무휴		Open all year round

마농 트로포

르 코르동 블뢰 숙명 아카데미를 졸업한 서정아 셰프가 지난 한남동에 2009년 오픈한 디저트 숍. 아이들을 위해 홈메이드 디저트를 자주 만들던 그녀의 오랜 취미가 직업이 됐다. 주택을 개조해 아늑한 분위기가 돋보이는 마농 트로포는 낮에 채광이 좋아 인근 거주자들이 모여드는 아지트다. 홀 입구에 색색의 디저트로 가득한 쇼케이스를 두고, 1층과 2층 홀 벽면에는 그녀가 평소 여행하며 모은 식기를 장식했다. "아이를 위해 디저트를 만들기 시작했기 때문에 좋은 재료를 쓰는 게 당연하다고 생각해요. 냉동 재료를 사용하는 게 아니라 계절 과일을 매장에서 직접 다듬어 사용하려고 노력하죠. 뉴질랜드산 천연 버터, 친환경 유정란과 유기농 밀가루, 동물성 생크림 등 아낌없이 쓰는 최고의 재료가 마농 트로포의 인기 비법인 것 같습니다." 서정아 셰프는 이곳의 시그너처 케이크로 초콜릿 크림을 겹겹이 바른 '홍차 애플'을 추천한다. 부드럽고 폭신한 두 개의 다쿠아즈 사이에 크림을 넣은 케이크로, 조린 사과가 상큼함을 더한다.

Ma Non Troppo

Ma Non Troppo is a dessert shop in Hannam-dong, started in 2009 by Chef Seo Jeong-A, who graduated from Le Cordon Bleu's Sookmyung Academy. She turned her long hobby of making desserts for kids into business. Its cozy and well-lighted ambiance in a remodeled family house has become nearby residents' favorite place. A showcase full with colorful desserts is placed at the entrance and a variety of dishes and glasses are displayed on shelves. Chef Seo's recommendation is Black Tea Apple Cake, her signature cake brushed with chocolate cream several times. This cake has cream between two soft, puffed dacquoises and boiled apple adds fresh flavor to it.

Address	용산구 한남대로20길 61-1	61-1, Hannam-daero 20-gil, Yongsan-gu
Contact	02-794-0011	82-2-794-0011
Web	cafe.naver.com/manontroppo	cafe.naver.com/manontroppo
Operation	11:00~23:00	11:00~23:00
Closed	설·추석 연휴	Holiday of Lunar New Year's Day & Chuseok

마카롱

전체 매출의 90퍼센트는 형형색색 보석처럼 아름다운 컬러와 바스락 부서지며 쫀득하게 씹히는 맛이 일품인 마카롱이 차지한다. 핑크색과 검은색이 어우러진 모던한 인테리어와 로고, 패키지 디자인까지 모두 오너 셰프인 루벤 얀 아드리안Ruben Jan Adriaan이 직접 담당했다. '피에르 에르메', '피에르 마르콜리니' 등에서 수석 페이스트리 셰프로 근무했던 그는 안국동 '아몽디에'에서 일한 것을 계기로 서울에 자신의 가게를 차렸다. 검은색과 스트라이프로 실내를 꾸며 마카롱의 밝은 색이 돋보이게 했으며 마카롱이 주인공이 되는 공간으로 꾸몄다. 홍대와 신사동 두 곳의 마카롱 숍과 샌드위치 매장 '루벤'을 운영하는 그는 새로운 메뉴에 에너지를 아끼지 않는다. "밸런타인데이에는 하트 모양의 초콜릿 케이크에 라즈베리 소스를 얹어냈지요. 늘 새로운 재료로 새로운 맛을 시도하는 것이 즐거워요. 밀푀유와 이스파한 아이스크림, 바닐라와 피칸, 캐러멜을 올린 슈 등 더 다양한 맛을 선사하고 싶습니다."

Macaron

Macaron's best-selling item is, of course, macarons. Its macaron is amazingly excellent with its dazzling color and crispy outside yet sticky inside texture. The owner and chef Ruben Jan Adriaan's touch is felt from its modern, pink-and-black interior, logo and package design as well as from his macarons. Black stripes on the wall make a bright color of macarons look outstanding. Chef Adriaan, running two macaron shops and one sandwich store 'Ruben' in Hongdae area and Sinsa-dong, always puts all his everything for a new item. He says, "For my customers, I would like to create more distinctive taste like mille-feuille & Ispahan ice cream, vanilla & pecan and choux topped with caramel."

Address	강남구 도산대로17길 12(신사동점)	12, Dosan-daero 17-gil, Gangnam-g
Contact	02-512-0815	82-2-512-0815
Operation	12:00~21:00	12:00~21:00
Closed	월요일	Mon

오뗄두스

영화 〈그랜드 부다페스트 호텔〉의 한 장면 속에 들어선 듯한 외관부터 눈길을 사로잡는 오뗄두스는 오랫동안 일본에서 활동한 정홍연 셰프의 디저트 숍. 마카롱과 구움 과자로 소문난 서래마을 '레꼴두스'를 시작으로, 작고 아담하지만 개성 있는 맛이 돋보이는 오뗄두스를 열었다. 일본 유학 시절 학비를 벌기 위해 아르바이트를 하다가 사장이 사준 점보 사이즈 슈크림이 그를 디저트의 길로 안내했다고. 진로를 바꾼 그는 도쿄 제과학교를 졸업한 후 동네 빵집부터 경력을 쌓았다. 오뗄두스는 화려한 색감의 마카롱, 쫄깃한 카늘레, 겉은 바삭하고 속은 부드러운 에클레어, 앙증맞은 머랭 쿠키, 촉촉한 롤케이크, 초콜릿까지 정홍연 셰프만의 개성 있는 디저트로 가득하다. 셰프의 추천 메뉴는 밀푀유와 크렘 당주. 하나의 메뉴가 나올 때마다 100번 이상 레시피를 수정한다. 오뗄두스는 100년 가는 가게를 목표로 디저트에 더욱 집중할 예정이다.

Hôtel Douce

The appearance of this store would make you feel like you are walking into the 'Grand Budapest Hotel' in the movie but it is a dessert shop of Chef Jeong Hong-Yeon who gained rich experience in Japan. While his first baking school cum café 'L'ecole Douce' offers a rather modest yet unique taste, Hôtel Douce is full of fancy macarons, chewy canelés, crunchy out, soft inside éclairs, adorable meringue cookies, moist roll cake and chocolates, in which Chef Jeong's own characteristic is well embodied. Chef's recommendations are Mille-feuille and Crémet d'Anjou.

Address 서초구 서래로10길 9(서래마을점)
Contact 02-595-5705
Web www.facebook.com/hotel.douce
Operation 10:00~21:00
Closed 연중무휴

9, Seorae-ro 10-gil, Seocho-gu
82-2-595-5705
www.facebook.com/hotel.douce
10:00~21:00
Open all year round

플랜트

이태원 시장 뒷골목에 자리 잡은 채식 베이킹 카페 플랜트는 미파와 요나, 두 명의 셰프가 함께 운영한다. 고등학교 때 섭식 장애를 겪어 식재료에 유독 까다로운 요나 셰프와 달걀과 꿀도 먹지 않는 채식주의자인 미파 셰프가 동물성 크림이나 버터를 넣지 않은 디저트를 만들자는 생각에 의기투합했다. 특히 미파 셰프는 평소 자신이 만들던 디저트를 블로그에 올리고 서울 시내 여러 카페에 케이크를 납품하며 미식가 사이에서 유명해진 인물. 우유 대신 두유를 사용하고 버터 대신 식물성 오일을 넣어 만든다. 작업실을 겸한 아늑한 플랜트에 들어서면 쇼케이스를 가득 채운 브라우니와 파이, 케이크를 만날 수 있다. 셰프가 추천하는 플랜트의 시그너처 디저트는 식물성 오일로 만든 촉촉한 당근 케이크. 당근과 각종 견과류의 고소한 맛이 어우러진 케이크로 여느 케이크와 달리 퍽퍽한 질감보다는 촉촉한 식감을 강조했다.

Plant

Plant, a vegan baking café, is run by Chef Mipa and Chef Yona together. Chef Yona, who became meticulous about choosing food materials after suffering from eating disorder, agreed with a vegetarian Chef Mipa to open a vegan bakery not using animal product including dairy products. Chef Mipa was a well-known blogger for her own desserts she posted on her blog and at the same time a famous cake supplier among epicures. She uses soybean milk instead of animal's milk and vegetable oil instead of butter. According to its chefs, Plant's signature dessert is Moist Carrot Cake using vegetable oil too. With well mingled carrots and diverse nuts, it has more moisture than other ordinary cakes.

Address	용산구 이태원로16길 20	20, Itaewon-ro 16-gil, Yongsan-gu
Contact	070-4115-8388	82-70-4115-8388
Web	www.facebook.com/STUDIOPLANT	www.facebook.com/STUDIOPLANT
Operation	11:00~20:00	11:00~20:00
Closed	일·월요일, 설·추석 당일	Sun & Mon, Day of Lunar New Year's Day & Chuseok

디저트리

2011년 겨울 신사동에 문을 연 이현희 셰프의 디저트리는 모던한 디저트 바다. 디저트리가 추구하는 것은 '예상 밖의 디저트'다. 보통 어떤 음식을 보면 맛을 상상할 수 있는 법인데 식재료의 컬러와 식감을 조합해 나름의 방식으로 재조합하는 식이다. 뻔한 건 싫어하는 이현희 셰프의 도전 정신으로 탄생한 대표적인 메뉴는 '오믈렛 노르베지엔느'다. 파리에 살던 시절 나이 많은 비스트로 셰프가 만든 음식을 새롭게 해석한 메뉴라고. 몰드에 아이스크림을 담아 얼린 뒤 달걀흰자로 만든 머랭을 아이스크림 표면에 바르고, 250℃로 예열한 오븐에 3분 넣었다가 꺼낸 후 향이 좋은 술을 끼얹어 먹는다. "그날 할머니 셰프가 만들어준 디저트를 잊을 수가 없어요. 놀랍고 행복한 것, 그게 저에게는 디저트입니다."

DesserTree

DesserTree is a modern dessert bar of Chef Lee Hyeon-Hee in Sinsa-dong, opened in 2011. DesserTree's goal is an 'unexpected dessert.' Usually we can imagine the taste of food from its appearance but DesserTree's creative and surprising recipe always goes well beyond our imagination. Its specialty, Omelette Norvégienne, is born based on Chef Lee's disposition of liking nothing predictable. She made this dish through her new interpretation on the food an old bistro chef made in Paris. It is made by freezing ice cream in a mould, brushing meringue made from egg white on the frozen ice cream and then putting it in an oven preheated at 250 degrees Celsius for 3 minutes. You should sprinkle some alcoholic beverage with good scents before eating it.

Address	강남구 도산대로51길 17	17, Dosan-daero 51-gil, Gangnam-gu
Contact	02-518-3852	82-2-518-3852
Operation	14:00~22:00	14:00~22:00
Closed	일요일	Sun

비 위치

패션 디자이너로 일하다 뉴욕으로 떠나 ICE에서 요리를 공부한 신지민 셰프가 가로수길에 오픈한 디저트 숍. 밀가루, 버터, 달걀, 사워크림, 과일 같은 몇 가지 안 되는 재료를 배합해서 다양한 케이크를 만든다. 고정적으로 만드는 케이크는 6~7가지 정도인데, 계절에 따라 호박, 딸기, 루바브, 황도 등 사용하는 재료가 달라진다. "과일은 디저트를 위한 최고의 재료예요. 설탕을 줄여도 단맛을 낼 수 있고, 여기에 밀가루나 부재료를 더한 뒤 우유 한 잔을 곁들이면 든든한 식사가 되죠. 당도를 조절하고 폭식하지 않는다면 디저트도 일종의 건강식이 된다고 생각합니다." 신지민 셰프가 추천하는 메뉴는 '레몬 버터 케이크'. 구겔호프 틀에 굽는, 질감이 빽빽한 케이크인데 버터와 설탕을 1 대 1 비율로 섞어 만든다. 레몬 제스트를 더해 상큼하면서도 부드럽다.

Be Witch

Chef Sin Ji-Min was a fashion designer before she became a chef. After studying cooking in ICE (Institute of Culinary Education) of New York, she opened this dessert shop in Garosu-gil. She makes various kinds of cakes using a few common ingredients like flour, egg, butter, sour cream and fruits with variations in its way of mixing. Be Witch serves six to seven cake steadily throughout the year but there are slight changes in their ingredients seasonally among pumpkin, strawberry, rhubarb and yellow peach. Chef Sin recommends Lemon Butter Cake. This cake uses butter and sugar at the same ratio and is baked in a kugelhopt mould. Lemon zest added on this cake imparts fresh and sour flavor.

Address	서초구 사평대로28길 82	82, Sapyeong-daero 28-gil, Seocho-gu
Contact	02-3445-0529	82-2-3445-0529
Operation	11:30~22:00	11:30~22:00
Closed	일요일	Sun

빠따슈

슈크림으로 알려진 빠따슈와 에클레어 중심의 디저트 숍. 온통 블랙으로 꾸민 빠따슈 매장은 여느 디저트 숍과는 분위기가 다르다. "보석이나 시계처럼 에클레어를 보여주는 부티크 스토어 콘셉트로 공간을 만들었습니다. 눈으로 먼저 즐기게 하고, 맛으로 한 번 더 즐거움을 주자는 것이 의도였지요." 의류 광고 크리에이티브 디렉터로 일했던 김민경 셰프의 말이다. 쇼케이스 안 검은색 돌 그릇 위에 올린 에클레어를 흰색 장갑을 낀 직원이 하나씩 꺼내 담아준다. 화려한 원색부터 골드, 브론즈 등 독특한 컬러가 눈길을 끌며, 장식적인 아름다움도 돋보인다. 빠따슈의 에클레어는 겉이 바삭하고 한입 베어 물면 입안 가득 촉촉한 슈크림이 퍼지는 것이 특징. 메뉴 개발은 김민경 셰프의 스케치에서 시작된다. 원하는 에클레어의 그림을 그린 다음 컬러에 맞는 재료 궁합을 고민하고, 테이스팅을 거쳐 최종 메뉴가 된다고. 초코슈를 제외한 모든 슈에 아몬드를 올려 고소한 풍미를 강조했고 파티시에가 직접 판매까지 담당한다. 한입 크기의 미니 사이즈도 판매한다.

Pâte à Choux

Pâte à Choux is a dessert shop specializing in éclair and pâte à choux (commonly known as choux cream). Its interiors in a black color give off rather different ambiance. "This store is adorned according to the concept of boutique store displaying jewelry or watch," said Chef Kim Min-Gyeong, who used to be a creative director. Its staff wearing white gloves puts éclairs one by one from the black stone plate in a showcase. Bright basic colors and gorgeous gold and bronze colors make éclairs look like jewelry or ornaments. Crunchy outside éclair is yet melted in a mouth with rich and moist choux cream. Except chocolate choux, choux are topped with almonds imparting savory taste to choux. Its patissier is also in charge of sales.

Address	강남구 강남대로 160길 37	37, Gangnam-daero 160-gil, Gangnam-gu
Contact	02-3446-4762	82-2-3446-4762
Operation	12:00~21:00	12:00~21:00
Closed	월요일	Mon

에클레어 by 가루하루

'국내에 없는 것, 한국 사람들이 편하게 느끼는 것'을 테마로 에클레어를 위주로 한 디저트 전문점. 2014년 오픈해 채 1년이 되지 않은 이곳은 오픈 시간 전부터 줄을 서고 몇 시간 지나지 않아 에클레어와 마카롱이 소진될 정도로 인기를 끄는 경리단길 최고의 핫 플레이스다. 그날 만든 메뉴를 모두 당일 판매한다는 원칙으로 보존료나 유화제 등을 배제한 엄선한 재료로 만들며 쇼케이스에 여덟 시간 이상 두지 않는다. 장식이 과하지 않고 적당히 달콤한 에클레어와 마카롱은 여행을 통해 메뉴 아이디어를 얻는 윤은영 셰프의 창작품. "먼저 눈이 즐겁고 입안에서 조화를 이뤄야 제대로 된 디저트라고 생각합니다. 일반적인 에클레어보다 바삭하고 너무 달지 않도록 설탕 옷을 입히지 않아요." 매장 한쪽에서는 핑크색 보냉백과 에이프런, 엽서, 에코 백 등 소품을 판매한다.

Éclair by Garuharu

Less than a year after it was opened last year, Éclair by Garuharu became the one of the most popular dessert shops in Itaewon. People are lined up in front of the store before its opening hours and all the éclairs and macarons are sold out a few hours after opening. They select food materials carefully and exclude everything including preservatives or emulsifier. For this reason they do not put their products in a showcase more than 8 hours and stick to their principle that there should be no products left in a showcase after closing hours. These modest and not too sweet éclairs and macarons are created by Chef Yun Eun-Yeong. On a corner of the store, they sell various goods like bag, apron, eco-bag and postcard.

Address	용산구 회나무로13가길 42	42, Hoenamu-ro 13ga-gil, Yongsan-gu
Contact	02-337-8090	82-2-337-8090
Web	www.garuharu.com	www.garuharu.com
Operation	12:30~20:30(판매 완료 시 종료)	12:30~20:30(It could be closed earlier if all products are sold out)
Closed	월요일	Mon

디시룸 by 도레도레

무지개색 케이크 시트, 독특한 케이크 이름으로 화제가 된 가로수길 '도레도레'가 2호점 디시룸 by 도레도레를 내면서 더욱 다양한 케이크를 선보이고 있다. 케이크의 주재료는 우유로 만든 동물성 생크림과 필라델피아 크림치즈. 가장 유명한 시그너처 디저트는 무지개색 시트 사이사이에 생크림을 바른 케이크지만 그 외에도 '행복해 케이크', '소중해 케이크', '진득해 케이크' 등 재치 있는 작명의 케이크가 골고루 사랑받고 있다. 최근에는 딸기를 갈아 넣은 생크림을 듬뿍 올린 '나이아가라 딸기 케이크'도 새롭게 선보였다. 주로 여러 파시티에가 모여 새로운 케이크를 구상하며 케이크를 디자인할 때는 '사람들이 즐거워하고 맛있게 먹을 수 있을까'를 가장 먼저 생각한다고.

Dishroom by Doré Doré

The main ingredients of Doré Doré's cake are fresh cream made from milk and Philadelphia cream cheese. Their signature cake is fresh cream cake with six layers, each of different color of the rainbow, but other cakes with unique names like "Happy Cake", "Precious Cake" or "Reliable Cake". Niagara Strawberry Cake topped with rich strawberry cream has newly been released recently.

Address	강남구 압구정로14길 34		34, Apgujeong-ro 14-gil, Gangnam-gu
Contact	02-511-2115		82-2-511-2115
Operation	10:00~23:00		10:00~23:00
Closed	연중무휴		Open all year round

줄리에뜨

딸기, 청포도, 자몽 등 새콤달콤한 과일 타르트로 유명한 서래마을 줄리에뜨의 오너 셰프 줄리에뜨 최. 그는 유학길에 오른 남편을 따라 프랑스 니스에 갔다가 프랑스 디저트에 빠져들었고, 후에 르 코르동 블뢰에서 직접 요리를 배우기에 이른다. 이후 캐나다 몬트리올의 빵집 등을 거쳐 2010년, 서래마을에 '엄마가 만들어주는 디저트' 콘셉트로 줄리에뜨를 오픈했다. 집에 있던 가구와 그릇을 그대로 옮겨 와 자신의 집 응접실처럼 꾸몄고 그날그날 가장 신선한 제철 과일을 선별해 천연 단맛이 나는 타르트를 만든다. 핼러윈이나 크리스마스에는 특색 있는 디저트를 판매하며, 오더 메이드 케이크도 제작한다.

Juliette

Juliette Choi is the chef cum owner of Juliette in Seorae Village, a dessert shop famous with her fruit tarts. When she went to France with her husband for his study she found true charms of French desserts and finally learned cooking in Le Cordon Bleu. After she came back to Korea, she opened Juliette in Seorae Village with the concept of 'mom's desserts' in 2010. Juliette makes tarts with natural sweet flavor with the freshest seasonal fruits every day. Some special desserts for Halloween or Christmas and order made cakes are available.

Address	서초구 동광로 178	178, Donggwang-ro, Seocho-gu
Contact	02-535-4002	82-2-535-4002
Web	juliette2.modoo.at	juliette2.modoo.at
Operation	월~토 09:00~22:00, 일 12:00~22:00	Mon to Sat 09:00~22:00, Sun 12:00~22:00
Closed	설·추석 연휴	Holiday of Lunar New Year's Day & Chuseok

마망 갸또

'엄마가 만든 과자'라는 뜻의 마당 갸또는 프랑스 르 코르동 블뢰에서 공부한 피윤정 셰프의 디저트 카페이자, 알찬 클래스로도 유명한 곳이다. 작은 오피스텔에서 시작한 작업실이 입소문을 타면서 2009년 가로수길에 문을 열게 된 것. 좋은 재료로 만드는 마망 갸또의 디저트는 웰빙 디저트로 인정받으며 자리 잡았다. 피윤정 대표는 오로지 홈메이드만 고집한다. 특히 캐러멜은 끓이는 시간과 정도에 따라 질감까지 달라지기에 가장 심혈을 기울여 만든다. 현재 숍에서는 캐러멜 치즈 케이크, 캐러멜 쇼콜라 무스 등 캐러멜을 주제로 한 다양한 디저트를 판매한다. 모든 디저트는 우유로 만든 동물성 버터와 우유 생크림, 그랑 크뤼급 초콜릿을 사용하는 것이 원칙이다.

Maman Gâteau

Maman Gâteau is a dessert café and famous baking academy of Chef Pi Yun-Jeong from Le Cordon Bleu Paris. This baking class that first started in her small studio became so famous and popular that it moved to a larger space in Garosu-gil. Fresh ingredients are paramount to Chef Pi and her sticking to this principle has made Maman Gâteau's well-being desssserts acknowledged by customers. As the name of store means 'Mom made cakes,' she tries to making desserts mom makes at home. A variety of caramel desserts including Caramel Cheesecake and Caramel Chocolate Mousse are presented on their showcase. Maman Gâteau uses butter and fresh cream made from milk and Grand Cru-level chocolates.Maman Gâteau uses butter and fresh cream made from milk and Grand Cru-level chocolates.

Address	강남구 압구정로10길 30-12(신사점)	30-12, Apgujeong-ro 10-gil, Gangnam-gu
Contact	070-4353-5860	82-70-4353-5860
Web	www.mamangt.com	www.mamangt.com
Operation	09:30~22:50	09:30~22:50
Closed	연중무휴	Open all year round

르와지르

2014년 여름 한남동에 오픈한 르와지르는 2층짜리 주택을 개조해 만든 아늑하고 밝은 분위기의 프랑스 디저트 숍이다. 〈마샤 스튜어트〉 매거진을 보며 취미로 베이킹을 하던 김수경 셰프가 나카무라 아카데미 서울의 디저트 과정을 졸업한 뒤 문을 연 곳. 다양한 메뉴를 선보이기 위해 한 가지 재료로 두 가지 이상의 디저트를 만들지 않고, 기본 재료일수록 좋은 것을 쓴다. 김수경 셰프가 자신 있게 내놓은 시그너처 메뉴는 '오렌지 얼그레이 생토노레'다. 생토노레 Saint-Honoré 는 슈와 푀이타주, 크림으로 이루어진 섬세한 디저트. 설탕을 넣는 대신 얼그레이 차를 우려낸 뒤 초콜릿을 배합한 크림과 커스터드 크림을 넣은 캐러멜 코팅 슈로 만든다. 슈에 오렌지 젤리와 필을 채워 상큼한 맛을 더한 것이 특징.

Loisir

Loisir is a French dessert shop. Its store is placed at a remodeled two-story house with bright and cozy ambiance. Their items have almost no overlap in its ingredients because Chef Kim Su-Gyeong does not use one ingredient for multiple desserts. Chef Kim's signature item is Orange Earl Grey Saint-Honoré. Saint-Honoré is a fine dessert made of choux, feuilletage and cream. Instead of sugar, custard cream and chocolate cream mixed with infused earl grey are put in its caramel coated choux. Orange jelly and peel in the choux imparts fresher flavor. Loisir's desserts are made based on Chef Kim's principle that the more basic the ingredient is, the better quality it should have.

Address	용산구 이태원로55나길 7		7, Itaewon-ro 55na-gil, Yongsan-gu
Contact	02-749-1128		82-2-749-1128
Operation	11:00~23:00		11:00~23:00
Closed	연중무휴		Open all year round

에이미 초코

신사동 가로수길에 위치한 카페 에이미 초코는 조미애 쇼콜라티에와 남편 김병현 대표가 함께 운영하는 곳. 신혼여행도 말레이시아 카카오 농장으로 다녀올 정도로 초콜릿의 매력에 푹 빠져든 조미애 셰프가 'all about chocolate' 콘셉트로 메뉴를 선보인다. 카페 1층에 카카오 로스팅 기기를 갖춰 테스트를 거듭하고 있고, 3층 작업실에서는 모두 수작업으로 그날 판매할 초콜릿을 완성한다. 에이미 초코에는 기본 초콜릿부터 브라우니, 케이크, 아이스크림, 음료, 초콜릿 피자까지 초콜릿의 묘미를 살린 다채로운 메뉴가 가득하다. "100퍼센트 카카오 파우더로 반죽하고 다크 초콜릿과 치즈를 넣은 다크 초콜릿 피자, 단호박과 화이트 초콜릿이 잘 어우러진 수프까지 초콜릿의 다양한 맛을 경험할 수 있어요." 모든 재료를 직접 만드는 그녀의 야무진 손길만큼 의외의 조합이 색다른 맛의 즐거움을 자아낸다.

Amy Choco

Chocolatier Jo Mi-Ae runs Amy Choco in Garosu-gil with her husband, Kim Byeong-Hyeon. Her love for chocolate is so particular that she stayed at a cacao farm in Malaysia even during her honeymoon. Amy Choco's slogan is 'All About Chocolate.' A cacao bean roaster set on the first story is used for endless testing and a workshop on the third story chocolate of the day is created by this meticulous chocolatier. Amy Choco's showcase is full of diverse items from basic chocolate, brownies, cakes, ice cream and beverages to chocolate pizza.

Address	강남구 압구정로10길 30-1	30-1, Apgujeong-ro 10-gil, Gangnam-gu
Contact	02-733-5509	82-2-733-5509
Web	www.amychoco.com	www.amychoco.com
Operation	11:30~23:00	11:30~23:00
Closed	설·추석 당일	Day of Lunar New Year's Day & Chuseok

에딸프

2014년 가을, 신사동에 문을 연 프랑스식 디저트 숍. 독특한 이름은 '플레이트plate'의 스펠링을 반대로 쓴 것이다. 심리치료사로 일하다 뉴욕의 ICC에서 프랑스 요리를 배운 송지선 파티시에는 극도로 섬세한 과정을 거쳐 완성하는 프랑스 디저트의 매력에 빠져 가게를 차리게 됐다. 에딸프 실내는 커다란 대리석 원형 테이블, 창가의 바, 화려한 샹들리에로 꾸며 우아한 보석 판매점 같은 분위기를 낸다. 송지선 파티시에는 쇼케이스 뒤쪽 넓은 오픈 키친에서 매일매일 디저트를 굽는다. 파티시에가 추천하는 시그너처 메뉴는 라벤더 케이크. 라벤더의 꽃향기와 복숭아 과일 향이 은은하게 배어 있어 특히 여성들이 좋아하는 메뉴다. 꽃과 허브의 독특한 조합도 매력적이다.

Étalp La Patiserie

Étalp is a French dessert shop in Sinsa-dong, opened by Chef Song Ji-Seon who worked as a therapist before attending French cooking classes in ICC (International Culinary Center in New York). What attracted her into the world of French dessert was its delicate and sophisticated element. This store looks like a fancy jewelry shop because of its round marble tables, bar next to window and delicate chandelier. You can find a large open kitchen behind a showcase, in which fresh desserts are baked every day. Étalp's signature item is Lavender Cake. The scents of lavender and peach made this cake popular especially with young women.

Address	강남구 논현로161길 39	39, Nonhyeon-ro 161-gil, Gangnam-gu
Contact	02-6010-7717	82-2-6010-7717
Web	www.etalp.com	www.etalp.com
Operation	11:00~22:00	11:00~22:00
Closed	월요일	Mon

삐아프

삐아프에는 테이블 하나 없이 뚜껑 없는 쇼케이스와 초콜릿 디저트를 보관하는 장식장이 전부다. 오직 초콜릿에 집중할 수 있게 하기 위해서다. 초콜릿 향을 풍부히 느낄 수 있도록 쇼케이스는 항상 열어두지만 온도와 습도 차에 특히 주의한다고. 전 과정을 손으로 작업하고, 초콜릿을 집는 부분을 천으로 감싸 상처가 나지 않도록 한 집게에 이르기까지 섬세하게 신경 썼다. 이곳의 시그너처 메뉴는 '더블 바닐라'. 타히티 바닐라의 플로럴 향과 마다가스카르 바닐라의 풍미가 어우러지며 마지막에는 옅은 신맛으로 마무리해 초콜릿 고유의 맛과 향을 제대로 느낄 수 있다고. 삐아프의 또 다른 매력은 밸런타인데이마다 선보이는 리미티드 에디션 패키지를 들 수 있다. 2013년 하트 모양의 패키지와 2014년 팝업 카드 형태 패키지에 이어 올해는 영화 〈그랜드 부다페스트 호텔〉의 그래픽 디자이너로 잘 알려진 애니 앳킨스 Annie Atkins와 함께해 화제를 모았다.

Piaf

Piaf's specialty is Double Vanilla. As it gives off first with the scent of Tahitian vanilla and flavor of Madagascar vanilla well mixed each other and then slight sour flavor, Double Vanilla would be the best item if you want to feel chocolate's own taste and smell. Piaf's limited edition package for Valentine's Day is also special. Following a heart-shaped package (2013) and a package with pop-up card form (2014), Piaf, for Valentine's Day of 2015, presented a package collaborated with Annie Atkins, a famous graphic designer of the movie <Grand Budapest Hotel>.

Address	강남구 압구정로4길 27-3
Contact	02-545-0317
Web	blog.naver.com/bulabog
Operation	11:00~19:30
Closed	월요일

27-3, Apgujeong-ro 4-gil, Gangnam-gu
82-2-545-0317
blog.naver.com/bulabog
11:00~19:30
Mon

글래머러스 펭귄

유년 시절을 캐나다에서 보낸 유민주 셰프는 홈 베이킹을 통해 처음 디저트를 접했다. 낯선 학교에 입학한 첫날 친구들과 친해지라며 어머니가 만들어준 블루베리 머핀, 동네 이웃들과 나눈 쿠키와 케이크를 통해 디저트의 매력에 빠져든 것. 본격적으로 캐나다 쿠킹 스쿨과 프랑스 알랭 뒤카스 파티세리에서 공부한 뒤 한남동에 글래머러스 펭귄을 오픈한 건 2012년 9월. 이곳의 시그너처 디저트는 뉴욕 '매그놀리아'의 바나나 푸딩을 업그레이드해 진한 단맛을 줄인 푸딩이다. 바닐라 크림과 부드러운 바나나 슬라이스, 달걀 과자, 케이크 시트를 겹쳐 부드럽고 촉촉하다. 프랑스 최고급 코코아 파우더를 쓴 레드 벨벳 케이크와 초콜릿 케이크에 가나슈, 마시멜로 머랭 프로스팅을 섞은 스모어 케이크도 추천할 만하다.

Glamorous Penguin

Chef Yu Min-Ju, who spent her childhood in Canada, had opportunities to see her mom baking treats at home. Mom's blueberry muffins, cookies and cakes she shared with her friends and neighbors in an unfamiliar country led her into a world of desserts. After she completed cooking classes in Canada and then in the Alain Ducasse Cooking School in Paris, she opened Glamorous Penguin in Hannam-dong in 2012. In Glamorous Penguin, you can taste a pudding not too sweet, an upgraded version of banana pudding of Magnolia Bakery in New York. This pudding has become Chef Yu's signature dessert. Red Velvet S'mores Cake using the finest French cocoa powder is also wonderful.

Address	용산구 이태원로49길 16		16, Itaewon-ro 49-gil, Yongsan-gu
Contact	02-790-7178		82-2-790-7178
Web	www.glamorouspenguin.com		www.glamorouspenguin.com
Operation	월~금 10:00~22:00, 토·일 11:00~22:00		Mon to Fri 10:00:00~22:00, Sat & Sun 11:00~22:00
Closed	연중무휴		Open all year round

듀자미

2009년 겨울, 신사동에서 시작해 2014년에는 삼청동에 2호점을 개설한 디저트 카페. 해외 출장을 자주 가던 홍승현 셰프와 불문학을 전공한 채혜수 셰프 부부가 함께 운영한다. "둘이 함께 르 코르동 블뢰 숙명 아카데미에서 제과 과정을 공부했어요. 디저트를 통해 인생이 바뀐 셈이지요." 홍승현, 채혜수 셰프 부부의 철학은 프랑스식 케이크에 동양의 식재료와 멋을 더해 듀자미만의 케이크를 만드는 것. 녹차, 밤, 단호박, 사과, 산딸기 등 우리나라 식재료를 활용해 아름답고 친숙한 맛을 내는 디저트를 다양하게 선보인다. 듀자미의 시그너처 케이크는 캐러멜 소금 케이크. 최고급 프랑스산 발로나 초콜릿으로 만드는 초콜릿 무스, 게랑드 천일염, 매일 일정한 농도로 끓이는 캐러멜의 조화가 훌륭하다.

Deux Amis

Deux Amis of Sinsa-dong was launched in 2009 and its second store of Samcheong-dong was opened in 2014. Chef Hong Seung-Hyeon and Chef Chae Hye-Su, a married couple, run these two stores together. "We attended baking classes of Le Cordon Bleu Sookmyung Academy together. Desserts changed our life somehow." This couple is focusing on making Deux Amis' own cake with native food materials of Korea based on authentic French cake recipes. Various ingredients like green tea, chestnut, sweet pumpkin, apple and wild berry make their desserts look beautiful and taste nice. Deux Amis' specialty is Salted-Caramel Cake, in which home-made caramel, Guérande sea salt and chocolate mousse made of the premium Valrhona chocolate are wonderfully harmonized.

Address	종로구 팔판길 22(삼청점)	22, Palpan-gil, Jongno-gu
Contact	02-733-9155	82-2-733-9155
Operation	11:30~22:00	11:30~22:00
Closed	연중무휴	Open all year round

전통 디저트 가게

대기업이 운영하는 떡 체인점은 물론 떡을 디저트처럼 판매하는 카페가 생겨나면서 떡을 손쉽게 접할 수 있는 곳이 늘어났다. 그중에서도 오랜 역사와 흉내 낼 수 없는 비법으로 맛과 멋을 아는 사람들을 매료시킨 최고의 떡집 네 곳을 소개한다.

TRADITIONAL KOREAN DESSERTS

A rice cake is a kind of traditional Korean dish and has been a common item of a dessert shop. From a chain store of a food service corporation to a dessert café, there are numerous places you can enjoy rice cakes as dessert.

동병상련

떡을 아끼고 좋아하는 사람들과 함께한다는 의미의 동병상련. 궁중음식연구원, 중국 상하이 요리학교, 전통병과원에서 다양한 경험을 쌓고 2004년 중요무형문화재 제38호 기능보유자로 지정된 박경미 대표가 운영하는 곳이다. 떡을 만들 때 쓰는 기본 곡류는 고시히카리종 멥쌀, 찹쌀, 발아 현미 등 국내산 재료만 사용한다. 그 외 색과 맛을 내거나 고명으로 올리는 재료로는 붉은팥, 수수, 검은콩, 유자, 깨, 꿀 등을 계절에 따라 선택해서 쓴다. 동병상련에서 가장 인기 있는 품목은 찰떡류와 한과류다. '현미 찰떡'과 '사과 찰떡'이 대표 메뉴. 그 외 '곶감 찰떡', '감귤 찰떡', '카스텔라 찰떡', '완두 찰떡'도 인기 상품이다. 견과나 뿌리채소, 생과를 꿀에 조리거나 재워 만든 정과류도 다양해 차를 마실 때 곁들이면 좋다.

Dong Byeong Sang Ryeon

This name, originally meaning 'sharing grief with others in a similar, miserable situation,' indicates here 'sharing rice cake with others who love it.' In 2004, its owner Park Gyeong-Mi was designated as one of the initiates of the Important Intangible Cultural Properties No.38 (Royal culinary art of the Joseon Dynasty) of Korea. The basic grains used for their rice cake are Koshihikari rice, glutinous rice and germinated brown rice, all cultivated in Korea. And a variety of grains and ingredients are used to add colors to rice cake or to garnish it. Their best seller is Hyeonmi Chaltteok (glutinous rice cake with germinated brown rice) and Sagwa Chaltteok (glutinous rice cake added with apple). Fruits preserved in honey would go well with a cup of tea. Diverse items for a gift set or return gift are also available.

Address	성북구 정릉로10길 42-6(본사)
Contact	02-391-0077
Web	www.ddock.co.kr
Operation	09:00~18:00
Closed	연중무휴

42-6, Jeongneung-ro 10-gil, Seongbuk-gu
82-2-391-0077
www.ddock.co.kr
09:00~18:00
Open all year round

비원떡집

조선왕조의 마지막 상궁이자 궁중 음식 기능보유자인 한희순 상궁에게 비법을 전수한 홍 씨 할머니가 1949년 낙원동 길가에 가게를 내면서 시작된 떡집. 현재 비원떡집은 그녀의 조카인 안인철 씨를 거쳐 그의 아들인 안상민 씨가 운영한다. 40여 종의 궁중 떡을 만날 수 있지만 다른 곳에서 흉내 낼 수 없는 비원떡집만의 시그너처 떡은 멥쌀로 만든 '갖은편'과 '쌍개피떡'이다. 전통 나왕나무 시루로 찌는 갖은편은 표면이 페이즐리 문양을 새긴 것처럼 화려하면서도 정갈하다. 백설기처럼 흰 떡과 대추를 고아 만든 대추고로 갈색을 낸 떡까지 네 종류가 있다. 고명은 대추, 밤, 잣, 석이버섯을 사용하는데 그중에서도 대추편은 씨를 뺀 통대추를 말린 뒤 전분을 묻혀 채를 썰고 다시 말리는 등 복잡한 과정을 거쳐 탄생한다. 쌍개피떡은 멥쌀로 만들었지만 절구로 치댄 반죽을 얇게 밀어 찹쌀로 만든 것처럼 쫄깃하다.

Bi Won

Madame Hong, who learned recipes from Court Lady Han Hui-Sun, the last court lady of the Joseon Dynasty and holder of royal culinary arts, started Biwon at the alley of Nakwon-dong in 1949. There are around 40 kinds of royal rice cakes but Biwon's specialty is Gajeunpyeon and Ssanggaepitteok. Gajeunpyeon, a kind of assorted rice cake, is made up of four kinds of rice cakes including white rice cake and jujubes-garnished rice cake. Ssanggaepitteok, though it is made from short grain rice less sticky than glutinous rice, is of much sticky texture.

Address	종로구 율곡로 20	20, Yulgok-ro, Jongno-gu	
Contact	02-765-4928	82-2-765-4928	
Web	www.biwon.net	www.biwon.net	
Operation	10:00~17:00	10:00~17:00	
Closed	일요일(예약 주문만 받음)	Sun(An advance order is possible)	

도수향

강정향 대표가 아들, 딸의 이름을 한 글자씩 모아 이름 지었다는 도수향. 모든 떡을 수작업으로 만들며 떡집 한쪽에 둔 빨간색 돌절구는 다른 떡집과 도수향의 맛을 차별화하는 비법 무기다. "다른 떡집은 보통 찹쌀가루 또는 멥쌀가루를 반죽해 떡을 만들지만 도수향에서는 밥을 찐 다음 절구로 찧어 떡을 만들지요." 강정향 대표의 설명이다. 떡에 밥알이 보이기도 하는데 이렇게 만든 떡은 밥을 먹는 것처럼 은근히 달면서 질리지 않는 것이 특징이라고. 메뉴는 '이북인절미', '흑임자 구름떡', '차 약식', '두텁 찹쌀떡', '말차 초콜릿 찹쌀떡', '흑임자 생강 찹쌀떡'까지 여섯 가지다. 도수향의 시그너처 떡인 이북인절미는 평양식 거피 팥고물을 손으로 쥐어 만든 찰떡 인절미다. 밥을 지을 때 설탕량을 조절해 은근한 단맛을 내는데, 부드럽게 으깨지는 팥고물이 별미다. 흑임자 구름떡은 찹쌀밥에 흑임자 고물을 넣어 구름 모양처럼 만든 것. 차 약식은 녹차의 쌉싸래한 맛을 살려 차와 함께 마셔도 좋다.

Do Su Hyang

A large red stone mortar in a corner of the store is a special tool for Do Su Hyang's rice cakes. Do Su Hyang has only six items including Ibuk-Injeolmi (North Korean style rice cake coated with bean flour), which is their signature item for its filling made from dehulled red bean. Heugimja Gureumttoek (cloud-shaped rice cake filled with black sesame) is also available. Cha Yaksik (sweet rice with nuts and jujubes flavored with green tea) is a good accompaniment of a cup of tea.

Address	강남구 논현로158길 33	33, Nonhyeon-ro 158-gil, Gangnam-gu
Contact	02-540-2939	82-2-540-2939
Operation	09:00~20:30	09:00~20:30
Closed	연중무휴	Open all year round

미정당

떡 본연의 맛에 충실한, 바른 맛을 선보이고 싶다는 강효성 대표의 떡집 미정당은 부암동주민센터 맞은편에 위치한 아담한 공간이다. 떡집으로만 운영하다가 2012년 10월 리뉴얼해 떡과 차를 즐길 수 있는 곳으로 거듭났다. 길가의 유리창 쪽에 작은 전시 공간을 마련해 매달 추천 떡을 전시하고 간단한 설명을 덧붙인다. 대추, 유자 등 한국 고유의 식재료로 떡과 정과를 만드는데 시그너처 떡은 '대추단자'. 일반적으로 대추채를 묻히지만 강 대표는 대추 특유의 거친 질감이 싫어 찹쌀가루에 부드러운 대추고를 넣고 잣고물을 묻혀 만든다. 추운 날 몸을 따뜻하게 해주는 대추와 머리를 좋게 한다고 알려진 잣을 사용한 약선 떡이라고. 식용 꽃을 얹은 '잣설기'는 반죽에 잣을 갈아 넣어 만들었고, '대추약편'은 멥쌀가루에 막걸리를 넣어 반죽해 뒷맛이 고소하다. 유자 맛이 관건인 '개성주악'은 거제도에서 공수한 유자로 맛을 내며, 카페에서 파는 유자차와도 잘 어울린다.

Mi Jeong Dang

Mi Jeong Dang is a small café serving rice cake, coffee and tea in Buam-dong. It was originally a retail shop specializing in rice cake but refurbished in 2012 as at present. As its owner says that Mi Jeong Dang pursues to keep natural taste of rice cake, it uses authentic Korean food materials for its rice cake and preserved fruits. Mi Jeong Dang's signature item is Daechudanja (rice cake ball with jujubes). They put soft jujube fillings into glutinous rice paste and then sprinkle pounded pine nuts on it, instead of usually used shredded jujubes.

Address	종로구 창의문로 146
Contact	02-391-9036
Operation	09:00~20:00
Closed	월요일

146, Changuimun-ro, Jongno-gu
82-2-391-9036
09:00~20:00
Mon

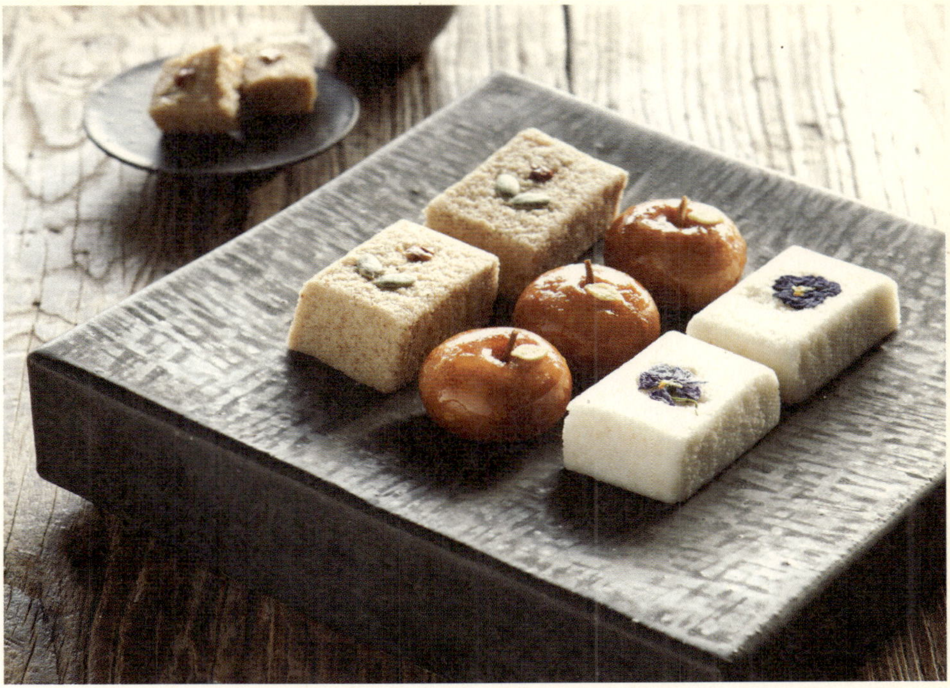

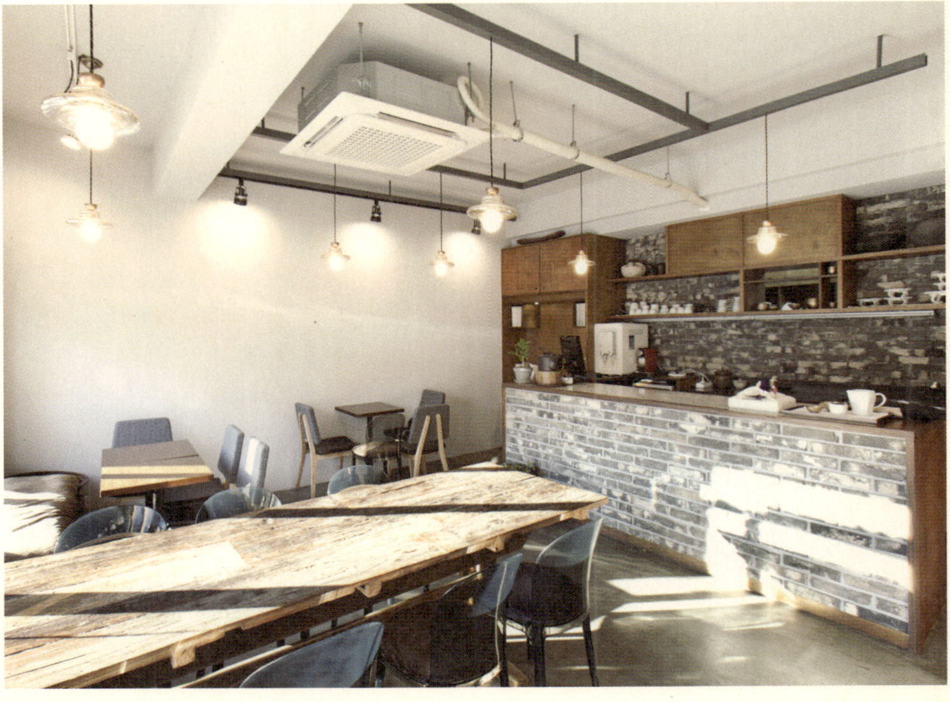

수제 맥주 펍

지금 서울에는 이태원을 중심으로 수제 맥주 열풍이 불고 있다. 홈브루잉 home-brewing에 관심을 가진 젊은 사장들이 직접 만든 수제 맥주를 판매하며 맥주 마니아들을 사로잡고 있는 것. 색다른 맥주를 맛볼 수 있는 공간을 소개한다.

CRAFT BEER HOUSE

Craft beer's popularity has seen immense growth in the past few years in Seoul. Many young brewers who are interested in home-brewing have opened craft beer houses around Itaewon and been attracting beer enthusiasts with their own craft beer. Here is a list of some beer houses providing a quality craft beer good.

라일리스 탭하우스

캐나다 출신의 맥주 소믈리에 트로이 치첼슈베르거 Troy Zitzelsberger가 2012년 오픈한 곳. 입구에 들어서면 창가와 카운터의 바, 널찍한 홀이 눈에 들어온다. 다양한 수제 맥주를 취급해 평일에도 북적이는 편. 대표 맥주는 페일 에일 중에서도 풍미가 강한 '제주 귤 인디언 페일 에일IPA'. 은은한 시트러스 아로마가 감도는 풍부한 향이 일품이다. 쓴맛이 덜해 여성들이 즐겨 찾는다고. 이외에도 생맥주로 제공하는 다양한 수제 맥주를 구비했으며 폭넓은 병맥주 리스트도 흥미롭다. 미국의 코나 브루잉 컴퍼니, 로스트 코스트, 앤더슨 밸리 등 여느 펍에서 찾아보기 힘든 맥주가 가득하다. 안주는 샐러드와 애피타이저, 홍합 요리와 샌드위치가 있다.

Reilly's Taphouse

Troy Zitzelsberger, a beer sommelier from Canada, opened a craft beer house called Reilly's Taphouse in 2012. Its large hall and bar seem nice to enjoy premium craft beers in a relaxed atmosphere. A wide range of quality beers are the biggest element, of course, to draw many people during weekdays. The Jeju Tangerine IPA with a rather strong flavor amongst pale ales is the representative of its beers. With its less bitter taste this beer is popular especially with women. Plus, various craft beers are served from its taps and an extensive list of bottled beers are available as well.

Address	용산구 이태원로 187	187, Itaewon-ro, Yongsan-gu
Contact	02-792-6590	82-2-792-6590
Operation	월~금 Mon to Fri 16:00~다음 날 The next day 01:00, 토·일 Sat & Sun 15:00~다음 날 The next day 02:00	
Closed	연중무휴	Open all year round

맥파이

이태원 경리단길에 위치한 맥파이는 취미로 홈브루잉을 즐기던 네 명의 미국인이 모여 오픈했다. 5~6명이 걸터앉을 수 있는 바와 테이블이 있고, 지하 펍에서는 테이블에 앉아 좀 더 여유롭게 맥주를 즐길 수 있다. 맥주를 만드는 주재료는 몰트와 홉, 이스트와 물 등 네 가지. 그중 몰트는 맥주의 컬러를, 홉은 특유의 쓴맛을 결정하고, 이스트는 맥주의 아로마를 결정한다. 맥파이에서 선보이는 맥주는 시트러스 풍미와 쌉싸래한 뒷맛이 일품인 페일 에일, 캐러멜과 몰트의 풍미가 진한 쿠퍼, 커피와 다크 초콜릿 아로마가 풍부한 포터까지 세 가지 스타일이다.

Magpie

Four Americans, just enjoying home-brewing as a hobby, started this craft brewery together at Gyeongridan-gil of Itaewon. On the first floor are a few tables and a bar with five to six seats but you would enjoy beers in more relaxed ambiance in the capacious basement. The main ingredients of beer are water, malted grain, hops and yeast. The malted grain is a key determinant of the color of the beer, hops contribute the bitterness and yeast has influence on the aroma. Magpie serves three styles of beers at large, that is, the pale ale with citrus aromas and bitter aftertaste, the copper with strong flavor of caramel and malt, the porter with rich aromas of coffee and dark chocolate.

Address	용산구 녹사평대로 244-1(이태원점)		244-1, Noksapyeong-daero, Yongsan-gu
Contact	02-749-2703		82-2-749-2703
Web	www.magpiebrewing.com		www.magpiebrewing.com
Operation	15:00~다음 날 01:00		15:00~The next day 01:00
Closed	월요일		Mon

크래프트웍스 탭하우스

경리단길 초입에 있는 크래프트웍스는 자체 공장에서 수돗물이 아닌 천연 지하수로 만든 신선하고 맛있는 맥주를 판매한다. 흥미로운 것은 맥주에 지리산, 한라산, 금강산 등 국내 명산의 이름을 붙였다는 점. '지리산 반달곰IPA' 맥주는 알코올 도수가 높고 드라이한 홉의 풍미를 살린 흑맥주다. '설악산 오트밀 스타우트' 맥주는 달콤한 커피와 초콜릿 풍미가 일품이며, '금강산 다크 에일'은 훈연 향과 견과류가 어우러진 독특한 스타일이다. '백두산 헤페바이젠'은 바나나와 정향의 아로마가 지배적이고, '한라산 골든 에일'은 질감이 크림처럼 부드러워 인기가 높다. 모든 종류의 맥주를 조금씩 맛본 뒤 메뉴를 고르고 싶다면 '맥주 샘플러'를 주문하면 된다. 글라스 단위로 판매하는 와인과 위스키, 리큐어 종류도 다양하게 갖췄다.

Craftworks Taphouse

Craftworks Taphouse, located at an entrance to Gyeongridan-gil, serves up fine beers brewed with natural underground water in its brewery, not with tap water. Interestingly, they name their beers after names of local mountains in Korea. Jirisan Moon Bear IPA is a sort of dark beer with a relatively high-proof and is characterized with good flavor of dry hops. The beer sampler consisting of their 7 beers is available as well. In addition to beers, they provide a wide range of wine, whisky and liquors in a glass.

Address	용산구 녹사평대로 238	238, Noksapyeong-daero, Yongsan-gu
Contact	02-794-2537	82-2-794-2537
Operation	14:00~00:00	14:00~00:00
Closed	연중무휴	Open all year round

주점 & 바

많은 사람에게 사랑받는 술집의 비결은 술맛을 증폭시키는 안주 리스트가 알차다는 것. 혹은 애주가들의 마음을 사로잡을 만한 '맛있는' 술을 갖추고 있기 마련이다. 훌륭한 안주 리스트를 선보이거나 싱글 몰트위스키 열풍을 이끌고 있는 근사한 바 일곱 곳을 소개한다.

BAR & PUB

A nice pub, popular with numerous people, would have a food menu with a great match for any alcoholic beverage. Or it would have alcoholic drinks to appease many alcohol lovers. It then would be perfect if there is any place to have both excellent food and terrific alcoholic drinks. Now we introduce a selection of bars and pubs with both of them including fine single malt whisky.

드슈

〈KTX 매거진〉에서 음식과 술 기사를 쓰던 기자가 차린 술집으로 주력하는 술은 전통주다. "전국 곳곳의 술도가를 취재하며 찾아낸 보석 같은 리스트를 혼자만 알기 아까워 직접 유통, 판매하기로 마음먹었다"라는 게 이주연 대표의 설명이다. 전통 방식으로 증류한 이강주, 문배주, 진도 홍주, 진도 백주 같은 소주와 면천두견주, 호산춘 같은 청주를 엄선해 판매한다. 맛은 물론 도수도 모두 다른 데다 생소한 브랜드도 많으니 꼭 추천받은 뒤 주문하길. 메뉴는 기본 식재료와 재료 모두 한식에서 영감을 얻었다. 어만두 샌드위치, 튀김옷을 입힌 참치 다다키 같은 메뉴는 도수 높은 소주나 청주를 마실 때 속을 든든하게 하기 좋다.

De Chou

A reporter who wrote articles on food and alcoholic beverage for KTX Magazine opened this pub specializing in traditional Korean alcoholic drinks. "I have found an endless list of fine breweries all over the country and really wanted to share it with others. This is the reason I opened De Chou,' said Lee Ju-Yeon, the owner of De Chou. This pub serves a selection of soju (Korean distilled liquor) and cheongju (refined rice wine) of each region, which are brewed in a traditional way. The taste and proof of these spirits are much different and there are many unfamiliar brewery brands as well. It would be easier for you to choose after you listen to their explanations first.

Address	강남구 강남대로152길 67	67, Gangnam-daero 152-gil, Gangnam-gu
Contact	02-514-2014	82-2-514-2014
Web	blog.naver.com/dechou	blog.naver.com/dechou
Operation	18:00~다음 날 02:00	18:00~The next day 02:00
Closed	일요일	Sun

커피 바 K

일본에서 탄생한 프랜차이즈 바. 클래식함과 모던함이 공존하는 고급스러운 분위기에서 전문 바텐더의 서비스와 추천을 받으며 다양한 싱글 몰트위스키를 마실 수 있다. 'ㄱ'자 형태의 창가 자리에서는 한남동 거리를 감상하며 술을 마실 수 있으며, 가죽 의자가 파티션 역할을 하는 안쪽 자리에서는 프라이빗한 분위기를 즐길 수 있다. 보리 경작부터 맥아 작업까지 수작업으로 진행해 맛이 깊고 부드러운 발베니 Balvenie, 화산섬 지대에서 제조해 숯과 스모키 향이 폭발적인 탈리스커 Talisker 등을 선택하면 블렌디드 위스키와 달리 맛과 향이 짙고 풍부한 싱글 몰트위스키의 매력을 제대로 경험할 수 있다. 올로로소 Oloroso 셰리와 PX 셰리를 숙성한 통에서 만드는 글렌드로낙 Glendronac은 전문가들이 '셰리가 만들어낸 괴물'이라 말할 정도로 벌꿀과 꽃, 나무의 강렬한 아로마가 이어지는 커피 바 K의 추천 위스키다.

Coffee Bar K

Coffee Bar K is a franchised bar that came from Japan, where you can taste a variety of single malt whisky with attentive service of an expert bartender in a classical yet modern ambiance. On a L-shaped table you can look out the street of the town and on inside tables with leather seats you would feel much relaxed in a private space. If you order Balvenie or Talisker, you could taste a real single malt whisky with richer flavor and aroma than blended whisky. Glendronach, acclaimed by experts as a monster made from sherry, is the finest whiskey Coffee Bar K recommends.

Address	용산구 독서당로 73(한남점)
Contact	02-796-9311
Operation	19:00~다음 날 03:00
Closed	일요일

	73, Dokseodang-ro, Yongsan-gu
	82-2-796-9311
	19:00~The next day 03:00
	Sun

페타테

고대 마야 어로 '평화와 균형'을 뜻하는 가로수길의 싱글 몰트위스키 바 페타테. 지하에 위치한 여느 바와 달리 테라스가 있는 2층에 위치해 가로수길의 활기찬 분위기를 느낄 수 있다. IT업계에 종사하던 최용남 대표가 싱글 몰트위스키와 사랑에 빠져 오픈한 이곳은 바와 테라스 쪽 테이블, 오디오와 책을 두어 미니 살롱처럼 꾸몄다. 구비한 싱글 몰트위스키는 약 80종. 초보자나 전문가 모두 만족할 만한 위스키 코스 메뉴가 이 집의 자랑이다. 안주는 카나페와 베이컨 꼬치구이, 크림치즈 나초 등 단출하지만 단골손님이 원하면 파스타나 볶음밥 등 원하는 메뉴를 뚝딱 만들어주기도 한다.

Petate

Petate means 'peace and balance' in the ancient Mayan language. This bar specializing in single malt whisky is located on the second floor and has a terrace good to look out lively streets of Garosu-gil. Petate was first started by Choi Yong-nam, who was and still is a huge whisky lover and used to work in the IT industry and now serves up over 80 single malt whiskies. Its whisky course to satisfy a novice or expert both is especially popular. Petate's food menu is very simple but sometimes it serves an extra dish upon a customer's request.

Address	강남구 압구정로14길 32 2층
Contact	02-516-3342
Operation	19:00~다음 날 04:00
Closed	연중무휴

2F, 32, Apgujeong-ro 14-gil, Gangnam-gu
82-2-516-3342
19:00~The next day 04:00
Open all year round

르쁘엥

캐주얼하고 편안한 프랑스식 안주를 다루는 르쁘엥은 최고의 와인과 푸드의 마리아주를 선보이는 와인바. 10년 넘게 정통 프렌치 레스토랑 '라 싸브어'를 운영했던 진경수 셰프가 지난해 새로 문을 연 곳이다. 1층에는 싱글 다이닝이 가능한 바와 테이블이 있고, 2층에는 널찍한 홀이 있어 모임이나 미팅 장소로도 적합하다. 메뉴는 프랑스의 부르고뉴 지역 레드 와인과 잘 어울리는 닭고기 간 요리와 푸아 그라 테린, 프랑스 남부 론 지역 레드 와인과 궁합이 좋은 매운 탈리아텔레 파스타와 프랑스식 삼겹살찜 등 전 세계 지역별 와인과 마리아주를 이루는 음식으로 구성했다.

Le Point

Le Point, famous for the greatest mariage of fine wine and excellent food, is a wine bar with a casual and relaxed ambiance. This is the second store of Chef Jin Kyung-soo, who is the owner cum chef of the French restaurant La Saveur. Le Point has a bar and tables for single dining on the first floor and a large hall for a large group on the second floor. It serves up a Chicken Dish or Foie Gras Terrine for red wine from Burgundy and spicy Tagliatelle Pasta or French-style Steamed Pork Belly for red wine from south France. These combinations are evaluated as the greatest mariage of wine and food.

Address	서초구 사평대로18길 38	38, Sapyeong-daero 18-gil, Seocho-gu
Contact	02-537-3339	82-2-537-3339
Operation	18:00~다음 날 01:00	18:00~The next day 01:00
Closed	일요일	Sun

로칸다 몽로

《어쨌든, 잇태리》의 저자이자 홍대 앞 '라꼼마', 이태원 '인스턴트 펑크'에서 이탈리아 음식을 선보인 박찬일 셰프가 문학과 지성사 사옥 지하에 새로운 음식점을 냈다. 무국적 술집을 표방하는 이곳은 이탈리아 어로 선술집을 뜻하는 '로칸다'에 꿈길이라는 뜻의 '몽로'를 조합한 것. 술맛을 돋울 만한 이탈리아식 안주를 다양하게 갖추었다. 문어와 골뱅이, 지중해의 붉은 새우로 만든 '문어 샐러드', 으깬 감자, 대구 살을 버무려 리치몬드 제과점에서 공수한 치아바타에 발라 먹는 '바칼라'는 화이트 와인과 최고의 궁합을 이룬다.

Locanda Mongro

Chef Park Chan-Il, who is the chef of Instant Punk and La Comma, fusion Italian restaurants, and also known as an author of Italy, Eataly, opened a new restaurant in the building of Moonji Publishing Company. Locanda Mongro styles themselves as a fusion pub. Their name is a compound word of 'Locanda', an Italian word meaning a stand-up bar and 'Mongro' meaning a path to dream in Korean.

As its name, they serve great Italian dishes to add more flavors to alcoholic beverage. Octopus Salad made with octopus, sea snails and Mediterranean red prawn and Baccalà made by spreading mashed potatoes and cod flesh on ciabatta brought from Richemont Bakery. These dishes boast a superb mariage with white wine.

Address	마포구 잔다리로7길 18 지하 1층	B1F, 18, Jandari-ro 7-gil, Mapo-gu
Contact	02-3144-8767	82-2-3144-8767
Operation	18:00~다음 날 01:00	18:00~The next day 01:00
Closed	일요일, 설·추석 연휴	Sun, Holiday of Lunar New Year's Day & Chuseok

루

조선 시대 외교 사절을 위해 연회를 베풀던 경회루를 모던하게 해석한 코리안 타파스 바. 이태원 '글램 라운지'를 설계한 김치호 디자이너의 감각으로 삼성동에 문을 연 루는 전통적인 문양과 소품, 현대식 조명이 절묘하게 어울려 독특한 분위기를 자아낸다. 메뉴는 조선 시대 왕이 즐겨 먹던 식재료에서 영감을 얻어 완성했다. '된장 맥적 피자', '간장 등갈비', '용안탕' 등 아이디어 넘치는 메뉴가 많다. 칵테일 역시 한식과 곁들여도 손색없는 메뉴를 자체 개발해 판매한다. '정1품', '강쇠', '슈퍼 석세스' 같은 유쾌한 이름이 시선을 끈다.

Lu:

Lu: is a Korean tapas bar, a kind of modernized version of Gyeonghoeru, a building to hold big banquet for a diplomatic mission during the Joseon Dynasty. Designer Kim Chi-Ho, who designed Glam Lounge in Itaewon, also designed this splendid restaurant where traditional patterns and decorations are amazingly balanced with modern lightings. Their dishes borros its concept from what kings of Joseon ate. So there are unusual dishes on its menu including Doenjang Maekjeok Pizza (pizza with broiled pork in soy bean paste) and Ganjang Deunggalbi (grilled back ribs in soy sauce). Self-developed cocktails to go well with Korean cuisines are also available.

Address	강남구 영동대로 513	513, Yeongdong-daero, Gangnam-gu
Contact	02-6002-2003	82-2-6002-2003
Operation	월~금 Mon to Fri 11:00~다음 날 The next day 01:00(Break 15:00~17:30),	
	토·일 Sat & Sun 11:00~다음 날 The next day 02:00(Break 15:00~18:00)	
Closed	연중무휴	Open all year round

가스트로 591

신사동 591번지에 위치한 와인 전문 주점. 와인으로 가득 찬 셀러를 지나면 아늑한 홀이 펼쳐진다. 홀 가운데에는 소믈리에와 대화하며 와인을 마실 수 있는 바가 있다. 약 200여 종에 이르는 와인 리스트를 나라와 지역별로 구분해뒀다. 프랑스는 보르도나 부르고뉴 외에도 론, 랑그도크 루시옹, 보졸레로 나눴고 이탈리아는 피에몬테와 토스카나, 스페인은 리오하, 라만차 등으로 세분화해 보기 쉽게 정리한 것. 레스토랑 매니저인 박문성 씨가 치즈, 하몬, 샐러드 등 와인과 어울리는 안주를 추천해준다.

Gastro 591

Gastro 591 is a wine bar located in 591, Sinsa-dong. Passing by a wine cellar which is full of a wide variety of wine, you can find yourself standing in a cozy hall. You can enjoy a glass of wine and a conversation with its sommelier at the bar placed in the middle of the hall. On their wine list, around 200 kinds of wines are classified according to each county and region. French wines are categorized into Bordeaux, Burgundy, Rhône, Languedoc-Roussillon and Beaujolais, Italian wines are into Piemonte and Toscana and Spanish wines are into Rioja and La Mancha. While enjoying wine, you can also taste side dishes, such as cheese, jamón and salad, best matched to each wine, with the help of a restaurant manager.

Address	강남구 논현로 824 지하 1층	B1F, 824, Nonhyeon-ro, Gangnam-gu
Contact	02-545-7448	82-2545-7448
Web	www.facebook.com/gastro591	www.facebook.com/gastro591
Operation	18:00~다음 날 02:00	18:00~The next day 02:00
Closed	일요일	Sun

credits

p18~25	한식에 대한 일곱 가지 상상
글 이영채, 조혜령 / 사진 이봉철 / 요리 그랜드 인터컨티넨탈 서울 파르나스, 롯데 호텔 서울,
W 서울 워커힐, 그랜드 하얏트 서울, 서울 웨스틴 조선 호텔, 파크 하얏트 서울

p26~69	외국인에게 소개하고 싶은 한식 레스토랑 46
글 이영채, 조혜령, 이영지 / 사진 염정훈, 황인우, 홍보라미, 정현석

p72~79	한국의 중국 음식 100년사
글 이영채 / 사진 김덕창, 민희기

p80~85	대륙의 맛을 아십니까?
글 조혜령 / 사진 민희기(요리사진 크리스탈 제이드 팰리스, 레드페퍼 리퍼블릭, 마오 제공)

p86~93	짜장에서 만찬까지, 중식 테이블
글 이영채 / 사진 김덕창 / 요리 서울 웨스틴 조선 호텔 홍연, 서울 신라 호텔 팔선 /
스타일링 이소영, 이승희(스타일링 하다)

p94~117	서울에서 가장 맛있는 중식 레스토랑 32
글 조혜령 / 사진 민희기, 홍보라미 / 요리 팔선생, 시안 청담점, 크리스탈 제이드 팰리스

p120~127	프랑스 요리는 어떻게 미식의 최고봉이 되었나?
글 정한진(창원문성대학 호텔조리제빵과 교수) / 일러스트 최익견

p128~133	프랑스 미식을 완성하는 기본 식재료
글 이영지 / 사진 김경수, 염정훈, 조정희

p134~139	식사 매너부터 코스 요리까지, 프렌치 테이블
글 이영채 / 사진 김경수 / 요리 서울 신라 호텔 콘티넨탈 / 스타일링 장문의, 박정희(7도어스)

p140~167	프랑스인도 인정한 프렌치 레스토랑 24
글 이영채, 정성갑, 이영지, 유선애 / 사진 이경옥, 이창화, 김정경, 배자경, 정현석

p170   이탈리아 음식의 역사는 서양 음식의 역사다
        글 이영채 / 사진 김동오 / 스타일링 민송이(7도어스)

p176~195   5년이 흘러도 건재하다, 믿고 가는 이탤리언 레스토랑 18
            글 이영채, 백문영 / 사진 이경옥, 김규한, 이창화, 이서린, 정푸르나, 김남우, 김도현

p198~215   기분 전환을 위한 세계 요리 레스토랑
            글 이영지 / 사진 김동오, 김용일, 이창화, 정현석, 조영수

p218   아시아 디저트 문화
        글 이영지 / 사진 김도현

p224~229   일상의 디저트 테이블
            글 이영채 / 사진 박찬우 / 스타일링 민송이, 민들레(7도어스)

p230~269   서울의 고급 디저트 숍 33
            글 이영채, 이영지 / 사진 김규한, 김동오, 박찬우, 이경옥, 이명수, 이우경, 이창화, 정현석

참고 도서   《중화요리에 담긴 중국》(매일경제신문사)
            《음식 잡학 사전》(북로드)
            《음식천국, 중국을 맛보다》(매일경제신문사)
            《짜장면뎐》(프로네시스)
            《가스트로노미》(비앤씨월드)
            《송희라의 177 테이블 매너》(세계미식문화연구원)
            《정통 이태리 요리》(백산출판사)
            《국수와 빵의 문화사》(뿌리와이파리)
            《엄마가 해주는 세계요리》(웅진닷컴)

eat, seoul
잇, 서울

1판 1쇄 발행   2015년 10월 15일

펴낸이   이영혜
펴낸곳   디자인하우스
             서울시 중구 동호로 310 태광빌딩
             우편번호 100-855 중앙우체국 사서함 2532

대표전화   (02) 2275-6151
영업부직통   (02) 2263-6900
팩시밀리   (02) 2275-7884, 7885
홈페이지   www.designhouse.co.kr
등록   1977년 8월 19일, 제2-208호

편집장   김은주
편집팀   박은경, 이수빈
디자인팀   김희정, 김지영
마케팅팀   도경의
영업부   오혜란, 고은영
제작부   이성훈, 민나영, 이난영

기획   <럭셔리> 편집부
글   백문영, 유선애, 이영지, 이영채, 정성갑, 조혜령
사진   김경수, 김규한, 김남우, 김덕창, 김도현, 김동오, 김용일, 김정경, 민희기, 박찬우, 배자경, 염정훈,
             이경옥, 이명수, 이봉철, 이서린, 이우경, 이창화, 정푸르나, 정현석, 조영수, 조정희, 홍보라미, 황인우

영문 번역   이성옥
교정·교열   이정현
출력·인쇄   M-print
Copyright ⓒ 2015 by 럭셔리

이 책은 ㈜디자인하우스의 콘텐츠로 출간되었으므로 이 책에 실린 내용의 무단 전재와 무단 복제를 금합니다.
㈜디자인하우스는 김영철 변호사·변리사(법무법인 케이씨엘)의 법률 자문을 받고 있습니다.

ISBN 978-89-7041-675-5 (13980)
가격 15,000원